New Mexico

Nancy Harbert
Photography by Michael Freeman

COMPASS AMERICAN GUIDES

New Mexico

LIBRARY OF CONGRESS CATALOGING IN PUBLICATION DATA
Harbert, Nancy.
    New Mexico / Nancy Harbert ; photography by Michael Freeman. —1st ed.
        p.   cm. — (Discover America)
    Includes bibliographical references and index.
    ISBN 1-878867-22-9 (cloth): $22.95   ISBN 1-878867-06-7 (pbk.): $15.95
        1. New Mexico—Description and travel—1981- —Guide-books.
I. Freeman, Michael, 1945-   II. Title.   III. Series.
F794.3.H37   1992   91-38896
917.8904'53—dc20   CIP

Series Editor: Kit Duane   Designers: David Hurst, Christopher Burt
Editors: Kit Duane, Deke Castleman   Map Design: Bob Race

First Published in 1992 by Compass American Guides, Inc.
6051 Margarido Drive, Oakland, CA 94618, USA
First Edition 1992

Production house: Twin Age Ltd., Hong Kong   .   Printed in Hong Kong
Cover: Taos Pueblo, New Mexico
Compass American Guides is an imprint of Fodor's Travel Publications, Inc.

ACKNOWLEDGMENTS

GRATEFUL APPRECIATION IS DUE to Fritz Thompson, a Wagon Mound native son, for his editorial comments and boundless knowledge of New Mexico's hidden treasures shared over numerous green chile enchilada lunches. Thanks also goes to Phoebe Latimer for her unwavering support, to Martin Frentzel for his professional guidance, and to Judge Tibo Chavez for sharing his knowledge of herbal medicines.

Recognition also goes to Kit Duane, my editor, for her patience and encouragement.

COMPASS AMERICAN GUIDES wishes to acknowledge the Museum of New Mexico for photos on pp. 21, 29, 60, 66, 67, 84, 96, 98, 107, 113, 118, 156, 166, 174, 180, 185, 191, 203, 204, 205, 229, 242-243, 246, 251, 253, 275; the Albuquerque Museum for the photos on p. 41; and the U.S. Forest Service for the photo on p. 222. The publisher also wishes to thank the following photographers for the use of their work: Paul Chesley, pp. 3, 14, 72, 73, 82, 150, 161, 165, 169, 172 (top), 173, 189, 192, 196, 197, 200, 209, 212, 213, 245, 260, 264, 265, 280, 281, 288, 306, 307, 320; Jack Olson, pp. 26, 43, 238-239.

To Jessica and Jack Harbert.
I hope this book brings you to New Mexico.

C O N T E N T S

Literary Excerpts

Sidebars

Maps

NEW MEXICO GUIDEBOOK
SECTION DIVISIONS

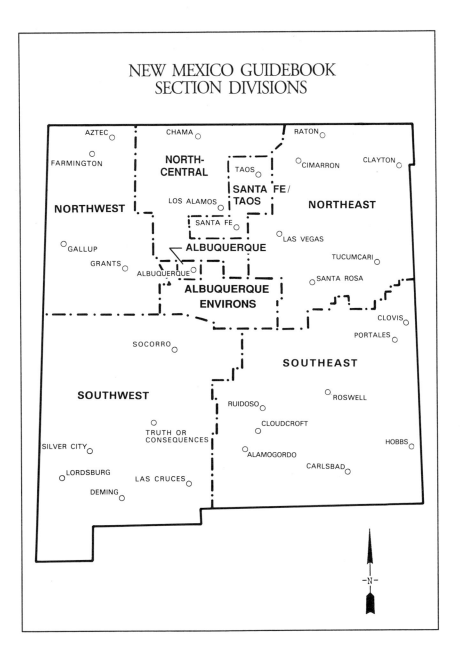

FACTS ABOUT NEW MEXICO
Land of Enchantment

CAPITAL: Santa Fe

ENTERED UNION: January 6, 1912

FIRST SETTLED: 1610

POPULATION: 1,515,000 (1990)

White	1,146,000
Hispanic	579,000
Indian	134,000
Black	30,000

STATE FLOWER: Yucca

STATE BIRD: Roadrunner

STATE TREE: Piñon

FIVE LARGEST CITIES:

Albuquerque	385,000
Santa Fe	56,000
Las Cruces	59,000
Roswell	43,000
Farmington	34,000

GEOGRAPHY:

Size: 121,593 sq. miles (fifth largest state)

Highest point: 13,161 feet (Wheeler Peak)

Lowest point: 2,842 feet (Red Bluff Reservoir)

Highest temp. recorded: 116°F in Orogrande on July 14,1934

Lowest temp. recorded: -50°F in Gavilan on February 1,1951

Wettest place: 33.43 inches (average annual) at Harvey's Upper Ranch in San Miguel County

Driest place: 6.76 inches (average annual) at Fruitland in San Juan County

ECONOMY:

Major industries: mining, tourism, agriculture

Chief crops: wheat, hay, sorghum, onions, cotton, corn

Minerals: copper, potash, construction sand and gravel

Per capita income: $13,191

Tourism: $2.3 billion spent by out-of-state visitors in 1990, or $1,447 for each resident

Education: Student-teacher ratio is 18.5 to 1

FAMOUS NEW MEXICANS:

Archbishop Jean Baptiste Lamy, Kit Carson, Billy (the Kid) Bonney, Peter Hurd, Nancy Lopez, Georgia O'Keeffe, Al and Bobby Unser, Tony Hillerman, Lee Wallace.

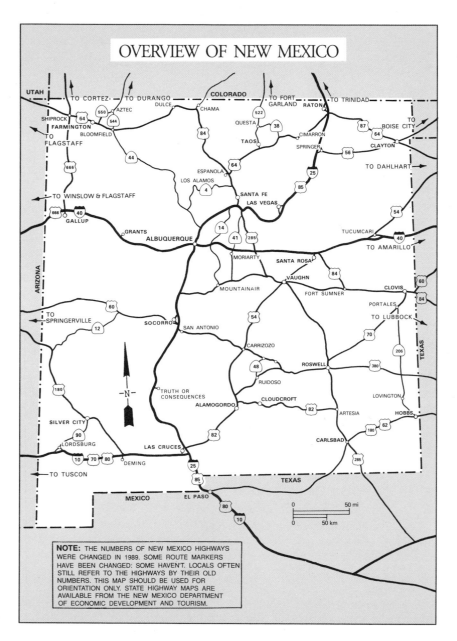

(following pages) Artist Ernest Blumenschein's studio in Taos is a perfect representation of the now popular "Santa Fe Style."

INTRODUCTION

NEW MEXICO'S MAGIC HAS BEEN INTRIGUING VISITORS FOR CENTURIES. Its natural beauty immediately captivates those who see it, and its elusive, indefinable character enriches all those who let it in. Space, light, purity have all been used to describe that latent quality that has attracted the travelers and settlers, artists and scientists, who've come in search of treasure, tangible and intangible.

In prehistoric times, Native Americans hunted game in New Mexico's mountains and farmed along its river banks. Pueblo Indians expressed their reverential relationship with the land through flat-roofed earthen architecture, drawings on rock faces, and rhythmic chants and dances. Spanish explorers followed, first in search of gold, then souls. The two cultures clashed, often violently. But eventually they came to tolerate each other and even to share their traditions. Pueblo Indians passed on their innovative uses for chile, beans, and corn, the main ingredients of what ironically has come to be known as Mexican food. In turn, the Spanish passed on their skill at metal work, which the Indians incorporated into intricate jewelry.

In the later half of the nineteenth century, determined groups of "Anglo" settlers began arriving via the Santa Fe Trail, bringing to New Mexico a third culture—Victorian, technologically emerging. In the early twentieth century, a new wave of immigrants of Italian, Lebanese, German, Irish, and Russian descent—also "Anglos" in New Mexican parlance—came to set up shops or work in coal, silver, and gold mines across the state.

Although the Anglos were the last of the three main cultural groups to arrive, they became the most influential. They mined the mountains for gold and precious metals, and uncovered vast deposits of coal, oil, and natural gas. They brought the railroad, the highway, and the atomic bomb. They came to capture the state's magic—on canvas, in photographs, and in their souls.

The state's Spanish community, once comprised mainly of descendants of the original settlers who came via Mexico, has expanded to include thousands of new Hispanic, or Spanish-speaking, immigrants from Central and South America. Today's Hispanics are responsible for a vitality and sensuality that has become part of New Mexico's mystique. Religion still permeates this culture and nearly every town honors its patron saint once a year in an exuberant fiesta. This sensitivity carries through in the imperfect sloping walls of adobe buildings, hand-punched tinwork, and strains of melodic *corridos* (love songs) that waft from open door-ways. Carved *bultos* and intricately painted *retablos* once adorned only church altars and walls, but now are found in gift shops and galleries.

Today, New Mexico's Indians often straddle two worlds: teaching math to fifth graders or arguing the First Amendment before a federal judge during the week, then returning to the reservation on weekends to participate in traditional dances where they exchange their button-down clothes for feathered headdresses and festive shirts.

The state's landscape is as varied as its cultures. The Rio Grande is the life-blood for much of this arid land, and serves as the natural east-west dividing line as it snakes through the mountainous north, skirting Albuquerque and providing the lifeline for the agricultural southwest before flowing into Texas at El Paso. Away from the river, pine and spruce forests blanket much of northern New Mexico. There you'll find pristine trout streams, bountiful hunting grounds, and world-class ski-slopes. A small section of the vast Navajo Reservation covers the northwestern corner of the state, and continues into neighboring Arizona. In the southwest is the 3.3-million-acre Gila National Forest, once home to the Mim-bres Indians, known for their distinctive black-on-white pottery decorated with geometric designs and animal motifs. East of the mountains lies the irrigated Mesilla Valley, with its acres of green chile, cotton, and onions.

On the vast plains of eastern New Mexico, lumbering herds of cattle and bands of sheep share windswept grasslands. Dryland farming has prospered in pockets of the Llano Estacado (Staked Plains), a western extension of the bountiful Great Plains that covers much of eastern New Mexico. To the west, rise the Sacramento Mountains, home to the Mescalero Apaches. One of the world's greatest natural wonders spreads out in massive rooms underneath a limestone ridge at Carlsbad Caverns.

New Mexico's cities are small, with the exception of Albuquerque, which holds one-third of the state's people and serves as its business, economic, and education center. A cursory glance might fail to distinguish it from any other spread-out Western metropolis, but most residents agree it's an unusually congenial place to live: traffic jams are few, the climate is ideal (mild winters and hot dry summers), and friendly smiles are everywhere.

Fifty miles (80 km) north of Albuquerque, the state capital of Santa Fe huddles in the shelter of the Sangre de Cristo Mountains. Here, narrow streets wind among centuries-old adobe buildings. You live in the right area of town if your adobe home sits on a dirt road. Students of acupuncture, massage, and natural healing mix amiably with long-time Hispanic residents and Indian artisans.

It's not a coincidence that New Mexico is known as the Land of Enchantment. The spells it casts are many and varied. For those who haven't yet experienced it, all it takes is to cross its borders to enter New Mexico's magical embrace.

MUSIC DEFINES THE DESERT

New Mexico has inspired writers, painters, and musicians. British composer George Benjamin described his piece Ringed by the Flat Horizon *as being inspired in part by a thunderstorm over the New Mexico desert.*

I wanted to portray an eerie tension as the landscape is overwhelmed by a vast storm. The work starts slowly and mysteriously with a succession of three textures that recur throughout the structure—weird, soft bell chords, a sustained semitone clash, and deep tremors in the lower registers of the orchestra that depict distant thunder. Piccolo solos surrounded by high violins follow, and fuller developments of the opening ideas, gradually transform the momentum to faster music.

Here a sonority of wind and muted trumpets, punctuated by wooden percussion is juxtaposed with quieter, more lyrical cello solos. These build up with increasing intensity, culminating in a massive climax, after which the music slowly descends to the bass register, subsiding in a solitary bass drum roll.

There follows a sequence of dark, ominous chords for full orchestra (a sound completely new to the piece), interspersed with solo melodic lines over deep tremors of the opening. For a moment the original semitone clash hovers motionless in the air, the thunder at last erupts in a violent explosion, and the work returns to a mood of unreal calm, ending as it began, with a soft bell chord.

—George Benjamin
program notes for the Berkeley Symphony Orchestra, 1987

Malpais National Monument region. (Paul Chesley)

H I S T O R Y

SHALLOW SEAS COVERED THE AREA NOW KNOWN as New Mexico for most of the Paleozoic Era, from 570 million to 245 million years ago. When they dried up they left behind brachiopods, trilobites, corals, and crinoid stems fossilized in limestone and shale. In southeastern New Mexico, the Capitan Reef grew to surround the Delaware Basin, a 10,000-square-mile (29,000-sq-km) sea. Vast deposits of oil and gas remain where the basin once was, along with gypsum, potash, and salt. During this time, volcanic explosions created mountain ranges and coated the earth with layers of lava that hardened into a jagged black landscape.

Eighty-million years ago, the Rocky Mountains jutted into existence, the southern end spilling into northern New Mexico. The seas dried up, camels, bears, large cats, and wild dogs replaced dinosaurs, and some of the state took on a lunar appearance of rugged mountains and vast plains covered with boulders and gravel.

Two fault zones cut across New Mexico from north to south. About 25 million years ago, the tension between the faults caused a long sliver of the Earth's crust to drop down in between them. This trough, known as the Rio Grande Rift, would eventually carry the waters of the Rio Grande from its headwaters in the Colorado Rockies 1,885 miles (3,016 km) to the Gulf of Mexico. The west side of the rift, where the crust had been stretched thin, erupted with violent volcanic explosions. One created the Jemez Mountains, centered by the 12-mile-diameter (18-km) Valle Grande caldera. Another fracture extended from present-day Quemado almost to Clayton, which produced Capulin, a volcanic mountain in northeast New Mexico, and El Malpais (the Badlands) lava flow south of Grants. Such widespread volcanic activity left behind rich mineral deposits scattered throughout the region, such as copper, lead, and zinc, as well as numerous geothermal pockets, some of which bubble to the surface as hot springs.

Beginning two million years ago during the ice ages, glaciers covered the state's highest mountains, and spread as far south as present-day Sierra Blanca. Later, large lakes filled basins in closed valleys in southern and central New Mexico. One of these bodies of water, Lake Lucero, evaporated, and winds blew its gypsum sediments into 50-foot (15-m) drifts, now known as White Sands. Glaciers probably still hung down from mountaintops and a few remaining volcanoes were still blowing their tops when the state's first human visitors arrived as early as 20,000 years ago.

■ EARLY INHABITANTS

Grasslands and forests covered much of New Mexico when big-game hunters followed mammoth, mastodon, sloth, bison, antelope, camel, and horse driven south by ice age glaciers that moved across much of North America. These early hunters chipped scrapers and spear points from flint, obsidian, jasper, and chert, then staked out their prey at watering holes.

By 10,000 B.C., the Clovis people regularly pursued the giant bison throughout southeastern New Mexico. Hundreds of miles away in the Sandia Mountains, the Sandia people, whom historians say were unrelated to the Clovis, hunted the same animals. Spear points up to three inches (8 cm) long and more finely honed than those of the Clovis or Sandia cultures were crafted in northeastern New Mexico by the Folsom people, appearing 1,000 years later than the earlier hunters. Mysteriously, no bones of these early people have been found, only the skeletons of prey pierced with their spear points.

As the glaciers melted, New Mexico warmed up and dried out. Piñon and juniper forests thinned, drought-resistant grama grass replaced lush grasslands, and cactus, mesquite, and creosote bush prospered. Large lakes near present-day Estancia and Lordsburg evaporated. Mastodons and mammoths disappeared, perhaps due to lack of food, disease, and over-zealous hunters.

■ THE INDIANS

The big-game hunters moved on, most likely to the Great Plains where they pursued smaller animals. They were replaced in New Mexico, beginning in A.D. 900, by the Desert Culture, whose hunters spread across western New Mexico in pursuit of elk, deer, antelope, turkey, and rodents. They fished in streams and gathered nuts, berries, the thirst-quenching fruit of cactus, and seeds. Noticing that seeds left in place grew into plants, these people soon added farming to their hunting and gathering. Later, because it was easier to care for crops by staying in one place, they established permanent settlements.

Two primary groups grew from the initial Desert Culture. In southwestern New Mexico, the Mogollon learned from their southern neighbors in present-day Mexico how to cultivate corn, squash, and beans, and how to fashion pottery. One branch, the Mimbres Indians, developed exquisitely stylized black-on-white designs based on birds and animals, as well as meticulous geometric patterns. The Mogollon's first homes were oval pits dug four feet (1 m) into the earth, covered with timber and dirt roofs. Built close together, these pit houses formed villages.

In northwestern New Mexico, the Anasazi culture borrowed agricultural and pottery techniques from the Mogollon, but developed more slowly. At their peak, however, the Anasazi displayed a sophistication far beyond that of their predecessors. By A.D. 900-1000, the Anasazi were living in stone dwellings built into the sides of high cliffs, and in free-standing multi-storied apartment buildings of finely fitting rock slabs held together with mud mortar. At Chaco Canyon, they designed a system of dams and ditches that directed the flow of water into fields. Roads connected far-flung pueblos. Men wore ornamental jewelry made of shell, turquoise, and other gemstones, and women wove textiles from cotton they grew in their fields. These ingenious people were the ancestors of today's Pueblo Indians.

About A.D. 1200, Athapascan-speaking tribes, including the Navajo and Apache, began making their way down from Canada into the Southwest. Decidedly different from the sedentary, agrarian Anasazi, the nomadic Navajo were adept traders, exchanging baskets, animal hides, and jerky with Pueblo Indians for corn, cotton cloth, and turquoise. Eventually, the Navajo built hogans, circular mud-plastered dwellings, and learned from the Pueblo Indians how to grow corn, beans, squash, and melons. They never completely gave up their wandering ways, even as they herded across the countryside small bands of sheep and goats, which were introduced by the Spanish. Families lived in clustered hogans, but villages as we think of them did not develop.

When the Apaches arrived in New Mexico, they separated into bands and never considered themselves a single tribe. The bands staked out their territory: the Jicarilla Apaches wandered across northern New Mexico and southern Colorado and learned how to cultivate corn from the pueblos; the Mescaleros stayed within southern New Mexico, and the Chiricahuas, who later became known for their fighting skills, roamed throughout southwestern New Mexico and southeastern Arizona. Like the Navajo, the Apache hunted bison and deer and gathered roots, nuts, and berries. Broad-faced with high cheekbones and a muscular physique, Apaches lived in thatched *wickiups* and animal-skin tepees. The women in the Mescalero bands roasted the meat of the mescal plant, an agave cactus, also known as a century plant, wove baskets from its fibers, and tanned buckskin and buffalo hides into silky smooth shirts and knee-high boots for the men and straight shifts decorated with beads for themselves.

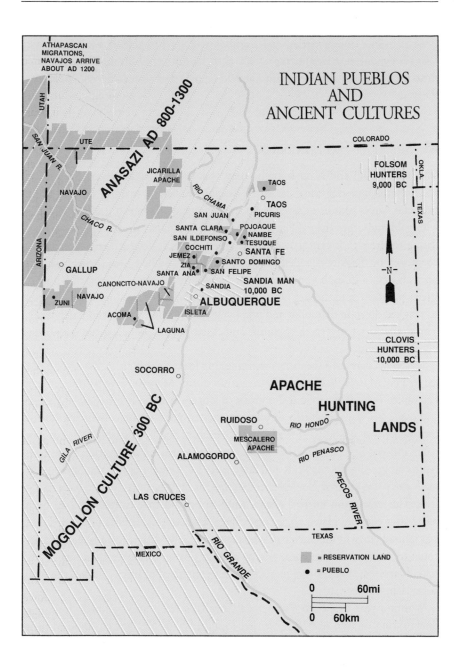

INDIAN PUEBLOS
AND
ANCIENT CULTURES

ATHAPASCAN MIGRATIONS, NAVAJOS ARRIVE ABOUT AD 1200

UTAH

SAN JUAN R.

ARIZONA

UTE

NAVAJO

ANASAZI AD 800-1300

CHACO R.

GALLUP

CANONCITO-NAVAJO

ZUNI

NAVAJO

ACOMA

LAGUNA

ISLETA

COLORADO

JICARILLA APACHE

RIO CHAMA

SAN JUAN

SANTA CLARA
SAN ILDEFONSO
COCHITI
JEMEZ
ZIA
SANTA ANA

TAOS

TAOS
PICURIS

POJOAQUE
NAMBE
TESUQUE
○ SANTA FE

SANTO DOMINGO
SAN FELIPE

SANDIA

SANDIA MAN
10,000 BC

ALBUQUERQUE

FOLSOM HUNTERS 9,000 BC

OKLA.

TEXAS

-N-

CLOVIS HUNTERS 10,000 BC

SOCORRO

MOGOLLON CULTURE 300 BC

GILA RIVER

APACHE

HUNTING

LANDS

RUIDOSO

RIO HONDO

MESCALERO APACHE

RIO PENASCO

ALAMOGORDO

PECOS RIVER

LAS CRUCES

TEXAS

MEXICO

RIO GRANDE

= RESERVATION LAND
● = PUEBLO

0   60mi

0   60km

At the same time a settled and sophisticated Pueblo culture thrived. When Spanish explorers arrived in the 1500s they found nearly 80 pueblos (many of these multi-storied) scattered along the Rio Grande and along adjacent streams to the west.

■ SPANISH EXPLORERS

The lure of gold and silver initially drew Spanish explorers to New Mexico. In 1521 after conquering the great Aztec Empire of Mexico, Spanish officials heard from the Aztecs rumors of seven cities in the uncharted lands to the north, laden with gold and other riches. The story wasn't too different from a Spanish legend dating to the eighth century, in which seven bishops, fleeing Spain after it was conquered by the Moors, sailed westward until they reached a land where each set up a church, and each church became fabulously wealthy. The legend told of streets paved in gold, houses bedecked with sapphires and turquoise, and natives so weighed down in diamonds and other valuable minerals they could barely walk. The similarities between the Spanish and Aztec myths propelled the conquistadores northward.

In 1539, a party of adventurers went looking for the seven cities. The group was led by Fray Marcos de Niza and by an extraordinary Moorish slave by the name of Estevanico (who had survived the wreck of a Spanish ship off the coast of Florida and made his way to Mexico through uncharted territory by convincing hostile Indians he was a God). Estevanico went ahead of the Niza party as an advance scout and was instructed to send back crosses to signal his discoveries: small ones representing insignificant finds and large ones for something of value. Before the main party had entered New Mexico, a cross "as high as a man" came back to the friar. The expedition hurried ahead, only to be told that Estevanico had been killed after entering Hawikuh, a Zuni village. Undaunted, de Niza proceeded, but was refused entry to the pueblo. Or he may only have viewed it from afar. His account to Antonio de Mendoza, viceroy of New Spain, as Mexico then was called, told of terraced, stone houses in a settlement comprised of seven villages, the total larger than Mexico City.

Within a year, Francisco Vasquez de Coronado was traveling north, leading a slow-moving caravan of 336 horsemen equipped with 559 horses, some of their wives and families, a few priests, and 100 Indians who tended small herds of cattle and sheep. They left Compostela, New Spain, on February 22, 1540, exactly 192 years before George Washington was born. Six months later, the entourage arrived at Hawikuh only to find small villages of mud huts.

Disappointed but not discouraged, Coronado headed east where he wintered at Alcanfor, known later as Kuaua, a pueblo on the Rio Grande near present-day Bernalillo. The following spring, he continued his eastward drive, this time in search of Quivira described, by a Pawnee slave whom the Spaniards named El Turco because he looked like a Turk, as another rich land with gold-paved streets and golden water jugs. Coronado's journey ended near Lyons, Kansas, at the grass huts of the Wichita Indians. A copper plate hung around the neck of the tribe's chief, and no gold was in sight. Furious with El Turco's deception, Coronado ordered the Indian's death, then returned to Alcanfor across the plains of eastern New Mexico. After another cold winter at the pueblo, the expedition returned empty-handed to New Spain, where Coronado stood trial for defrauding his country of immeasurable wealth and of abusing the natives. He was cleared, but never recovered his pride or his status. Coronado died in 1556 a broken man.

Coronado party arrives in New Mexico. Mural by Gerald Cassidy, 1921. (Museum of New Mexico)

■ SPANISH SETTLERS

Despite their curiosity about the land to the north of Mexico, the Spaniards' first attempt to settle New Mexico wasn't until the Juan de Oñate Expedition in 1598. Oñate, the son of a wealthy Zacatecas miner, led a caravan consisting of 83 *carretas* hauled by oxen, 129 soldiers, 7,000 head of cattle, a handful of clergy, and 400 settlers, some with families. Following the Rio Grande northward, the weary travelers encountered one pueblo after another, receiving the wide-eyed stares and forced hospitality of Indians whose lives would forever be changed by these newcomers.

Six months after they left Mexico, the thirsty, ragged, and demoralized colonists came to an arable river valley near the confluence of the Rio Grande and Chama River. With the slate-blue Sangre de Cristo Mountains as a distant backdrop, construction began on San Gabriel, New Mexico's first capital. Nearby, residents of San Juan Pueblo guardedly observed the Spaniards, many of whom were disappointed to find no gold jewelry accenting the simple clothing of the Indians.

After establishing the colony, Oñate continued to explore and claim the far reaches of the state for Spain, leaving behind the settlers. But instead of working the soil and planning for a future, they spent their time searching for precious metals. Having failed both as farmers and as miners, the colonists returned to New Spain. Even Oñate admitted defeat and on October 7, 1604, left San Gabriel.

Six years later, Pedro de Peralta led a second group of settlers into the area. With dreams of riches carefully tempered, he chose a high valley tucked into the shadows of the Sangre de Cristo Mountains alongside a narrow stream. De Peralta named the new capital La Villa Real de la Santa Fe de San Francisco, ultimately shortened to Santa Fe (Holy Faith). An able administrator, De Peralta marked municipal boundaries, assigned house and garden lots to colonists, and supervised construction of government offices, which he forced Indians to help erect.

As the capital was being established, church officials wasted no time in reciting the virtues of God and the Catholic church to their new neighbors. For the next 70 years, 250 Franciscan friars circulated among the state's pueblos, converting the Indians and forcing them to adopt a Spanish lifestyle. Disregarding their religion and culture, the Spanish required Indian men to wear pants and shirts and women to wear skirts and blouses. Indian marriages became monogamous, and weddings followed Christian rituals. Indians also were forced to construct large mission

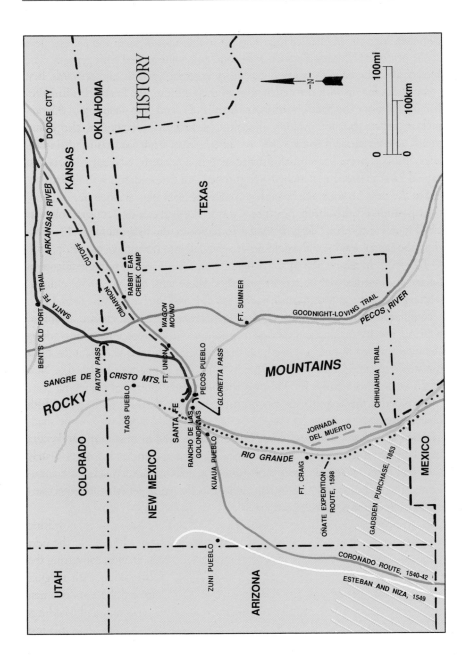

churches. Men cut and hauled huge logs for roof beams. Women and children laid adobe bricks, which they plastered with mud and whitewashed with gypsum. The Indians also labored in the workshops, barns, vegetable gardens, and orchards.

By 1680, fed up with the destruction of their culture, the Pueblo Indians prepared to remove the Spanish intruders from their land. On August 10, they attacked settlers, burned mission churches, destroyed holy statues, and killed priests at their altars. Led by Popé, a medicine man from San Juan Pueblo, the angry Indians proved too much for the surprised Spanish, who surrendered the capital 12 days later and marched—frightened and defeated, south to El Paso.

For the next 11 years, the Spanish stayed away from New Mexico, reevaluating their position on the unruly province—was it worth the cost? By 1691, they decided it was and chose Diego de Vargas to recapture the battered land. After two trips, the capital was his and would never again fall into Indian hands.

To ensure harmony, the Spanish made concessions to the Indians. They no longer destroyed sacred objects or punished those who did not attend church. Throughout the eighteenth century, the Spanish and Pueblo Indians settled into a complacent existence, accepting their differences and even sharing farming, weaving, jewelry-making and carving techniques. With the province secure, more colonists traveled in caravans north on the Camino Real, also known as the Chihuahua Trail, a 533-mile (853-km) trade route that connected the Mexican city of Chihuahua with Santa Fe. This was the only trade route that led out of New Mexico, since the Spanish Crown prohibited Santa Fe from trading with the United States.

Lured by vast tracts of land, these homesteaders lived in small settlements and grew corn, wheat, beans, chile, and cotton, and grazed cattle and sheep. Life was basic and hard, made even more challenging by unannounced attacks of Apache, Comanche, Navajo, and Ute Indians who usually made off with livestock and occasionally captured or killed settlers.

JORNADA DEL MUERTO

There's a stretch of desert in southwestern New Mexico that most early explorers would have preferred never to have seen. This 90-mile (144-km) expanse of sandy prairie strewn with spiny mesquite trees, black grama grass, and creosote bush starts north of Las Cruces and ends south of Socorro. It has earned the name Jornada del Muerto, or Journey of Death. Luckily today no one will double dare you to cross it, because a portion of it is within the confines of White Sands Missile Range, and therefore off limits to adventuresome travelers seeking to relive the horrors of the past.

But in the seventeenth century, Spanish expeditions regularly crossed this near-waterless portion of El Camino Real. They had the option of taking a more circuitous route, thick with deep arroyos and dense vegetation, along the Rio Grande. Most opted for the direct Jornada because it was easier on their wagons and could be crossed in three long days—or nights, which was the preferred time of day to travel. In addition to the absence of water, weather extremes ranged from 100-degree F (38°-C) days in the summer to minus 20-degree F (-38°C) nighttime temperatures in the winter. Then there were the bands of Apaches who seldom failed to miss a move of the noisy caravans. Unlike the European travelers, the Apaches knew the location of every water hole and where to hunt jackrabbits, antelope, deer, and bighorn sheep. They also knew when the travelers would be at their weariest and most susceptible to attack.

The first Spaniard to cross the Jornada was Juan de Oñate, who set out in 1598 to colonize New Mexico and cash in on the riches Francisco Vasquez de Coronado failed to find 50 years earlier.

The day before Oñate headed into the unknown desert, a foreboding incident occurred—one of his men, Pedro Robledo, died and was buried at the base of a mountain that today bears his name. Undaunted, the explorer and his entourage left behind the Rio Grande Valley as scheduled. Oñate was hoping the route would curve back to the Rio Grande. Instead, the Jornada passed in between the Caballo and Fra Cristobal mountain ranges on the west and the San Andres range to the east, and access to the river was severed.

Within one day, water ran short and animals began to die. The party crept along, spread out for miles. On the evening of the second day, a resourceful dog returned to camp with mud on its paws and muzzle, and probably saved the expedition. One of the soldiers followed pawprints in the sand to a nearby spring, which he named *Los Charcos del Perrillo* (the Pools of the Little Dog). This site became a regular stop on the trail for future travelers, and its name was shortened to Perrillo.

Refreshed, the settlers continued, and Oñate and a few horsemen pushed on ahead. A few days later, they arrived at present-day Socorro, exhausted, dehydrated, and certainly dispirited. Oñate spied the sun-dried adobe walls of Pilabo, a Piro pueblo where he found long-haired men and women planting fields of corn, beans, and squash. They were probably startled at his unkempt appearance, but he nevertheless convinced them to provide corn and water for himself and the other hungry travelers who were behind him.

After Santa Fe was settled in 1610, the Chihuahua Trail became a major trade route between Chihuahua, Mexico, and the New Mexico capital. The Jornada remained the most dreaded portion of the trip. Apaches, increasingly upset by the invasion of their territory and realizing the vulnerability of the wagon trains, increased their attacks. Countless Spaniards died in this God-forsaken expanse. Even Oñate's family wasn't spared. During a return trip to Chihuahua, the governor fought in vain to protect his son, who was killed in an Indian ambush.

After the Pueblo Revolt of 1680, an estimated 2,500 colonists fled the Indians, assembling at present-day El Paso. On their trek across the Jornada del Muerto, as many as 573 Spaniards died before help reached them a few miles north of Perrillo.

Indian raids continued to be the major hazard along the Jornada. In 1854, Fort Craig was built at the northern end of the trail and in 1865 Fort Selden at the southern end. After the railroad arrived in the early 1880s, paralleling the trail, horses and wagons no longer crossed the feared Jornada. Cattle replaced the early travelers, finding plenty to eat in patches of desert grasses.

On July 16, 1945, the Jornada once again became a topic of conversation when the world's first atomic bomb was detonated at its far northeastern edge. Today only military trucks and jeeps travel a network of gravel roads that crisscross the desolate range.

*Tombstone at Ponil Park Cemetery
in Carson National Forest. (Jack Olson)*

■ UNDER MEXICAN RULE

In 1821, Mexico gained its independence from Spain, taking New Mexico along with it. Little changed, except that Mexican leaders allowed Santa Fe to trade with the United States. This new situation proved fortuitous for William Becknell, a famed Indian fighter who arrived in New Mexico amid independence celebrations, laden with brightly colored cloth, kettles, knives, and looking glasses he hoped to exchange with Indians. Instead, the Missouri trader sold his wares to Spanish settlers in Santa Fe and quickly returned to Missouri for more. Thus, the Santa Fe Trail was born.

At first, the trail was used by daring tradesmen, who hauled tools, cloth, shoes, and nails across the prairie. Soon, mountain men were dropping down to trap beaver and hunt deer in New Mexico's mountains. Once word spread of a new frontier, settlers from the United States (Anglos) headed for New Mexico.

For 25 years, Mexico ruled the state from afar; while officials there regarded the Anglos suspiciously, they mostly took a hands-off approach to the province, permitting the New Mexico governor to run the show. In 1846, war broke out between Mexico and the United States, the culmination of a disagreement over the U.S. annexation of Texas the year before, which Mexico refused to recognize. The two countries also disputed Texas' southern boundary—the U.S. claimed it was the Rio Grande, but Mexico deemed it to be the Nueces River. Added to the situation was a growing expansionist movement in the U.S. led by President James Polk, who wished to acquire New Mexico and California.

General Stephen Watts Kearny was given the task of seizing the Southwest, but was warned not to frighten its residents. With the support of 1,600 troops, he crossed the Mountain Branch of the Santa Fe Trail that wound into Colorado before dropping into New Mexico. Kearny met no resistance at Las Vegas, where he announced from a rooftop that New Mexico was now part of the U.S. On August 18, the general peaceably claimed the capital of Santa Fe for his homeland, promising its citizens that their property rights and religion would be respected and that their new country would protect them from hostile Indians.

A month later, Kearny moved on to California, leaving a portion of his Army of the West to manage the transition to the government of the Americans. He appointed trader Charles Bent as New Mexico's first U.S. governor. Another segment of Kearny's troops, led by Col. Alexander Doniphan, marched across the state, signing a peace treaty with Navajo Chief Zarcillos Largos and defeating a Mexican force on the Rio Grande south of Las Cruces at the Battle of Brazito. The troops captured the city of Chihuahua the following February.

Back in New Mexico, however, not everyone wanted to be an American. In mid-January, on a visit to his home in Taos, Governor Bent was scalped and killed by an angry mob of colonists and Indians. The insurgents were swiftly trapped inside a mission church at Taos Pueblo. A bloody battle ended with the capture of the rebels, followed by speedy trials and executions of their leaders. Thus ended opposition to the new government. For the next year, New Mexicans lived by American rules, but did not officially become part of the U.S. until the signing in 1848 of the Treaty of Guadalupe-Hidalgo, which ended the war. Even then, the southwestern corner of the state remained part of Mexico until the Gadsden Purchase in 1853 brought into the U.S. the fertile fields of the Mesilla Valley and the cactus-pocked desert west of the Rio Grande.

■ THE ANGLOS

Across the Santa Fe Trail they came—German-Jewish merchants eager to tap a wide-open market; a French bishop, Jean Baptiste Lamy, prepared to lead the territory's Catholic church; and lawyers seeking to snatch up New Mexico's valuable land and gain a foothold in its fledgling political arena.

Military officials honored Kearny's promise and erected forts across the state. In addition to providing a refuge from marauding Apaches, Comanches, Navajos, and Utes, these army posts also helped to secure stagecoach routes through the Southwest.

When the Civil War broke out in 1861, New Mexico found itself in the middle of the conflict: Mesilla Valley settlers identified with the Confederates, but northern residents sided with the Yankees. Officially, the state remained part of the Union.

In February 1862, Brig. Gen. Henry Sibley led a small Confederate army of 2,600 men up the Rio Grande. Sitting proudly astride their range-raised Texas horses, the soldiers met little resistance until they reached Valverde, a tree-shaded ford on the Rio Grande. Here, on February 21, Sibley was greeted by 3,800 Union troops led by the West Point pal who had served as the best man at his wedding:

Col. Edward Canby, commander of federal forces in New Mexico. Brandishing squirrel rifles, double-barrel shotguns, pistols, and Bowie knives, the Rebels charged across the river, overrunning the inexperienced Union troops. By day's end, Canby's troops were retreating south toward Fort Craig. Sibley led his men northward where they hoisted the Confederate flag above defenseless Albuquerque and Santa Fe. Both cities were devoid of troops, which had shifted north to join forces with Fort Union soldiers and a group of Colorado Volunteers.

A month later, at Glorieta Pass, a wide swath of grassland bordered at either end by steep cliffs, Sibley's army was outsmarted. Major John Chivington and a group of Colorado Volunteers crept behind Confederate lines, destroyed ammunition supplies, burned 73 wagons, and killed 600 horses and mules. Often referred to as the Gettysburg of the West, this battle marked the beginning of New Mexico's expulsion of Confederate troops. Sibley retreated, pursued by Canby and his regrouped army, until Sibley slipped out of the territory.

While U.S. soldiers were preoccupied with the Civil War, New Mexico's Apache and Navajo stepped up their raids on settlers, driving off sheep and cattle. The Indians met little resistance until Gen. James Carlton and his California Column arrived in 1862, following the withdrawal of Confederate troops. After enlisting the help of Col. Kit Carson in negotiating with the Navajo, the general rounded up 400 Mescalero Apache in southern New Mexico and moved them to the new Bosque Redondo Reservation. The reservation spread alongside the cottonwood-shaded banks of the Pecos River near Fort Sumner, a new installation built to supervise the Indians' relocation. Carlton's idea was for the Apaches—warriors and hunters whose nomadic way of life was a part of their self definition—to settle down as farmers.

Kit Carson. (Museum of New Mexico)

Over in western New Mexico and eastern Arizona, Kit Carson was unable to make peace with the semi-nomadic Navajos. Thus, a campaign began in which Carson's men relentlessly burned hogans and butchered sheep, chopped down peach trees, and destroyed fields of corn. Weakened and demoralized, the Indians finally acquiesced in 1864 and agreed to relocate to Bosque Redondo. What followed was the "Long Walk," in which thousands of Navajos trudged across 300 miles (450 km) of desert covered with yucca, cholla cactus, and hardened lava beds. This brutal march so affected the Indians that they date historical events by referring to whether the events occurred before or after the Long Walk.

At the reservation, 8,500 Navajos failed to mix with their historic enemies, the Apache. Both tribes resented their imprisonment. Disease ravaged their ranks, and the crops were destroyed by parasites. A few years later, Carlton admitted failure. In 1868, the Navajos were given 3.5 million acres amid the red-rock canyons and piñon mesas of their homeland. In 1873, the Mescaleros received 460,177 acres among the forested slopes of the Sacramento Mountains.

To reward the Pueblo Indians for remaining neutral throughout the Civil War, President Abraham Lincoln in 1863 presented each of the 19 pueblos with a black ebony cane crowned with silver and inscribed with his signature. These symbols of

Kitchen of Hacienda Martinez near Taos.

the pueblos' sovereignty, along with silver-tipped staffs given to the pueblos in 1620 by the Spanish government, are brought out every January and ceremoniously conferred upon a new governor as he takes office.

Comanches and Kiowas remained a threat on the eastern plains, raiding caravans and sometimes brutally murdering travelers on the Santa Fe Trail. Chiricahua Apaches, led by Victorio, his son-in-law Nana, and Geronimo, attacked soldiers and looted settlements along the southern Rio Grande and in Arizona. The raids of these nomadic Indians came to an end when the final rails of the Santa Fe Railroad were laid, connecting the territory to the rest of the country. Their horses couldn't keep up with the moving cars, and travelers were safe inside the metal cocoons.

Once the Indian threat was removed, settlers crowded onto trains bound for the vast Southwest territory, where they expanded railroad camps into thriving towns, established enormous sheep and cattle ranches on the eastern plains, and irrigated acres of farmland with annual snowmelt and the water from small streams. Drovers escorted thousands of longhorn cattle up from Texas through the Pecos River Valley on into Colorado, establishing the Goodnight-Loving Trail. Miners arrived to search for gold and to work in the coal mines near Gallup, Raton, and Madrid, as well as the silver and copper mines near Silver City.

Many of New Mexico's immigrants during the late 1800s were the sort who took the law into their hands. Saloons outnumbered churches in many towns, and the law of the smoking gun often prevailed over that of men with badges. Range wars erupted, along with violent struggles for power. Cattle rustlers operated freely, and Anglo lawyers who received their fees in property benefited most in disputes over land-grant boundaries.

■ STATEHOOD

Soon after Stephen Kearny raised the stars and stripes above Santa Fe in 1846, debate began over whether or not New Mexico would be better off as a state or as a territory. But every time the statehood issue reached the halls of Congress, it was defeated. Eastern politicians feared the strong Hispanic influence and uncivilized character of the Southwestern frontier.

That attitude changed after the 1898 Spanish-American War. Determined to demonstrate New Mexico's dedication to the Union, Gov. Miguel Otero called for

340 cowboys to ride with the Rough Riders cavalry unit led by Theodore Roosevelt. Never did these men, many of Spanish ancestry, hesitate as they sweated and struggled up San Juan Hill on foot after their horses failed to receive a transport to Cuba.

Still it took another 14 years for statehood to finally arrive in 1912. Immediately, New Mexico's powerful politicos jockeyed for seats in the new state legislature and vied for positions in Congress. But most of its nearly 300,000 citizens held onto a well-rooted ambling way of life: Pueblo Indians maintained their intimate relationship with Mother Earth, dancing in thanks for bountiful crops and their health, while learning the language and customs that would help them get along in the Anglo world. Hispanics devotedly filled Catholic churches and danced whenever they had a reason to schedule a fiesta—for a wedding or a saint's day.

In the 1920s, New Mexico's clear air and uncluttered landscape attracted a new wave of eastern Anglos, some of whom were sent by their doctors to recover from tuberculosis, and others by the military to establish air bases on the expansive prairie. Another group of Anglo immigrants worked tirelessly to capture the soft red glow of the desert sunsets and the square jaws of New Mexico's native citizens in photographs, on canvas, and in the written word. Once exposed to the state's ever-changing skies, these artists rarely looked elsewhere for their subjects.

An isolated plateau at the edge of the Jemez Mountains, blanketed in volcanic ash and tall pines, in 1943 lured a small group of scientists who worked in secrecy for two years. Families lived in near-seclusion at what had been the Los Alamos Ranch School, a private boys' institution. In the early-morning hours of July 16, 1945, before the parched earth heated up for the day, the result of the scientists' efforts was unearthed amid the cholla and yucca cactus of the Tularosa Basin in central New Mexico: the detonation of the world's first atomic bomb. This event set the state on a direct path toward a nuclear future. Los Alamos National Laboratory, Sandia National Laboratories, and White Sands Missile Range were since created to fabricate and test this potent technology.

Scientists have since mixed with the state's other residents, who continue to alter its makeup. Regardless of the numerous influences wrought by history, New Mexico remains rooted to tradition and the Earth: adobe construction first used by the Pueblo Indians remains a status symbol; Spanish rolls off tongues in offices, fields, and schools; and brilliant sunsets that bathe mountain slopes and tall-grass prairies in a rosy light continue to attract those who love beauty.

A L B U Q U E R Q U E

ALBUQUERQUE IS A STUDY IN CONTRASTS. Long ago it was no more than a dusty frontier outpost of the Spanish colonial empire, an isolated enclave of rudimentary adobe homes along the banks of the Rio Grande. Today, it is the most vital city in New Mexico, spreading 12 miles (19 km) east of the river to the foothills of the Sandia Mountains and 3.5 miles (6 km) west to a rugged volcanic escarpment. A major scientific and high technology center, Albuquerque serves as the state's economic, education, and transportation core. With a population approaching 500,000, it is also a melting pot for the state's three primary cultures: Native American, Hispanic, and Anglo.

The Rio Grande, shaded by leafy cottonwoods, cuts a north-south swath through the city. Five dormant volcanic cones, the Sleeping Sisters, mark the city's western edge, and a shrub-covered mesa spreads out under their shadow. Between this mesa and the cactus-covered foothills of the Sandia and Manzano mountains, Albuquerque stretches forth in a shimmering sea of asphalt and flat rooftops.

To early Spaniards, the Sandia (Watermelon) Mountains resembled a wedge of watermelon, especially at sunset, when they took on the color of its pulp. The Manzano (Apple) Mountains received their label not because they are green and round, but because an apple orchard was planted on their eastern flank as early as the nineteenth century.

Sandia Crest rises 10,678 feet (3,249 m) from the valley floor, and its cool summit is within easy reach via an 18-minute tram-car ride. From it you can see a breathtaking panorama of the city, river, and mesas that extend toward 11,000-foot (3,300-m) snow-capped Mt. Taylor, 70 miles away. In the skies overhead you may see red-tail hawks, golden eagles, hot-air balloons, hang gliders, or fighter jets from Kirtland Air Force Base.

To someone driving through (or flying over), the city might seem just one more homogeneous, sprawling, western metropolis, with streets set out in a grid pattern and shopping malls at nearly every major intersection. But those with a little more time will find there's much to discover. Because Albuquerque is not a congested city, it's easy to take a leisurely drive through its neighborhoods. In the mostly Hispanic, rural **South Valley,** which follows the river south of Old Town, billboards advertising cigarettes read "El Sabor Rico y Suave" ("A Mild, Rich Flavor"), and in autumn newly harvested green chiles roasting outside fruit and vegetable stands saturate the air with a nose-tingling aroma. **Northeast Heights** and **Southeast Heights** are made up of new developments and contain a heavy proportion of the city's businesses. In the **North Valley** tall grass grows along Rio Grande Boulevard as it winds beside horse farms and orchards. At the original Albuquerque townsite, restored as **Old Town,** horses and buggies still transport shoppers through narrow streets.

Even though the city contains one-third of the state's residents and is New Mexico's largest contribution to urban America, Albuquerque retains the informality of a small town. Among shopkeepers and folks on the street, friendly smiles are the norm. Albuquerque doesn't tolerate pretensions, and its citizens don't concern themselves much with desert visions or astral planes. Residents are down to earth and readily accept, and even thrive on, their city's normalcy.

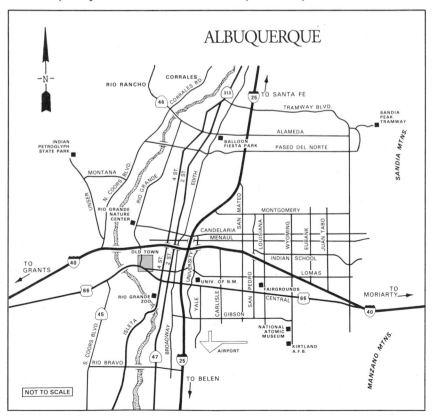

■ HISTORY

The first people to scale the granite outcroppings of the Sandia Mountains and look out over the future site of Albuquerque probably arrived at the end of the last Ice Age, about 12,000 years ago. Hunters, they came in pursuit of mammoths, mastodons, bison, and antelope. Over the course of their sojourn in the valley, the hunters left behind spear points and scrapers in Sandia Cave, a deep cave on the northeastern flank of the mountains. The people who used it for protection were therefore referred to as Sandia Man.

Thousands of years after these primitive hunters moved on, ancestors of today's Pueblo Indians began living along the Rio Grande in settlements which date from A.D. 500. By about A.D. 1300, these Indians were cultivating beans, maize, and squash, coiling pottery, and living in four-story pueblos they built of *terrones*—sod squares made with twigs, grass, dirt, and water. Men wore deerskin shirts, and when they wished to marry, they wove a blanket and placed it in front of the woman of their choice. A woman accepted by wrapping the blanket around herself, thereby becoming a wife.

This was the world that Spanish conquistador Francisco Vasquez de Coronado stumbled upon when he arrived in the autumn of 1540 at the pueblo of Kuaua, 17 miles (77 km) north of present-day Albuquerque. (The Spanish referred to the pueblo as Alcanfor.) He was looking for a place to winter his entourage of 336 soldiers, 100 Indians, and slaves from Mexico, and thousands of horses and mules. During the two winters and one summer he based himself at the pueblo, Coronado searched tirelessly for gold around the state and as far north as Kansas. In 1542, he returned empty-handed to the city of Mexico in the Spanish colony of New Spain.

Despite a few subsequent Spanish expeditions into New Mexico and a settlement in Santa Fe to the north, the area around Albuquerque remained largely free of European influence until the last years of the sixteenth century. By that time the Pueblo Indians (if not the Apaches) were more or less subdued, and with increasing numbers of Spanish settlers arriving in the New World to seek their fortune, the Spanish crown began issuing land grants at the far northern perimeter of its empire.

Typically, a land grant was a small plot near a water supply. On it, settlers built a rustic home and grew corn, wheat, beans, chile, and fruits. They cultivated cotton for cloth and sewed their own clothes. Cattle and sheep were grazed on *ejidos*—larger parcels of common land shared by grant recipients. If life was grueling and very basic, the Spaniards believed they were investing in a provident future: then, as today, land represented freedom and independence.

These individuals were a hardy lot. Women helped with planting, spent long hours grinding corn on well-worn *metates,* fashioned their own brooms from meadow grass, and of course bore and raised many children. Men braved blinding windstorms and cold winters to herd their cattle and sheep, and felled tall ponderosa pine trees to fabricate furniture. Because metal was scarce, they designed wooden plows, hoes, and shovels. They also built the only vehicles used in the state during the 1700s and early 1800s—two-wheeled, wooden, oxen-drawn carts known as *carretas.*

The entire family worked in the fields, breaking the soil, planting seeds, pulling weeds, and harvesting crops. The men dug and maintained irrigation ditches called *acequias.* Transferring water from the Rio Grande to fields in the Albuquerque area, these *acequias* were so wide that small bridges were built across them. Homes were constructed of five-inch- (13-cm-) thick, handmade, adobe bricks that weighed 50 pounds (23 kg) each. For insulation, thick mud was plastered in between the bricks. At the more isolated ranchos, often targeted by Apache attacks, defensive *torreons* were built—round, rock-walled towers equipped with a few small windows.

In 1706, Francisco Cuervo y Valdes, provisional governor of New Mexico, moved 30 families from the trading center of Bernalillo (where a number of haciendas flourished adjacent to Kuaua) to a spot 17 miles (27 km) south in the middle Rio Grande Valley, which boasted steady water, good soil, grassland, and timber. To flatter the Duke of Alburquerque, then viceroy of New Spain, Valdes named the new community after him, and it later became known as the "Duke City." (The additional "r" was later dropped.) Settlers cleared the land, cut the timber, and baked bricks, building their squat mud houses and small adobe church around a central plaza, today known as Old Town. Ten soldiers were assigned to protect the new villa from Indian attacks. No walls or fortification were constructed at the new settlement of Albuquerque, but as Indian raids increased homes were built closer together and closer to the plaza. Some original family *ranchos* today have been incorporated into the city as neighborhoods, such as Duranes, Los Poblanos, and Los Griegos.

These early residences weren't much to look at, but their adobe construction provided natural insulation: warmth in the winter and relief from a glaring summer sun. By day, they looked dreary. But in the evening, when the sun sank below the West Mesa, a rosy-red and golden glow that bathed the nearby mountains also fell across the townsite, giving it the appearance, albeit fleeting, of a prosperous village.

ARRIVAL OF THE RAILROAD

The town of Albuquerque remained huddled for protection around its plaza for more than 170 years—until the arrival in April 1880 of the Santa Fe Railroad. Built across the desert two miles (3 km) east of the original villa, the railroad soon sprouted a second settlement—New Albuquerque—which rose up along the tracks. Because many of the new residents came from east of the Mississippi River, their homes reflected the Victorian architecture of the Midwest—gabled wooden houses. These two-story, pitched-roof homes were far less amenable to life in the desert than those of naturally insulating adobe bricks built low to the ground.

This period also brought to Albuquerque its first African-American residents, who came to work for the Santa Fe Railroad. Today, their South Broadway

San Felipe de Neri church, Albuquerque.

neighborhood remains a center of black cultural life, and its public library branch serves as the city's media center for Black Studies.

With the arrival of the railroad, Albuquerque's population skyrocketed and so did its vitality. The city's first entrepreneur was Peter "Shorty" Parker who opened a saloon by staking out space in a vacant lot and erecting a bar that consisted of a board placed across two upended barrels. Soon 14 new saloons (with roofs) and gambling houses sprang up between First and Third streets on Railroad (now Central) Avenue. Men stood along the wooden bars, paying 15 cents for a shot of whiskey. Respectable women listened from afar to songs played on a honky-tonk piano or accordion. The White Elephant, whose solid mahogany bar could accommodate 50 men at one time and whose glassware was imported from Belgium, served the town nabobs. One block away, the no-frills Bucket of Blood catered to the railroad workers; when a man drank away his paycheck during the weekend, owners John and Mary Boyle made sure he was sobered up in time to report to work on Monday morning. Another of these early taverns, the Silver Dollar, embedded its namesake in the floor.

Street fights, murders, and hangings were commonplace, as were stories like this one: In 1881 someone fired a shot into the air at the same time a railroad carpenter by the name of Charles Campbell was crossing First Street. A bystander said it was the carpenter who fired the shot, so the town's marshal, Milt Yarberry, and his friend, Monte Frank Boyd, pumped 12 bullets into Campbell to teach him a lesson. Two years later, Marshal Yarberry was hanged for murder in front of 100 people, some of whom had paid $1 to witness the event. One newspaper related that the marshal had been "Jerked to Jesus."

The era's showpiece was the Huning Castle, with its five-foot-thick (1.5-m) wood-veneered sod walls dug from a nearby meadow. A flat roof trimmed with ornamental grille work and a tower decorated with balconies gave the two-story home the feeling of a castle, which is what owner Franz Huning called it. Huning, one of Albuquerque's prominent Anglo merchants, was a German immigrant. (By 1955, the architectural novelty was considered an embarrassment by its neighbors and was torn down.)

Along with the debauchery brought by the railroad came education, first in the form of public schools in 1884, followed by parochial schools the next year. In 1889, the University of New Mexico was founded a mile (1.6 km) east of the railroad tracks on a sandy yucca-filled tableland. The university's third president,

William Tight, was responsible for transforming the desert into a shady oasis. He transplanted hundreds of trees and native plants from nearby mountains, dug a well so they could be watered, and imported squirrels from his previous home in Ohio. Presumably, it is the descendants of these squirrels who still romp among the trees today.

President Tight was so impressed by the surviving Pueblo Indian culture that he envisioned a campus that would reflect the Indians' unique architecture. He quickly saw to the construction of flat-roofed adobe buildings with portals and *vigas*, and went so far as to remove the gables and to plaster adobe over Victorian-style Hodgin Hall. Soon, public outcry over Tight's attachment to "primitive" architecture grew so loud that he was removed from office. (In later years, however, Tight's vision was resurrected and much is seen today in the work of famed Santa Fe architect John Gaw Meem, a major proponent of the Spanish-Pueblo style. As university architect for 25 years, Meem designed many of the campus' finest examples of that style, including Zimmerman Library and Scholes Hall.)

By the turn of the century, the high desert city of Albuquerque was becoming a haven for tuberculosis patients. Seventeen tuberculosis centers were built, including Lovelace Clinic, founded by tuberculosis patient William Randolph Lovelace. Today it is a full-service medical facility involved in state-of-the-art medical research.

In 1926, Route 66, the much ballyhooed national highway that linked Chicago with the West Coast, passed through Albuquerque's central business district. As a result, Central Avenue blossomed with a highway culture of tourist courts, diners, and storefronts. Many of these establishments retain a down-home ambiance in hospitality and architecture, as well as dazzling vintage neon signs.

In 1939, up-and-coming financier Conrad Hilton turned his attention to his home state. A native of San Antonio, a rural hamlet 86 miles (138 km) south of Albuquerque, Hilton was convinced Albuquerque was destined for growth and designated the downtown lot of the former Trimble Livery Stable as the site for his next project. He set about building a 10-story Hilton Hotel, with an airy two-story lobby accented with carved corbels, a Mexican tiled floor, and white-washed arches. In 1942, Hilton married Georgia Gabor (later known as Zsa Zsa Gabor) in Santa Fe, and they spent a few nights at the Albuquerque Hilton. The hotel escaped the ravages of 1960s urban renewal and was restored in the 1980s. Today, no longer a Hilton, it operates as La Posada de Albuquerque.

(above) Original Victorian-style Hodgin Hall at the University of New Mexico, and Hodgin Hall redone in the Pueblo Revival style (below). (Albuquerque Museum)

MILITARY AND AVIATION HISTORY

Nothing better suits an airplane pilot than clear sky, and since Albuquerque enjoys an abundance of it, the United States Army Air Corps designated the city as a service station for military planes in 1940. The following year, as the U.S. seemed about to become embroiled in World War II, the Air Corps Advance Flying School was established on land adjacent to the municipal airport. This school was expanded, and in 1942 became Kirtland Field, a major defense installation.

You can catch a glimpse of **Kirtland Air Force Base** if you drive to the **National Atomic Museum** set inside its borders. This museum traces the history of the top-secret Manhattan Project, centered in the isolated mountain hideaway of Los Alamos. On display is a copy of a letter written by Albert Einstein to President Franklin D. Roosevelt encouraging him to develop the atomic bomb.

At the end of World War II (but paradoxically the beginning of the Cold War), the nuclear research begun at nearby Los Alamos continued unabated, and expanded to Sandia National Laboratories, created during the war for munitions development. Together, Kirtland Air Force Base and the labs are Albuquerque's largest employers, with more than 18,000 workers between them. Among their employees are some of the world's foremost experts in the science of destruction, as well as in those aspects of high technology that may significantly enhance life. At Sandia, scientists have developed a method of using concentrated sunlight to destroy pollutants in water. A trough of parabolic mirrors focuses ultraviolet radiation onto a long glass tube, through which contaminated water and titanium dioxide flow. The radiation reacts with the titanium, which in turn breaks down hazardous dyes and solvents into environmentally safe components.

BALLOONING

Another aspect of flight that has captured the imagination of Albuquerqueans is hot-air ballooning. In the early 1970s, pioneer baloonists Sid Cutter, Maxie Anderson, and Ben Abruzzo first fired up propane burners and injected heat into 60-foot-high (18-m) nylon balloons attached to wicker baskets. Soon they were gracefully lifted upward, flying thousands of feet above a silent panorama of the desert. In 1972, Cutter established the **Albuquerque International Balloon Fiesta**, which today is one of the largest balloon gatherings in the world, attracting up to 500 balloons for 10 days every October.

The Albuquerque Balloon Fiesta is the largest such event to take place annually in the U.S. (Jack Olson)

Anderson and Abruzzo, meanwhile, chose adventure. The two pilots, along with Larry Newman of Phoenix, Arizona, won worldwide fame in 1978 when they completed the first trans-Atlantic helium balloon flight. By using helium instead of propane, they were able to fly at higher elevations and for longer periods. Abruzzo and Anderson also participated in the first trans-Pacific helium balloon flight. Both Anderson and Abruzzo died in flight accidents: Anderson at a 1983 West German balloon race and Abruzzo in a private plane crash two years later.

■ SIGHTS AND ATTRACTIONS

OLD TOWN

Old Town offers a refuge from the encroaching monotony of Albuquerque's modern-day malls and suburbs. All it takes is a few steps inside to become immersed in the flavor of the past. A well-used, jet-black stagecoach carries you through the narrow streets of the city's original townsite, passing by adobe buildings that have been whitewashed or tinted in colors from beige to chocolate-brown. Wooden doorways and windowsills are livelier—painted in magenta, turquoise, and navy blue. The original **San Felipe de Neri Church** was begun in 1706, but disentegrated after years of weathering and neglect. Its replacement (1793) is impeccably cared for. Outside, its flower beds are tidy and bright; inside, a pressed-tin ceiling rises above wooden arches and dark wooden paneling and pews. No stained glass graces San Felipe's windows, but flickering lights from votive candles reflect an atmosphere of reverence.

San Felipe Church overlooks a central plaza, once a dirt-covered square well known to settlers and adventurers, and soldiers preparing to fight the Indians. Later, Confederate and Union armies alternated possession of the outpost, and today two Civil War cannons still sit in the plaza. A whitewashed wooden and cement gazebo now serves as a bandstand for musicians and dancers, and tall, broad-leafed cottonwood trees provide welcome shade for picnickers and shoppers resting on wrought-iron benches.

All of the original homesites that face the plaza have been transformed into shops, galleries, and restaurants. An example is La Placita Dining Rooms, originally built in 1706 as the Armijo family home. Today the smell of hot *sopaipillas* (deep-fried bread dough) and tortillas frying in oil wafts from the old home, whose rooms meander throughout the restaurant. Out front, local artisans line the brick sidewalk with blankets upon which they display handmade jewelry and weavings.

Away from the plaza, narrow backstreets weave among adobe buildings nearly 300 years old. If time is limited and you want to know where to find authentic Navajo rugs, Acoma pottery, and hot-air-balloon cookie cutters, pick up a map at the visitor center at the northwest corner of the plaza. But if you already have been bitten by the mañana bug and aren't in a hurry, stroll among the 160 shops, restaurants, and galleries. Find out for yourself which shop sells jalapeño jelly beans, green and red chile pasta, tortilla-shaped potholders, and the finest Chinese-made bow-and-arrow sets. Some stores have remodeled, carpeted interiors, while others retain solid oak display cases and creaky wooden floors. Just about every clerk will ask where you're from.

If you happen to be wandering the streets on Sunday afternoon, you might suddenly find yourself diving for cover when gunshots ring out, signifying the beginning of the weekly Romero Street fight. Gunslingers wrangle over women and money, and before long prone bodies are spread around the street. Then everyone gets up and walks away.

While Old Town receives most of its visitors during the warm summer months, those willing to brave the brisk temperatures of a chill Christmas Eve will find the neighborhood transformed into a world of shimmering light. On that evening, in traditional Hispanic style, Old Town's citizens set out more than 500,000 *farolitos* (votive candles placed in a handful of dirt in a small brown paper bag). These are set along sidewalks, adobe walls, and rooftops as a sign of rejoicing and festivity. Some people say the twinkling brilliance symbolizes illuminating the way for Mary and Joseph when they were in search of a bed for the night.

MUSEUMS AND GALLERIES

Albuquerque's museums reflect the region's unique heritage and rich history, natural or not. Leading the way in innovation is the **New Mexico Museum of Natural History,** which opened in 1986 at the northern edge of Old Town. At the front door, Spike the *Pentaceratops* and Alberta the *Albertosaurus* stand guard. Inside, a *Quetzalcoatlus* soars over a *Camarasaurus,* an *Allosaurus,* and a life-size model of *Coelophysis*—the New Mexico state fossil, so small you can look him straight in the eye. If some exhibits resemble those found at Disneyland, that's not surprising because many were designed by Disney artists.

A walk through 4.6 billion years of New Mexico's geologically tumultuous past immerses you in a tropical seacoast environment complete with sharks and sea anemones, takes you inside an active volcano, and leads you through the grassy plains of eastern New Mexico 12,000 years ago when primitive hunters roamed the region. An "evolator," which suspiciously resembles an elevator, whisks you through 38 million years in time.

Just across the street from the Natural History Museum, you will find the **Albuquerque Museum of Art, History, and Science,** which should be a stop on your tour. Documenting 400 years of the state's history, the huge museum offers a wealth of artifactual information on the culture of the Spanish settlers. Don't miss the revolving *Así Es la Vida* (This is Life) exhibit, featuring the work of local grammar and high school students, or the museum's theater, which regularly shows films on Albuquerque's history.

For an inside look into the Southwest's native cultures, the **Maxwell Museum of Anthropology,** located on the university campus, invites you to walk through four million years of human evolution. You'll see a life-size (3-foot 7-inch, or 1-m) reconstruction of your average three-million-year-old woman. In a glass case facing her, primate jawbones (complete with teeth), start with a chimpanzee and progress to modern man. The artwork of our more recent ancestors is reproduced in a cave whose walls are decorated with horses, bison, and wolves painted red and black and resembling those found at Lascaux, France. A new two-story gallery shows off items from the museum's permanent collection of Mimbres and Pueblo pottery, Navajo weavings and textiles, American Indian basketry, *kachina* dolls, and jewelry. And you can try your skill at grinding corn the Indian way by using a *mano* (hand stone) in a *metate* (stone bowl).

The **Spanish History Museum** is tucked into a storefront space at Lead Avenue near Harvard, SE. A result of the vision of the museum's founder, Elmer Martinez, its two rooms house photos and relics of Hispanic history from the time of Christopher Columbus to the present day. Photos and short biographies of early Spanish dignitaries, sheriffs, and lawmen line a wall. The stern, serious, and confident faces of the early twentieth-century Hispanic signers of the New Mexico Constitution gaze out from photographs that hang nearby. Of special interest is Martinez's own research into Spanish coats of arms. Having traced the 250 families that came to New Mexico with Juan de Oñate in 1598, he sells their brightly painted family crests, as well as a history of these coats of arms.

An inside look at the creative, social, and historical aspects of New Mexico's Pueblo Indians can be found at the **Indian Pueblo Cultural Center,** at the corner of 12th Street and Indian School Road. The two-story center is operated by the All-Indian Pueblo Council, a coalition of the governors of the state's 19 pueblos. Most weekends and holidays Indians wear traditional dress and dance to the gentle, rhythmic beat of animal-skin drums in a central courtyard. Its walls are covered with murals of eagle and buffalo dancers and of horses roaming atop mesas.

Don't miss the museum in the center's lower level, with its exhibits on Native languages and lifestyles. For example, in the warm months, men and children wore little except for sandals woven from yucca fibers, and women wore a miniskirt made of string. In the winter, they all donned soft robes of tanned deerskin or rabbit fur. Men kept their hair long, but women cut theirs to make cords and ropes. Also of interest are instructions on how to bake bread in a *horno* and a video in which famed San Ildefonso Pueblo potter Maria Martinez demonstrates, step-by-step, the process by which she achieved her distinct black-on-black glaze. Each pueblo has its own display case. Sandia Pueblo exhibits its red clay pots and buckskin moccasins; San Felipe its Heishi necklaces made from semi-precious and precious stones; and Isleta its clay storyteller sculptures.

Upstairs, Indian pottery, jewelry, and rugs are for sale, and a restaurant serves a selection of Indian cuisine, from frybread to tamales.

Across from the University, behind an ordinary storefront at 108 Cornell, SE, the **Tamarind Lithography Institute and Gallery** offers a two-year course in lithography. Since its founding in 1970, some of the world's foremost modern artists, including John Cage, Sam Francis, Jasper Johns, Robert Motherwell, Frank Stella, Claes Oldenburg, and Roy Lichtenstein, have processed prints of their work here. Tours are offered the first Friday of every month.

PARKS

Albuquerque has grown out instead of up, and now encompasses 125 square miles (324 sq km) of high desert. More than 145 city parks help break up the urban sprawl. The finest of them is **Rio Grande Zoological Park,** set in a grove of ancient cottonwood trees about a mile (1.6 km) south of downtown. More than 1,200 exotic animals from around the world live within the zoo's walls: a snow-white polar bear splashes in a giant pool that only he can make appear small, and a black-spotted cheetah wanders through sandstone cliffs and outcroppings. In the reptile house, iguanas, skinks, and crocodiles enjoy their own natural environment thanks to special controls that vary each species' temperature and seasonal day-length changes. Zoo personnel also are active in the preservation of many endangered species, such as the Mexican gray wolf and the pink pigeon. When a recent drought drew scores of hungry and thirsty black bears from the mountains to the city, animal control officers shot them with tranquilizers, then returned them home. One mother was injured during her capture, so zoo personnel provided a home for her and her cub to recuperate for a winter. The following spring they were dutifully delivered back to the mountains.

At **Rio Grande Nature Center** on Candelaria Road near Rio Grande Boulevard, two miles (3 km) of trails along the river lead through a riparian environment or *bosque* (woodlands) that attract pheasants, roadrunners, toads, beavers, and skunks. The visitor center is built partially underground, and the unobtrusive design enables visitors to watch bird life both above and below the surface of a three-acre pond. During the migration months of May and October, Canada and snow geese, sandhill cranes, and an occasional whooping crane stop at the center to rest. Free guided walks along the park's trails are conducted every weekend.

Across the river on the West Mesa, along a boulder-strewn volcanic escarpment beneath the five Sleeping Sisters, are at least 15,000 **petroglyphs,** which date as far back as A.D. 1300. A walk among the craggy boulders takes you past drawings of long-legged birds, animated dancers, snakes, and shields etched in dark basalt. Standing in front of any one of them, it's hard not to wonder about the world of these artists. What were they thinking and what were they trying to say? Most scholars agree the designs were symbolic and not meant to represent actual events. "It is not a language. You can't read them," says Polly Schaafsma, author of *Indian Rock Art of the Southwest.* "They are a graphic expression of ideas from their world, how they describe and define their world and how they put value on it." For years **Petroglyph State Park** preserved a fraction of the figures. But in 1990, **Petroglyph National Monument,** the nation's first designated site for the protection of prehistoric rock art, was established. The 17-mile-long (27-km) glimpse into the creative world of early Indian inhabitants won't be fully opened until the mid-1990s. In the meantime, it protects at least some of this ancient art from the encroachment of housing developments.

RESTAURANTS

At most Albuquerque restaurants, food still spills over the edges of the plates because Albuquerqueans are cowboys at heart who expect to get their money's worth. Lately, too, creativity is creeping into the city's cooking. At **Restaurant Andre,** New Mexico's indigenous green chile is stuffed inside a chicken breast along with monterey jack cheese. You'll also find chiles in the corn bread at **Casa Chaco,** in the pasta at **Mama Mia's,** and available as a topping at every pizza parlor in town. Piñon nuts are found in ice cream, tarts, and muffins; at **Scalo Northern Italian Grill,** it's not just European pine nuts that grace pasta dishes, but local pine or piñon nuts as well.

Ethnic restaurants have taken this frontier town into the international mainstream. Come to Albuquerque now and you can enjoy Thai, East Indian, Vietnamese, and Mediterranean cooking. But Albuquerque hasn't forgotten how to make New Mexican food. At **Sadie's,** located in the North Valley, try guaco-chicken tacos or a meat-bean burrito à la carte. (Finish a dinner plate and call a friend to roll you out the door in a wheelbarrow.) At **El Patio** on Harvard Drive across from the University, the green chile chicken enchilada plate is a favorite, and their honey-laden *sopaipillas* made with honey are tops. At the downtown **M & J Sanitary Tortilla Factory,** lines often extend out the door at lunchtime as students, lawyers, and artists vie for mismatched vinyl booths. The food is good, but the atmosphere is even better. The walls are covered with local artwork and letters of appreciation to Jake and Bea Montoya, the friendly owners who bustle about making sure you have enough fresh salsa and iced tea. When they're not too rushed, the Montoyas enjoy finding out all about their customers.

As for breakfast, Albuquerque finally has more to offer than cowboy coffee and a pot of mush at daybreak. Good, strong coffee is preferred, and you can find cappuccinos and croissants. If, after you've spent some time in New Mexico, you find yourself wanting chile first thing in the morning, try the breakfast burrito—a flour tortilla wrapped around scrambled eggs, bacon or *chorizo* (spicy sausage), cheese, home-fried potatoes, and chile. More cheese and chile are poured on top. You won't have to eat the rest of the day.

For more specific information, see "Restaurants" in "PRACTICAL INFORMATION."

CHILE V. CHILI

In New Mexico, when folks believe in something, you'd best believe it, too.

Take, for example, the spelling of 'chile.' A small matter, you might say, but not for New Mexicans, who refuse to accept the way the rest of the country spells it—'chili.' Chile, the Spanish spelling, is found on menus, in stores, and in newspapers throughout the state.

New Mexicans are so adamant about the spelling that in 1983, they directed their senior U.S. legislator, Senator Pete Domenici, to enter into the Congressional Record the state's stand on the spelling.

"New Mexicans consume mass quantities of this magical and lifegiving fruit from birth, and labels on chile products, descriptions of dishes at New Mexican restaurants and billboards and advertisements all reinforce the fact that chile is spelled with an 'e' and not an 'i.' A naiveté exists among native New Mexicans who wrongly assume that everyone spells it with an 'e.'

"Even the dictionary makes the error, stating that chili is defined as the pod of any species of capsicum, especially *Capsicum frutescens*. Chili is the preferred spelling and chile is only mentioned as an alternate spelling. Knowing that criticizing the dictionary is akin to criticizing the Bible, I nevertheless stand here before the full Senate and with the backing of my New Mexico constituents state unequivocally that the dictionary is wrong.

"Native New Mexicans are extremely sensitive about this spelling, for the *Capsicum frutescens*, commonly known as green chile, and when dried in the autumn sun in great strings called *ristras*, becoming red chile, is New Mexico's most famous agricultural product. Though the chile can be grown in other parts of the country, it is known worldwide that the New Mexico soil produces a chile pod with a mouth-watering flavor that none can even brag about coming close to.

"New Mexicans know that 'chili' is the inedible mixture of watery tomato soup, dried gristle, half-cooked kidney beans, and a myriad of silly ingredients that is passed off as food in Texas and Oklahoma. The different tabascos and jalapeño sauces added to the mixture do little good and in most cases simply cause a casual visitor to suffer great gastrointestinal distress.

"Contrast this to New Mexico, where ordering a bowl of chile is a delightful experience. Hospitable as we are to all visitors, we have chile that is mild enough to make a baby coo in delight, or hot enough to make even the strongest constitutions perspire in a sensual experience of both pleasure and pain.

"I could go on and on about the wonders of red and green chile, but in reality, all I wanted to do was inform Congress on the correct way to spell the word."

Ristra *of chiles (chilis).*

NIGHTLIFE

Albuquerque's nightclub circuit runs the gamut of musical tastes: there's rock and roll, rhythm and blues, Latin, acoustic, piano bars, and, of course, country and western. Most of the country bars offer free dance lessons on weeknights, and you'll see men with their names engraved into their leather belts and women in full skirts heading toward them, determined to learn the two-step, polka, waltz, jitterbug, and cotton-eyed joe.

The Nob Hill shopping district is nothing more than that by day, but by evening it's lively. Restaurants with outdoor seating fill up with patrons, and coffeehouses featuring exotic java and desserts are abuzz with conversation. Window shopping is a great way to walk off the food.

Other evening events include stand-up comedy clubs in **Northeast Heights,** and amateur plays at the **Vortex Theatre** on Central near the University and at the **Albuquerque Little Theater** near Old Town. The University, with a student population exceeding 28,000, brings in Broadway plays and international speakers. In addition, at the KiMo Theater (following), you can see something different almost every night of the week

KiMo THEATRE

Electric eyes beam from garlanded horned buffalo skulls, installed as sconce lights. Plaster-of-Paris Indian shields grace inside and outside walls. Wrought-iron balusters resemble stylized waterfowl on stairways leading to the balcony. Plastered ceiling beams are textured to look like wooden *vigas* and decorated with painted thunderbirds, butterflies, and geometrical designs. Chandeliers are shaped like war drums, and air vents are disguised as Navajo rugs. Everywhere you turn are visions only described by an exotic vocabulary.

This is the KiMo Theatre (the name means "Mountain Lion" in one Pueblo dialect). It reflects the vision of Oreste Bachechi, an Italian-American immigrant who sought to honor the community that had made him a successful liquor and grocery dealer. Desiring to build a premier motion picture palace he hired Hollywood architect Carl Boller to create a theater that would combine the traditions, arts, and culture of New Mexico and the American Indian. Boller traveled extensively throughout the state, visiting Acoma and Isleta pueblos, and the Navajo Reservation. Back in Albuquerque, he fused traditional Indian designs with Spanish mission styles and certain flamboyant motifs of the day into a new—but short-lived—architectural style called Pueblo Deco. He took months choosing colors, and making sure Native American interpretations were properly represented in minute detail. For example, red portrays the life-giving sun, white the approaching morning, yellow the setting sun of the west, and black the darkening clouds from the north.

Bachechi paid $150,000 to build the magnificent theater, which opened in 1927. He spent an additional $18,000 for the elaborate Wurlitzer organ, which was played by Frances Farney during each silent film showing.

The KiMo also served as a major stepping stone for local talent. Albuquerque resident Vivian Vance, who gained fame as Ethel Mertz of the "I Love Lucy" television series, worked at the theater. Other Hollywood stars to grace its stage were Sally Rand, Gloria Swanson, Tom Mix, and Ginger Rogers.

Through the years, the KiMo has been altered several times to keep up with current theater trends. By 1968, it closed as a movie house. During the next decade, it served as offices for Commonwealth Theatres and occasionally hosted local performing arts groups. The city purchased the theater and reopened it in 1977 as a public performing space. Interior renovation has been slow, with voters consistently rejecting bond issues. In 1989, a non-profit group organized to help preserve the historical theater provided financial assistance to restore the murals, including those in the lobby ceiling painted by Albuquerque artist Carl von Hassler. One of the larger ones, however, had been destroyed.

Today, the theater is open almost every night for performances that range from regional professional productions to traveling shows of all kinds, from Ballet Folklorico to tap dance revues.

SANDIA PEAK

In just 18 minutes, one of two cars at the **Sandia Peak Aerial Tramway** whisks passengers through four of Earth's seven life zones, rising nearly 4,000 feet (1,200 m) to the top of the mountain known as Sandia Crest. On its silent 2.7-mile (4.3-km) journey, the tram quickly leaves behind clusters of cholla cactus and ascends above jagged granite outcroppings until it reaches the windy pine-covered summit of the Sandia Mountains. From the top, the city and surrounding desert stretch to the horizon, sliced by the greenbelt of the Rio Grande. Hikers and backpackers can set off along forested trails to enjoy cool relief in the summer. In the winter, skiers glide along cross-country trails or schuss the groomed slopes of **Sandia Peak Ski Area,** carved from the forest on the mountain's eastern flank. During summer and fall, one of the ski area's chairlifts carries sightseers over grassy slopes. Deer and

rabbits dart for cover in nearby stands of pines. This ride is especially enjoyable in the fall when the aspen's green leaves turn golden and shimmer in the sunlight. Dusk is the most dramatic time to be atop the 10,600-foot (3,200-m) peak. When the sun disappears behind the West Mesa, it casts a rosy glow across the city, followed by the gradual birth of a man-made sea of twinkling lights.

At the summit of Sandia Peak, the High Finance Restaurant serves steaks and hot chocolate, and provides luxurious shelter from gusty winds that often buffet the mountaintop. A one-mile (1.6-km) trail along the edge of the ridge leads to Sandia Crest House, a small gift shop and snack bar. Sandia Peak Aerial Tramway operates daily from 9 A.M. to 10 P.M.

(opposite) Art deco detail of facade of the KiMo Theatre, Albuquerque.

HARVEY GIRLS

When the railroad snaked its way into New Mexico in the late 1800s, connecting the southwestern frontier with the eastern United States, little thought was given to the comfort of the passengers who would be riding the iron horse. Towns, if you can call them that, consisted of a few canvas tents and flimsy wooden shacks, one designated as the depot. Another wooden shack served as a very basic dining hall for train passengers. Inside, they ate greasy meat, canned beans, rancid bacon, and eggs preserved in lime and shipped from the East Coast. Worst of all, passengers had 20 minutes to gulp down this unsavory repast before they reboarded, resuming a jolting journey at 20 mph (32 kmph) across the dusty desert. To avoid this unpleasant eating ritual, seasoned travelers either headed for a saloon, which was amply supplied and more comfortable than the dining shack, or they brought along apples, bread, and cheese, hoping it would last throughout their trip. Often, it didn't. This mediocrity failed to concern railroad executives, but one young entrepreneur knew customers deserved better and would pay for food they could digest.

Fred Harvey was born in London. After emigrating to New York City at 15, he spent years working in restaurants. He knew the value of quality food and service and he was convinced a network of classy restaurants along a rail line was not just a good idea, but a great one. In 1878, he talked officials at the Atchison, Topeka and Santa Fe Railway into giving him a shot. That was all he needed, for Harvey and his Harvey Houses brought a refinement to the Santa Fe Railroad unsurpassed by other rail lines.

In New Mexico, 16 Harvey Houses graced the tracks. Usually they were two-story brick buildings with dining rooms on the main floor and staff living quarters upstairs. Situated in isolated communities such as Clovis, Deming, Belen, Vaughn, and Raton, these welcome whistlestops also served as social centers for area residents. In addition, five of the railroad's showpiece hotels lined the tracks in New Mexico: the Montezuma and Castañeda in Las Vegas, La Fonda in Santa Fe, the Alvarado in Albuquerque, and El Navajo in Gallup. (The Alvarado and El Navajo have since been demolished.)

Unlike the Spanish or Mission Revival style of most of the Harvey Houses, El Navajo opened in 1923 as a tribute to the American Indian. Furniture was upholstered in Navajo weaving designs, and Navajo sand paintings adorned walls of the elegant restaurant and hotel.

Many of the women who worked for the chain received their training at El Navajo. Midwesterners between the ages of 18 and 30, most from poor families, left Missouri towns and Kansas farms and headed West, not so much for the adventure, as for the much-needed job. Although their duties were strictly to serve customers, these women never were referred to as waitresses. They were known proudly as Harvey Girls. Immaculately attired, they served a four-course meal in less than 30 minutes, usually three times a day, to rail passengers.

Rules were rigid: no makeup, no jewelry, hair pulled away from the face atop the head. They wore starched black-and-white skirts, white aprons, high-collared shirts, black shoes and stockings, and hairnets. Introduced in 1883, this uniform changed little during the next 50 years. If they spilled anything on their precisely pressed uniforms, no matter how small a spot it left, they were instructed to change into a fresh outfit. And they were forbidden to marry while under contract with Fred Harvey.

No matter where they were sent—the windswept plains of Vaughn, the heart of Indian country at Gallup, or the bustling state capital of Santa Fe—most of the women loved the West. Many married rail workers or fellow Harvey House employees and raised families in their adopted towns.

ALBUQUERQUE ENVIRONS

IN THE IMMEDIATE AREA AROUND RAPIDLY EXPANDING ALBUQUERQUE lie ancient Indian pueblos, the site of explorer Coronado's first winter encampment in New Mexico, lovely countryside, and the Turquoise Trail. All are worth a day or two of pleasurable meandering.

■ TO BERNALILLO

The sleepy village of **Alameda,** north of Albuquerque on Fourth Street, was once a Tiwa Pueblo. After the 1680 Pueblo Revolt, the pueblo was abandoned for 15 years, at which time a small group of Spanish colonists moved in. Today, an adobe church fronts the street, along with copper-brown homes and businesses. North of Alameda, the street becomes NM 313 (old US 85) and slices through the Sandia Indian Reservation, paralleling railroad tracks and irrigation ditches. Fifteen miles (24 km) north of Albuquerque is **Bernalillo,** one of the oldest European towns in the United States.

Ceremonial kiva, Bandelier National Monument.

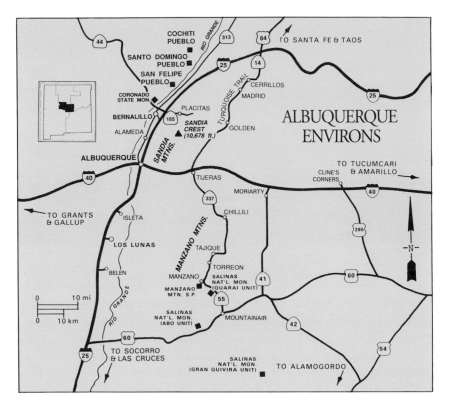

Before Francisco Vasquez de Coronado wintered just north of Bernalillo at the Kuaua Pueblo in 1540, the area was home to Tiwa Indians who had drifted down from Chaco Canyon around A.D. 1300. At the 1,200-room pueblo built along the banks of the moody Rio Grande, which flows muddy in the spring and deep-green in the winter, these Indians grew beans, squash, and corn. Women gathered in a special building to grind corn by rhythmically moving a small stone (*mano*) across a rectangular stone trough (*metate.*) Once the corn was made into meal, they pounded it into flat bread, a staple of their diet. While they worked, a man would sit at the door, playing a flute carved from an eagle bone, as the women sang to his music.

These people built several underground ceremonial *kivas*, which they entered by ladder through an opening in the roof. On the walls of one *kiva* they painted

*Corn Dance photographed by Nathan Kendall in 1913 at
Santo Domingo Pueblo. (Museum of New Mexico)*

black fish, masked kachinas dressed in yellow shirts with black skirts and white sashes, white rabbits, white clouds, seed and corn, and white-tipped red arrows. Near the end of the seventeenth century, the Indians abandoned the pueblo, probably moving south, and sands drifted over Kuaua's mud walls, burying it for the next 250 years.

When archaeologists excavated the pueblo in 1935, they discovered 85 layers of adobe plaster inside the *kiva*, 17 of which contained painted symbols of the Indians' complex relationship with the earth and the heavens. Some of these original murals are encased in glass inside the visitor center at **Coronado State Monument**, which was created in 1940 to preserve the pueblo ruins. Reproductions of the paintings line the walls of a reconstructed *kiva*, which you can enter by climbing down a solid wooden ladder into the cool subterranean interior.

Outside, tumbleweeds wedge themselves into corners of the crumbling rock walls of the pueblo. A trail winds among cholla cactus, four-wing saltbush, and clumps of grass alongside the low, eroding walls that divide the pueblo's rooms. In the distance, the craggy ridges of the pale-green Sandia Mountains loom against the eastern sky and, closer in, ducks float atop the gently flowing Rio Grande, which passes by rust-colored reeds and sweet-smelling Russian olive trees in front of the pueblo. Adjacent to the monument is Coronado State Park, a collection of picnic shelters and campsites set atop additional ruins, some older and some newer than Kuaua, and the charred remains of a Spanish *hacienda* that was burned during the Pueblo Revolt.

Even though Coronado was unimpressed with the fertile greenbelt of present-day Bernalillo, other Spaniards recognized its value and many made their homes along the river there in the late sixteenth century. Unlike most pioneers to the north who built simple homes and tended their own small farms or ranches, these upper-class Bernalillo colonists received large land grants. The Montoyas, Bacas, Castillos, and Pereas hired *paisanos* to tend the new crops they introduced to the region, such as grapes, Castillian wheat, plums, and peaches, and to look after their vast herds of cattle and sheep. The Gonzales-Bernal family owned the largest spread, and the town was named for them.

These *hacendados,* or wealthy land barons, lived in 40-room homes and protected their privacy by fencing their immaculately kept grounds with high adobe walls. Inside their houses were finely carved tables and tall cupboards that were hauled up from Mexico over the Chihuahua Trail. They ate with silver knives and forks, sometimes off of silver plates. Men trimmed their clothes with silver buttons, silk sashes, and silver buckles, and women adorned bright skirts with ribbons, silk, lace, and velvet. Their field workers, along with servants and their families, lived in Las Cocinitas (Little Kitchens)—a barrio of squat adobe houses whose ruins may be seen today at the south end of Bernalillo.

Diego de Vargas spent a night at the settlement during his reconquest of New Mexico after the Pueblo Revolt; three years later, in 1695, he founded Bernalillo. Nine years later, while on a campaign against Indians, he died there, probably from wounds received in a skirmish. From the beginning, Bernalillo flourished as a trading center where local hacienda owners exchanged vegetables, wool, and meat for iron tools, shoes, paper, and sugar from caravans heading north on the Chihuahua Trail.

In 1871, Nathan Bibo opened a branch of the Bernalillo Mercantile Company, which already had stores in the lumber town of Porter and the gold-mining settlement of Bland, along with trading posts near Acoma and Laguna pueblos. No item was too large or too unusual for Bibo to stock. He sold coffins, harnesses, overalls, tractors, Studebaker wagons, feathers, spittoons, loggers' hooks, blue cornmeal, and dolls. Customers could rent rooms at the "Merc" while they waited to have their wheat ground or to sell their sheep. Today, the refurbished building sells hardware and groceries.

SPANISH COLONIAL LIFE:
THE WEDDING FEAST

*A*t last all was ready, and the engaged youth and maiden, who though under the same roof since their betrothal had kept away from one another, now met again and before the altar in the evening, accompanied by their godparents. They were married in candlelight, with the handshaped earthen walls of their family about them, and a burden upon them of solemn commitment. Tensions broke when the vows were done. All gathered in the sala for the wedding feast. Now a river house had put forth another reach of growth and promise of the future, all in proper observance of ways that were as old as memory. In her white silk wedding dress the bride went on the arm of her husband in his rich silver-braided suit and his lace-ruffled shirt. Everyone came past to embrace them, and then the feast began. Roast chickens basted in spiced wine and stuffed with meat; piñons and raisins; baked hams; ribs of beef; fresh bread of blue meal; cookies, cakes, sweets; beakers of chocolate and flasks of wine; bowls of hot chile; platters of tortillas, all stood upon extra tables draped to the floor with lace curtains. All feasted.

Then came music, and dark eyes fired up. The sala was cleared, while the musicians tuned up on two or three violins, a guitar and a guitarron, or bass guitar. Servants came to spread clean wheat straw on the earth floor to keep dust from rising, or stood by with jars of water from which to sprinkle the floor between dances. In the candlelight the faces of the woman, heavily powdered with Mexican white lead, looked an ashen violet, in which their eyes were dark caves deeply harboring the ardent emotion of the occasion. The orchestra struck up . . .

While the dancing went on, the bride had an obligation to fulfill. Retiring from the floor in her wedding dress, she reappeared presently in another gown from her trousseau, and later in another, and another. Everyone was eager to see what she had been given. Politely and proudly she gratified them. They fingered her silks and examined the set of jewels given her by the groom—matching earrings, necklace, bracelets, combs, brooches, and gold inlaid with enamel, or seed pearls, rose diamonds, amethysts or garnets.

Before midnight the bride retired not to reappear. Her maiden friends and her godmother went with her. The groom drank with the men in whose company he now belonged, while boys watched and nudged. The dancing continued, and humor went around. The groom's father calling above the noise in the hot, hard-plastered room, urged everyone to keep right on enjoying themselves. Presently the groom managed to slip away. In the bridal chamber the ladies admitted him and left him with his bride. Across the patio the merriment continued. Voices were singing. Someone shouted a refrain. The violins jigged along in a remote monotonous sing, and the gulping throb of the guitarron was like a pulse of mindless life in the night.

—Paul Horgan, *Great River: the Rio Grande in North American History,* 1954

Bernalillo's decline began in 1878 when five well-tailored men disembarked from a stagecoach to meet with José Leandro Perea, the leading *patron* of the day. The men had selected the town as the site of the main offices and chief division point for the Atchison, Topeka & Santa Fe Railroad, which soon would wend its way into the region. Perea, however, saw no need for the noise and clutter the operation would bring. He over-priced plots requested by the rail line—charging $425 an acre for land that was worth maybe $3 an acre. The men returned to their coach and headed to Albuquerque, where the main offices were constructed, spurring the growth of what went on to become the state's largest city. Bernalillo received a red-painted frame depot, a railroad siding, and a grade crossing. As its southern neighbor grew, Bernalillo remained unchanged. Today, nearly all streets have Spanish names, and single-story, tin-roofed adobe homes are preserved at the north end of town. These are the work of Abenicio Salazar, a local carpenter who built hundreds of adobe buildings in the early 1900s.

Every summer, townsfolk spend many weekends and evenings rehearsing for the annual **Fiesta de San Lorenzo.** During the three-day event in August, they share great spreads of chile, tortillas, bread, and desserts, and some of them turn into actors and perform Los Matachines, a dance-drama traced to medieval Europe. The colorful dance reflects Spanish, Moorish, and Aztec influences and has probably been performed every year since the 1600s.

The story pits good against evil as Montezuma, last emperor of the Aztec Empire, is Christianized during the dance. La Malinche, a young girl dressed in white to emphasize her goodness, is said to be Doña Marina, an exiled Aztec princess who spoke both the Mayan and Aztec languages and served as interpreter and later mistress to Hernando Cortez. El Toro is the evil force, and some interpretations have him as Cortez. El Monarca, as the Montezuma figure is known, leads in dance other monarchs dressed like himself in brightly colored shawls draped over street clothes. Red, pink, yellow, and blue ribbons cascade down their backs. They wear tall headgear, known as *coronas,* decorated with silver belt buckles and jewelry, striped brocade, beads, and Christmas ornaments. In one hand these men carry a gourd rattle and in the other a three-pronged wooden ornament known as a *palma.* Plaintive strains from fiddles and guitars create a somber mood. Providing comic relief are the *abuelos* (grandfathers) who act as clowns and threaten the town's children with whips to keep them in line.

■ INTO THE SANDIAS

Across I-25 east of Bernalillo, NM 165 winds its way among gently rolling hillsides covered with bushy piñon pines and junipers, passing through the tiny village of **Placitas**. Once home to 21 families, recipients of the 1745 San Antonio de las Huertas Grant, Placitas is evolving from a rural, once-popular hippie haven into an up-scale subdivision of Albuquerque. Multi-level designer adobe homes with walls of windows, high *viga*-and-*latilla* ceilings, and indoor hot tubs have been built on spacious lots overlooking the Rio Grande Valley, the slate-blue Jemez Mountains rising to the west and the majestic Sandias a closer backdrop to the south.

Once past Placitas, NM 165 winds up the Sandia Mountains, following the tree-lined banks of Las Huertas Creek. The gravel road passes under tall pines, locust, and elder trees and alongside granite outcroppings covered with orange lichen. A turnout marks **Sandia Man Cave** where prehistoric spear points and scrapers were discovered in 1936 by Dr. Frank Hibben, then an anthropology student at the University of New Mexico. These tools were chipped by hunters who pursued bison and woolly mammoth throughout the middle Rio Grande Valley nearly 12,000 years ago. Known as Sandia Man, these early people were contemporaries

Heavy winter snowfall is common in the mountains of northern New Mexico.

of Clovis Man, another group of hunters who roamed southeastern New Mexico. It was through this cave's opening that small prehistoric hunters once came to seek protection and probably a place to eat their food in peace.

Today, an easy one-half mile (1 km) trail leads to the cave, but once there a concrete staircase followed by a 12-foot (4-m) spiral of metal steps scales the sheer rock face up to the opening. Inside, the narrow shaft has been sealed off to protect would-be explorers from getting stuck crawling on their bellies 300 feet (91 m) to its end.

The narrow road continues weaving its way up through scrub oaks, ponderosa pines, and aspen groves until joining NM 536, a paved road that scales the mountain's eastern flank. Because of deep snow and a scant shoulder, NM 165 is closed during winter months.

ANCIENT PUEBLOS

North of Bernalillo, NM 313 passes by the modern stuccoed homes of **Santa Ana Pueblo** before meeting up with I-25, which veers away from the Rio Grande as it

Kossa clowns play an important role in the Rice Corn Dance. These performed at San Juan Pueblo in 1935. (Museum of New Mexico)

heads north toward Santa Fe. Through this region, the river courses alongside three Keres-speaking pueblos: San Felipe, Santo Domingo, and Cochiti. While these pueblos share a language, each has its own dialect and is known for a special tradition: San Felipe for its Christmas Eve dances; Santo Domingo for its August 4th Corn Dance, and Cochiti for its pottery. San Felipe and Santo Domingo are both very traditional pueblos, forbidding cameras and tape recorders. Remember to ask permission at the governor's office before walking around the communities and striking up conversations with residents.

Though many of **Santo Domingo's** ceremonies are closed to the public, on August 4th visitors are welcome to view the elaborate Corn Dance. It begins in mid-morning when the comic Koshare appear painted in black and gray stripes to warn the pueblo of attackers who are on their way to the village. Having done that, the dancers pantomime the ensuing battle, in which the Indians defeat the invaders. A steady drumbeat announces the arrival of the singers, about 50 Pueblo men who slowly walk into the enormous dirt plaza, chanting rhythmically. As they arrange themselves along one side, a line of dancers, both male and female, enters

Corn dancers at San Ildefonso Pueblo. Notice headdresses worn by women in center of photograph. (Museum of New Mexico)

(following pages) More than 1,500 people once lived at Gran Quivira at Salinas Pueblo.

from the south after emerging from a *kiva* where they have huddled since early morning. This is the squash or pumpkin group, whose bodies are tinted in orange-tan colors. With measured steps, they move gracefully to the mesmerizing drum beat, shaking turtle and gourd rattles. This group moves out and is replaced by the turquoise group, dancers painted in blue who enter the plaza from the southeast. The men in both groups of dancers, which alternate their performances throughout the day, are dressed in kilts adorned with a foxtail at the waist and skunk skins and bells around each ankle. Women wear one-shouldered black dresses and colorfully painted stiff boards (*tablitas*) atop their heads. After a break for midday feasting on breads, pastries, chile, potato salad, and beans, the dancing continues until the sun sinks below the Jemez Mountains.

At **Cochiti Pueblo,** outsiders always are welcome to view the Church of San Buenaventura, its interior displaying tin candlesticks brought from Chihuahua and a larger-than-life painting of the patron saint that adorns the center wall above the altar. The pueblo also is recognized for its pottery, especially red-and-black "storyteller" dolls that depict little children crawling and clinging to an open-mouthed grandmother or grandfather figure.

Just north of Cochiti Pueblo's water tanks (painted to look like animal-skin drums), the Rio Grande backs up behind Cochiti Dam, creating a swimming hole and a haven for windsurfers. Don't bring a powerful motorboat in the hopes of waterskiing. Wakes behind boats are prohibited, leaving the waters to small sailboats and fishermen trolling for bass, crappie, and pike.

■ TURQUOISE TRAIL

Over a thousand years ago Pueblo Indians in the Cerrillos Hills south of Santa Fe were using stone hammers to mine for turquoise—highly prized for its beauty, as well as its purported ability to ensure good fortune and a long, healthy life. This stunning blue mineral found its way to Canada and Mexico where, according to legend, Montezuma II, the powerful Aztec emperor, proudly displayed his pendants and necklaces of Cerrillos turquoise.

Later miners coaxed gold, coal, silver, lead, and zinc from the Ortiz and San Pedro mountains that extend south to Tijeras Canyon, a passage that bisects the Sandia and Manzano mountains east of Albuquerque. Today NM 14 connects these long dormant mining districts, now called the Turquoise Trail.

Tall yellow-green grasses mix with an occasional cholla cactus as the two-lane road leaves behind the bedroom communities of Cedar Crest and Sandia Park, once rural oases from Albuquerque, which sprawl on the opposite flanks of the Sandia Mountains. The air is scented with juniper berries, and hills are dotted with piñons and junipers, a refreshing change from Albuquerque's gas stations, burger stands, and auto parts stores. The snowcapped peaks of the Sangre de Cristo Mountains appear behind corners as the road wends its way to **Golden,** once a bustling gold-mining district on the northern edge of the San Pedro Mountains.

A general store and gift shop sit on the highway along with a few homes constructed of adobe, rock, and galvanized iron. Piñons sprout from the ruins of rock homes that proliferated in the mid-1800s when the town was booming with 22 stores and 100 houses. Still, nobody got rich because there wasn't enough water to wash the gold dust from the sand.

Golden's most impressive building is a little mission church atop a hill at the northern edge of town. Built in the late 1830s soon after the gold rush began, the adobe church honored St. Francis of Assisi. A hand-carved and carefully detailed figure of the church's patron saint was displayed inside for more than 130 years, until it was moved to the cathedral in Santa Fe. The well-worn saint was brought by *carreta* from Mexico to Golden in the early 1700s. A newer St. Francis has replaced the original, along with two statues, one a five-foot (1.5-m) St. Peter. Services are conducted at the simple church twice a year—on June 29th for the Feast of St. Peter and October 4th for the Feast of St. Francis. To see the interior of the church, stop at La Casita, a gift shop at the north end of town and ask Beatrice for the key.

The slate-blue swell of the Sandia Mountains rises to the southwest, the ski runs of Sandia Peak Ski Area appearing from the distance like fairways divided by the deeper green pine trees. Pale-green lichen cover rock outcroppings as the road penetrates the Ortiz Mountains, then descends into the once-thriving coal mining district of **Madrid.** Charcoal-gray and pinkish-red tailings pile up underneath bare slopes, reminders of an era that began in 1889, when the mines produced 500 tons of coal a day, two-story wooden cabins lined the main street, and white picket fences protected groomed lawns and well-tended flower gardens. Company-owned Madrid boasted tennis courts, a seven-hole golf course, a shooting range, and a 30-piece brass band that marched in an annual July 4th parade.

In the 1930s, Madrid was so famous for its annual Christmas display that TWA pilots made detours to catch an aerial view of the town's 150,000 lights. Christmas decorations covered every inch of the main street, and the city ballpark was transformed into a giant toyland in which a miniature train carried children past the House that Jack Built and Peter the Pumpkin Eater.

During World War II, Madrid shipped 20,000 tons of coal to the secret mountain community of Los Alamos, where scientists were busy developing the world's first atomic bomb. By 1947, with the demand for coal dwindling, the mines closed down.

In 1975, tired of waiting for another boom or a buyer for the entire town, owner Joe Huber sold Madrid piece by piece. It took 16 days. Artists, craftsmen, and back-to-the-earth characters purchased the 150 dilapidated buildings for between $1,500 and $7,500 each. Today, many of the miners' cabins and hillside adobe homes sport new roofs and windowpanes. Galleries and gift shops face NM 14. Mexican folk art, custom clothing and toys, jewelry made by Santo Domingo Pueblo craftsmen, and locally crafted pottery line the shelves of the quaint shops. You can still descend into an old mine shaft at the Old Coal Mine Museum. And in the summertime, strains of bluegrass and jazz waft from the ballpark during Sunday afternoon concerts.

A few more bends in the road and **Los Cerrillos** appears beneath leafy cotton-

North-central New Mexico continues to support a host of artisans. (Paul Chesley)

woods. Its boom days long over, this sleepy hamlet resembles a movie set, with its few faded storefronts, dirt streets, and rundown exteriors. In fact, movies continue to be filmed here, the most recent being *Young Guns*. In the late 1800s, when Los Cerrillos still offered lodging at hotels and saloons filled with miners seeking their fortunes in gold, Thomas Edison paid a visit. He tried to extract gold from sand and gravel using static electricity, but he wasn't able to do it.

Today, the Turquoise Trail Trading Post sells tie-dyed T-shirts, petrified shark's teeth, and miniature adobe bricks, and features a homespun petting zoo in which goats, sheep, and burros await the caress of—and a hand-out from—soft hands. The Clear Light Opera House is now a recording studio.

If you're heading on in to Santa Fe, you might want to take a detour west on NM 586 to the Millennium Turquoise Mine where some of the world's highest-grade turquoise was first mined in A.D. 500. Once known as the Tiffany-Cerrillos Mines when the Tiffany Company of New York was part-owner, the site no longer is open to the public. But you can stand at the fence along this lightly traveled highway, gaze at the distant Jemez and Ortiz mountains on either side of you, and imagine those ancient Indian miners cracking the rocks with crude picks as they looked for turquoise.

Trading posts such as this serve as an outlet for the artisans of New Mexico. (Paul Chesley)

■ EAST AND SOUTH OF ALBUQUERQUE

East of Albuquerque, I-40 bisects the Sandia and Manzano mountain ranges through Tijeras (Scissors) Canyon on its way to the eastern plains. One of the state's more interesting drives curves along the eastern foothills of the Manzano Mountains on NM 337 (old 14). Leaving Tijeras Canyon, the road climbs and dips, sometimes hugging lichen-covered granite outcroppings and other times passing through wide-open meadows of yellow wildflowers. Interspersed along this route is a collection of villages created as nineteenth-century land grants, with names such as Chilili, Tajique, Torreon, and Manzano. In 1829, at the mountain range's southern end, Spanish settlers built a small fort for protection from Apache attacks. They named their community Manzano, after a thriving apple orchard established there in 1800. Still bearing fruit today, this orchard is the oldest in the country. Manzano remains a sleepy community of tin-roofed adobe homes, some with horses in the yard, and a stuccoed adobe church. Two gravel roads wind away from the town, one leading to Capilla Peak and the other to a shady campground at the base of Manzano State Park, the starting place for hikers who wish to scale the mountains on foot.

South of Manzano, the rolling slopes of junipers and piñons give way to the meadows of the Estancia Basin, traveled by prehistoric nomadic hunters who camped on the shores of a huge lake that filled the basin 12,000 years ago. Settlement came in the tenth century, when Mogollon Indians established villages alongside dependable streams and fresh springs. These early inhabitants grew corn, beans, and squash, hunted antelope and deer, and gathered piñon nuts and wild berries in nearby hills. They fashioned simple red or brown clay pottery and lived in pit houses, which later were replaced by *jacales*. Nearly 200 years later, the Anasazi arrived, bringing with them their stone and mortar architecture and multi-level homes.

The Anasazi mined salt at nearby salt lakes and beds, which they bartered, along with corn, beans, squash, piñon nuts, and cotton goods, for buffalo meat, hides, flints, and shells from Plains tribes to the east and Rio Grande pueblos to the west. This area, at the southern edge of the Manzano Mountains, served as a major trade route, connecting tribes throughout the region. By 1300, outside influences had crept in: these Salinas Valley Indians raised turkeys and added bison and rabbit to their diet. Men wore breech cloths and bison robes. Both men and women wore antelope and deer hides and wrapped themselves in decorative blankets they wove of cotton and yucca fibers. They adorned themselves in turquoise and shell jewelry.

Juan de Oñate visited the area in 1598, but Spaniards didn't move in until Franciscan priests settled alongside Indians in the early 1600s. The missionaries wasted no time converting the pueblo residents to Christianity and forcing them to build churches. Indians hauled heavy slabs of limestone and sandstone from nearby outcroppings and laid them out to make smooth flagstone floors for the 40-foot-high (12-m) stone churches with four-foot-thick (1-m) walls. Initially the Franciscans tried to prohibit Indians from practicing their native religion, but their efforts failed, and the Indians eventually frequented both churches and their traditional *kivas*. The Spanish also taught the Indians how to tend orchards, vineyards, and wheat fields, and forced them to herd cattle, goats, and sheep.

Three of these pueblos, separately situated in a 25-mile (40-km) radius of the ranching center of Mountainair, have been preserved as **Salinas National Monument**. At Punta de Agua, a sleepy hamlet on NM 55, a gravel road veers off to the west, leading to the mission ruins at Quarai. Sandstone walls still loom 40 feet (12 m) above a grassy plain, much as they did in 1630 when the church of La Purisima Concepcion de Cuarac was completed. A well-marked trail passes by the unexcavated mounds of pueblo dwellings, covered with patches of grass. Entering the nave of the church, you are walking on some of the original flagstone set down by the pueblos. The dirt roof is gone, replaced by an azure sky. At the altar, you can picture the colorful altar screen that once decorated the wall, filled with *retablos* painted in red, blue, and yellow, and embellished with bits of reflective mica. Outside, a *kiva* is submerged into the earth. Additional rooms that stretch to the mission's far walls, which surrounded the pueblo, most likely served as stables, hay and storage sheds, and animal pens. Close by the settlement, a grove of towering cottonwoods indicates the springs that were so vital to Quarai's survival. Today, these trees provide shade to picnickers who sit at tables and gaze over at the imposing church, perhaps speculating about what the original residents might have had for lunch—beef jerky and corn tortillas with beans, washed down with goat milk?

Seventeen miles (27 km) southwest via NM 55 and US 60, Indians at Abo erected their mission church in the late 1620s atop a rise in a wide valley surrounded by hillsides covered with piñon and juniper trees. Built of bright red sandstone, the **Abo church** is 30 feet (9 m) high. Stone buttresses support two-foot-thick (.5 m) walls, an unusually sophisticated building technique for seventeenth-century New Mexico. The church also contained an organ, which was accompanied by a choir during services. The narrow Abo River gently flows nearby the Indians' three-storied rock-walled homes, now covered with red soil and patches of pale-green desert grass. Only partial walls show above the earth.

South of the town of **Mountainair**, NM 55 crosses vast fields of cholla cactus and brilliant orange-red Indian paintbrush. An occasional truck rattling along a lonely road disturbs the silence, and an occasional hawk floats in the sky. Then, looking up, you see the partial walls of the mission church at **Gran Quivira** rise majestically atop a distant mesa.

Early Spanish visitors who arrived with Juan de Oñate in 1598 named the community Pueblo de los Jumanos (Pueblo of the Striped Ones) for a stripe the Indians painted across their noses. Later explorers gave it its current name. Once, 1,500 people lived at Gran Quivira, growing beans and squash in fields that were well-served by rain. Though no water source is known within 30 miles (48 km), historians believe the Indians captured rainwater in natural limestone cisterns or tapped a spring that has since dried up. The Indians here also hunted bison, and fashioned pottery that they painted with black and white stripes.

In 1659, Indians erected the massive Mission of San Buenaventura, with 30-foot-high (9-m) gray-blue limestone walls that were six feet (2 m) thick. Nearby, they worshipped their traditional gods in underground *kivas*.

You can view generations of homes as you peer down into the multi-level ruins of the pueblo. At the lowest level, the rock walls are ill-fitting compared to well-crafted ones in the upper levels. Stone *metates* lie among grass that has grown up between low rock walls. After walking through the ruins and the immense church, you might want to sit on a stone bench, look out across the vast plains, and imagine children playing hide-and-seek among nearby stands of juniper trees or think of the woman who once ground the day's cornmeal on one of those worn *metates*. From atop this windswept mesa, the snow-capped peak of Sierra Blanca looms to the south and the deep-blue outline of the Manzanos to the north.

In the 1670s, besieged by Apache attacks and drought, the Indians of the Salinas Valley left their homes to take refuge at pueblos along the Rio Grande.

A **visitor center** for these three restored pueblos is in Mountainair, inside the Shaffer Hotel—itself worth a visit, the visitors center is only one reason to venture inside the white-washed building near the center of what once was known as

For centuries bells have called the faithful to worship.

the Pinto Bean Capital of the World. Orange and black squares and black swastikas (Indian symbols for happiness) adorn the exterior which is a magnificent example of Pueblo Deco architecture. You can't get a room at Clem "Pop" Shaffer's place, built in 1929—they are rented out as offices. But you can get a good Mexican meal or a piece of homemade apple pie at El Pueblo Cafe, where wooden trim carved in whimsical geometric patterns is painted in bright reds, blues, yellows, and greens, and antique metal light fixtures hang from the ceiling.

ISLETA PUEBLO

One of the oldest missions in the United States, **St. Augustine Church,** lies about 18 miles (29 km) south of Albuquerque off I-25 in Isleta. Surrounded by adobe homes and rough shacks, the church has an other-worldly quality. Outside, the walls are high, white, and irregular; inside, a sense of mystery hovers among paintings of saints.

The pueblo itself dates from the sixteenth century and is one of the oldest and largest in New Mexico. Its history followed the generally tragic course of most Southwest Indian villages. Although its population acquiesced fairly amicably to the imposition of the Catholic faith and Spanish culture, this didn't protect them from being decimated by disease, conflict, and forced relocation. A thriving town when the Spanish first arrived, by 1692 Isleta was home to only a handful of Indians—many of those refugees from other pueblos. Today, the pueblo has a population of 3,000.

TIME ENDING

One morning in the spring of 1942 I walked to the edge of the canyon and sat dreaming for awhile under the branches of a fir tree. The air was gossamer. A haze of subdued light lay over rock and tree. I watched thunderheads build up in the north over Tsacoma, the sacred mountain. A tiny spider spun a web from the twig of a barberry to my knee and back again.

But roughly upon the edge of peace that day an airplane droned, circling back and forth among the clouds, from the river to the mountain, south along the flowing hills on the horizon, out of sight, and then suddenly back again. It flew low, methodically. The sunlight glinted from its silvery structure. It was then I first knew without doubt that a time was ending. Not even here on these mesas was isolation possible. We too were vulnerable to change. The narrow trails cut in the ancient rock could not be defended against the invading future.

On the first of May we waked to the sound of an extraordinary wind. The sky that had been limpid at daybreak darkened. The sun was muffled, though there were no clouds. The bright air was choked with dust that stung our faces and burned our eyeballs. We women were too restless that day to stay alone in our houses. Each went to seek some neighbor for reassurance, and as we walked we leaned against the wind like ghosts. Tarpaper ripped from roofs whirled past our windows. Sheds were overturned. Paths and doorways were blocked by fallen trees. Before it died at evening the wind cut a wide swath of destruction across mountain and mesa.

When I next rode on the trail up the Guaje ridge northwest of Los Alamos I became for the first time in my life almost hopelessly lost. Trees lay scattered as though spilled from a giant matchbox. Great roots had been flung upward out of pits of earth. Picking my way through the ruined landscape I lost all sense of direction. My confused mare balked and trembled till at last I got off and led her. I knew that for the animal's sake, if not my own, I must not panic. I talked to her gently and turned from time to time to lay my hand on her sweating neck in reassurance. At the peak of despair I stumbled across a shattered root. Exposed in the gaping earth shone a black piece of carved obsidian. That unexpected pattern of symmetry could only have been formed by the hand of man. I picked it up and held it in my hand, an ancient spearhead, and suddenly felt that I was not alone. An age-old human instinct for finding order in the midst of chaos came to my rescue. In a few moments I found myself back on the homeward trail.

—Peggy Pond Church
The House at Otowi Bridge: The Story of Edith Warner and Los Alamos, 1960

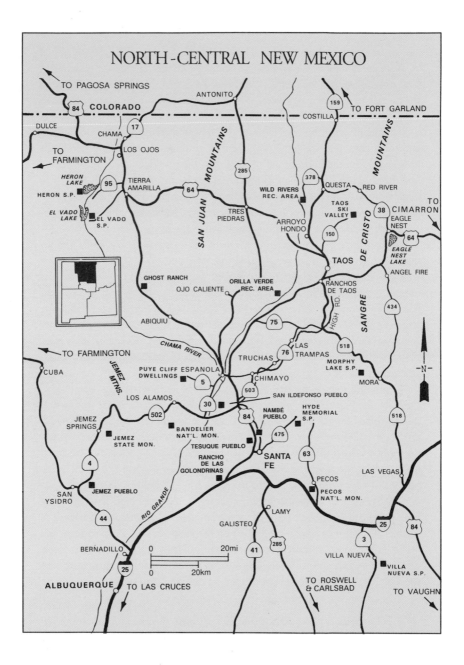

NORTH-CENTRAL NEW MEXICO

N O R T H - C E N T R A L
N E W M E X I C O

PINE FORESTS, ASPEN GROVES, AND THE CRAGGY PEAKS of the Sangre de Cristo and San Juan mountains combine with the gentler slopes of the Jemez Mountains to frame the north-central region of New Mexico. In between are the russet-tawny-lavender cliffs near Abiquiu and the placid Chama River and the more turbulent Rio Grande. Within this rugged, mountainous region, the state's spell is cast daily —in sunsets that transform deep-green hillsides into golden, and then rose-red, portraits. Coyotes howl and owls hoot as the slate blue of evening begins to blanket the high country and lights switch on in the tiny villages.

Long ago, Indian agricultural communities flourished in the soft, crumbly tuff formed from volcanic ash and cinders left behind when a volcano exploded, creating the Jemez Mountains. Some of these communities are preserved at Bandelier National Monument and the Puye Cliff Dwellings. Today, a majority of the state's Indian pueblos spread throughout this region, alongside and near waterways that flow from snowpacked mountains. These villages look like other rural New Mexican towns, with low-slung adobe buildings arranged around a central plaza. The northern-most pueblo is also the most spectacular: Taos Pueblo, a stunning multi-level structure that has been occupied since A.D. 1350.

Hispanic culture is pervasive here. Spanish is spoken as often, if not more, than English. Even the smallest hamlet displays a well-tended Catholic church, usually built of sturdy adobe, and some isolated ranches have their own chapels.

The Rio Grande makes a dramatic entrance into New Mexico from its headwaters in southern Colorado, cutting a 650-foot-deep (198-km) gash through a sagebrush plain. The blue-green water kicks up through the Rio Grande Gorge, churning itself into roiling rapids and deadly drops. One bridge passes over the deep volcanic chasm along US 64; another rugged gravel road with no designation follows the Rio Hondo, slicing through the gorge's middle. The only other access to the river here is by steep trails.

Once through the gorge, the Rio Grande mellows. Towns such as Velarde and Alcalde tap its water to irrigate apple orchards before the river piles up behind Cochiti Dam. The Rio Grande also flows past Española, which bills itself as the Low Rider capital of the world, and Bandelier National Monument.

Another of New Mexico's major waterways, the Chama River, enters the state at the western edge of this region. This gentle river, winding between alpine meadows and pine forests, backs up behind El Vado and Abiquiu dams before joining the Rio Grande north of Española.

North-central's magical setting has drawn scores of artists who have been coming since the 1920s to paint, sketch, and write about its sandstone bluffs, silent, sagebrush plains, pine forests, and modest people rooted to the earth. Georgia O'Keeffe and D.H. Lawrence are the best known, but hundreds more have settled here. Galleries can be found in most small towns, showing off paintings, pottery, weavings, and jewelry of local artists.

■ INDIAN HISTORY

Beginning in A.D. 1300, the Anasazi Indians began leaving their multi-tiered homes in Chaco Canyon in northwestern New Mexico and southern Colorado. Most likely, they had despaired of unreliable seasonal storms needed to water their crops, so they began heading toward water they could count on. Most ended up along the Rio Grande or one of its tributaries. In some cases, these farmers joined tribes already growing corn and beans in the fertile lowlands.

*Navajo pottery.
(Paul Chesley)*

(opposite) Pueblo Bonito, Chaco Canyon.

Others formed new communities, building multi-family dwellings and practicing irrigation methods developed at Chaco Canyon, such as diverting river water to crops through ditches. Some of these transplanted natives constructed their buildings with a new organizing principle, breaking from earlier traditions of carving out homes in canyon walls or lining a valley floor with multi-storied structures. These new homes were built along streets and around open plazas.

During this transition, known as the Regressive Period, which lasted until 1450, ceremonial *kivas* varied from pueblo to pueblo, some remaining traditionally round, while others were rectangular. Also, pottery styles changed from black-on-white vessels to black- or white-on-red. Designs differed from pueblo to pueblo. By 1500, the Indians were concentrated in the Acoma-Zuni area and the Rio Grande Valley.

Sixteenth-century Spanish explorers found nearly 80 pueblos scattered throughout northern New Mexico, some with as many as 300 residents. They were impressed with the ingenious way each upper level was built behind the lower one so that access could be gained by climbing outside ladders. These flat-roofed buildings placed around plazas reminded explorers of the towns of their homeland which is why they named their new settlements after pueblos.

Pueblo Indians used whatever materials were available to build a series of rectangular rooms with a central fireplace and a corner for grinding corn. Lower

The carreta *was the most common vehicle of transport in Spanish colonial New Mexico. This one photographed at Tesuque Pueblo in 1890. (Museum of New Mexico)*

storage rooms were entered through the roof by a ladder, while additional ladders led to upper-story rooms, themselves entered through four-foot-high (1.2-m) doorways. Along the river where building rocks were scarce, the Indians prepared adobe by mixing water with the clay and sandy soil, then spreading this paste over a framework of sticks and brush.

Indian religion reflected a deep reverence for nature: the sun and moon were gods, while clouds, thunder, and wind were Pueblo spirits. Religious ceremonies dominated their lives. In the summer they centered on the growing of crops; in winter on hunting. Produce consisted of beans, squash, melons, and a large variety of corn: yellow, blue, white, pink, red, and deep purple. Fresh vegetables were a treat in the fall, but most were dried and stored for the cold winter. Likewise, the meat from buffalo was dried into jerky, and hides were used as blankets and coats.

■ SPANISH HISTORY

Juan de Oñate arrived in New Mexico in 1598 to settle the land for the Spanish crown. His slow-moving cumbersome caravan followed, more or less, the Rio Grande until it reached San Juan Pueblo, situated in a small valley near the confluence of the Chama River and the Rio Grande. The Indians were friendly, and the settlers at first considered living alongside them, but eventually they opted for a site on the west bank of the Rio Grande that offered more room for expansion. On a low hill with the densely wooded Sangre de Cristo Mountains as a distant backdrop, the settlement of San Gabriel was carved out. It would be nine more years before English colonists established their first permanent settlement at Jamestown, Virginia.

Eleven years later in 1609, King Philip III of Spain designated New Mexico a royal colony, which placed it under direct control of the Spanish crown. Under this new designation, the Spanish government would pay the colony's expenses, along with those incurred by missionaries in their efforts to spread the Catholic faith. Pedro de Peralta was dispatched the following year from New Spain, with orders to establish a new capital. He chose a spot 30 miles (40 km) south of San Gabriel in a grove of junipers and piñons, beside which ran a narrow stream that meandered down from the nearby Sangre de Cristo Mountains (named "Blood of Christ" for the rouge-red color they turn in the setting sun). At an altitude of

(following pages) Taos Pueblo, a magnificent structure dating from A.D. 1450.

7,000 feet (2,134 m), the new capital, La Villa Real de la Santa Fe de San Francisco enjoyed crisp, clean mountain air and looked to the west at juniper-covered mesas and the soft curves of the Jemez Mountains.

De Peralta proceeded to establish a town council, assign house and garden lots to citizens, and order construction of the Palace of the Governors, a walled compound that contained the governor's residence, government offices, and council chambers. From this fortress, 60 successive Spanish governors ruled New Mexico. All of this activity bore a sense of permanence, and Santa Fe to this day remains the capital of New Mexico, making it the oldest state capital in the country. The Palace of the Governors, now a museum, is the nation's oldest government building.

During the next 65 years, aptly called the Great Missionary Period, 250 friars of the Franciscan Order traveled among the pueblos, building churches and tirelessly working to turn the Indians into devout Catholics. Missions sprung up from Pecos to the western villages of the Hopi in eastern Arizona. Soon, the simple pueblo dwellings were dwarfed by colossal churches. Indians were ordered to erect these structures, assembling 30-foot-high (9-m) walls with adobe bricks that weighed 60 pounds (27 kg) each, and topping them off with *latillas,* heavy *vigas,* dirt roofs, and a bell tower.

Church leaders didn't stop at converting the Indians. The Spaniards also taught them painting, Latin, blacksmithing, carpentry, weaving, and how to play small pipe organs that had been transported in wagons from Mexico. As the friars and priests focused on "civilizing" the natives, they also set out to destroy Indian civilization, raiding ceremonial *kivas,* desecrating altars, and burning masks, prayer plumes, and fetishes in the plazas. Soon they had outlawed all Pueblo religious rites, singing, and dancing.

The crackdown on Pueblo religions came to a head in 1675 when Gov. Juan Francisco Trevino ordered the arrest of 47 medicine men, whom Spanish priests regarded as little more than devil worshipers. Three were hung, another hung himself, and the rest were whipped and jailed. A group of Tewa warriors then descended upon the capital, demanding the release of the prisoners. Though Trevino obliged, the seed of revolt had been planted and Pueblo activists began plotting an uprising against the oppressive Spanish.

In 1680 that day came. Runners delivered knotted yucca cords to each pueblo. A knot was untied each day, until none were left, signifying the day for battle. Led by Popé, medicine man of San Juan Pueblo and one of those humiliated five years earlier by Trevino, Pueblo Indians across New Mexico attacked settlers, burning their homes and killing entire families. Years of tyranny-caused frustration welled up in the warriors as they directed their greatest wrath at the churches, where they killed priests at their altars and destroyed holy symbols, smearing them with human excrement. Eleven days later, Gov. Antonio de Otermin surrendered Santa Fe and led a string of battered, frightened settlers southward. The Indians let them go.

The shattered Spanish settlers retreated 300 miles (480 km) to El Paso, but within a year, they had regrouped and were making attempts to retake the territory. Armed Indians turned them back three times during the next decade. With the Spanish safely deposed, Popé encouraged the Indians to shed all ties to the Europeans and to return to their traditional ways. He ordered everyone to wash in the river with soapweed to remove the taint of baptism. All Spanish influences were to be discarded, such as clothing, tools, livestock. Unfortunately for Popé and his followers, many Indians couldn't remember much about the days before the Spanish and their cattle, sheep, and horses. But at each pueblo, natives did revive the independence they had given over to the Spanish. Old feuds resurfaced, Popé lost his grip, and the nomadic Apaches, now on horseback, renewed raiding on pueblos to a degree not seen since the onset of Spanish rule.

In 1692, when Diego de Vargas, accompanied by 60 soldiers and 100 Indian helpers, marched northward from El Paso, he passed by one deserted pueblo after another before arriving in Santa Fe, which he found in a shambles. The Palace of the Governors had been converted into a pueblo.

The Indians initially countered his entrance into the city with a few bold refusals. But after a good long look into a couple of Spanish cannons, they surrendered, embracing de Vargas's promises of pardons and an unconditional return to the Catholic Church.

Despite this bloodless retaking, the next decade was rocked by more Indian uprisings—all unsuccessful. Thousands of Indians abandoned their Rio Grande homes rather than return to Spanish rule, and many of these rebels moved in with the Hopis in eastern Arizona. Some eventually returned to the river, but others stayed on in Arizona. The Hopis never did return to Spanish rule. As New Mexico's Indians readjusted to their Spanish conquerors and resumed their subservient roles, the church leaders likewise compromised: no longer did they raid sacred *kivas,* destroy religious symbols, or severely punish those Indians who embraced Christianity but retained their traditional religious practices.

Still, with their freedom gone forever, the Indians' spirits flagged. Diseases introduced by the Spanish continued to take their toll on the natives who had no resistance to measles, whooping cough, cholera, and smallpox. By the end of the 1700s, the pueblos had lost one-half the population of 100 years earlier. Only 19 pueblos remained of the nearly 80 that were flourishing when the Spanish arrived.

By contrast, the Spanish thrived. Land grants were issued to entice colonists to the untamed province. They settled in villas laid out in fertile river valleys, and on small ranches where they raised cattle and sheep, planted apple orchards, and cultivated squash, peas, and melons in fields irrigated by the Rio Grande, Chama River, and numerous streams that flowed from the mountains. As years passed, relations between the Indians and Spanish became more cordial. Indian women shared their traditional methods for cooking bread, corn, beans, and chile. Both cultures traded herbs and healing plants, and pottery-making and weaving methods. The Spanish adopted the pueblos' flat-roofed architecture. And the two groups intermarried.

Today, mud-brick buildings blend into the chamisa-covered earth, corn stalks reach for the sky, and sheep munch on grass in small villages with names such as

(above) Rancho de las Golondrinas built by Spanish colonist Miguel Vega y Coca in 1710 (about 15 miles south of Santa Fe), and (opposite) North Building at Taos Pueblo reflect varieties of fine adobe architecture.

Abiquiu, Canjilon, Vallecitos, Santa Cruz, and Tierra Amarilla. These towns, which never prospered, appear much as they did 100 years ago. Ansel Adams brought fame to Hernandez, with his world famous photo, "Moonrise Over Hernandez." A small cluster of adobe homes just north of Española, Hernandez's winter heating fires spread the sweet smell of piñon smoke across the valley. After a disappointing autumn day of photographing the northern New Mexico landscape in 1941, Adams was passing through Hernandez when he noticed a full moon hovering high above the snowcapped peaks of the Sangre de Cristos. Standing atop his station wagon, he snapped a shot in which the moon cast an eerie light on the town's church and houses, illuminating crosses in its cemetery. "Moonrise Over Hernandez" proved to be the photographer's best-known work.

■ PUEBLO CULTURE TODAY

Despite a similar culture, history, and physical appearance, Pueblo Indians are not a single tribe that speaks a common language. Today, 19 pueblos remain, sharing three language groups. Zuni is spoken at Zuni Pueblo. Keres is the language at Laguna, Acoma, Santo Domingo, Cochiti, Santa Ana, San Felipe, and Zia pueblos. The remaining 11 pueblos speak dialects of the Tanoan language family: Tiwa is spoken at Taos, Picuris, Sandia, and Isleta pueblos; Tewa is spoken at San Juan, Santa Clara, San Ildefonso, Pojoaque, Nambe, and Tesuque pueblos. Jemez Pueblo is the only one where Towa is spoken.

Pueblo Indians, stocky in build with piercing dark eyes, are reserved and very polite. They don't go for small talk, feeling that silence is part of the concentration that produces results. Therefore, many of their rituals are cloaked in silence. Because towns have sprung up near most of the northern pueblos, many tribal members work at city jobs, returning to the pueblo on weekends and for ceremonies. This balancing of traditional demands with modern-day pressures often creates inner turmoil as people struggle to exist in two distinctly different worlds.

Pueblo Indians carry on their creative traditions, many centuries old, weaving willow wickerwork baskets, beargrass and yucca bowls, and colorful cotton belts and headbands. They fashion beadwork jewelry and leathercraft, and painstakingly shape pottery without the aid of a potter's wheel. Clays usually are dug from sandstone mesas, then strengthened with volcanic ash. After shaping a piece into a pancake for a base, a potter patiently lays on rolls of coiled clay, one atop the other, until the desired shape and size are reached. Using a smoothing stone, the artist smooths out the coils. Pots are polished to a deep red before firing, which is done outdoors over an open fire. If a red glaze is desired, the potter fires the pots with an oxidizing flame. To achieve the black-on-black pots made famous by San Ildefonso potter Maria Martinez, cow dung is piled around and over the upside-down pottery, permitting the carbon to permeate the porous clay. To decorate the wares, the artist uses spiked yucca or soapweed leaves that have been chewed until only the stiff fibers remain.

"Everything we do is sacred," says Craig, son of Blue Corn, a well-known San Ildefonso potter. He paints the designs on his mother's black- and earth-colored pots. "All designs have meanings. You learn by watching and memorizing the designs. Some designs take days to get the feelings. The design will come into your head and after that you try and work it onto the pot."

Most pueblos also host a few silversmiths who continue the tradition of jewelry-making. Although metals were not commonly used until the nineteenth century, Pueblo craftsmen have for centuries been carving turquoise, shell, and other gemstones for adornment. Turquoise, once plentiful in the knobby volcanic rock of the Cerrillos Hills south of Santa Fe, is said to contain benign powers: even a bead of the blue-green gemstone tied in an Indian's hair prevents disaster and ensures general well-being.

Another form of Indian artistic and religious expression can be found in *kachinas,* or *katsinas,* small doll-like figures carved from a single piece of pine. They are painted in bright colors, and dressed in deerskin, fur, feathers, and cloth. Each *kachina* is unique and a constant reminder of the "real" *kachinas,* supernatural beings who live in the mountains, lakes, and clouds. These messengers dispense blessings, such as rain and good crops. All *kachinas* wear masks. Doll-like figurines of buffalo, deer, eagle, and snake dancers are not *kachinas,* although they often are sold alongside them.

Dances, held regularly, are the major measure by which Indians express their deep respect for nature. They dance to help the seasons follow one another in proper succession. They dance to promote fertility of plants and animals. They dance to encourage rain and ensure hunting success. Participation in these ceremonies is a duty and privilege of all Pueblo people, who are trained to take part from early childhood. Every item of clothing and adornment has a special significance, from hand-carried spruce or fir twigs that symbolize physical longevity and everlasting life, to feathers and tufts of down and cotton that are cloud and sky symbols.

At Jemez Pueblo, as at many of the state's pueblos, Christmas Day is spent dancing. Leading a throng of reindeer are three buffalo dancers—two men and a woman—who move steadily up and down the plaza to the beat of drums and a chanting chorus of pueblo men. The buffalo woman wears a black skirt, a one-shouldered top called a *manta,* and white moccasins. The men paint their skin dark brown and wear mustard-yellow shirts and dark pants. All don bushy head-dresses with horns and bells around their waists, and each carries eagle feathers and shakes a gourd rattle. Behind them are a few rows of reindeer dancers of all ages. They are decked out in white garments with red, black, and green woven trim and wear turquoise deer heads that seem to be made of papier maché. Each reindeer dancer leans on two sticks, meant to serve as front legs, and spruce boughs deco-rate their attire. Swooping around the animal dancers are a group of eagle dancers, comprised of teenage boys adorned with eagle feathers. Another animal group, young boys dressed as antelope, join in the dancing, then disappear into the pueblo's maze of earthen homes, only to reappear later. They wear tawny falcon or hawk feathers. Sometimes, Santa Claus even accompanies the drummers and cho-rus and hands out candy canes to spectators.

While some dances are open to the public, every pueblo has its own policy regarding guests. Some don't permit cameras or tape recorders, and those that do require approval from the governor's office. Ceremonies are highly sacred to the pueblos and customs must be respected. Guests should stay clear of Indian per-formers or spectators, enter homes only when invited, and speak in hushed tones. Approach these ceremonies as if visiting a church of which you aren't a member.

■ ABIQUIU

Abiquiu began as a farming and cattle center on the banks of the Chama River and later served as a stop on the Old Spanish Trail, the tortuous trade route from Santa Fe to Los Angeles. Shortly after Abiquiu's settlement in the 1740s, Spanish officials moved in a group of *genizaros* to help tame the barren land. These people were non-Pueblo Indians with Spanish surnames. Some had been captives of no-madic Apaches and Navajos who were sold to the Spanish as laborers and servants.

At Abiquiu they struggled alongside Spanish settlers, regularly fending off attacks of Ute Indians who came down from Colorado to terrorize the colonists. Arable land was scarce and could only be cultivated as far back from waterways as irrigation ditches could be maintained. Timber was difficult to harvest because it had to be hauled long distances across open country. In between attacks, Ute Indians paid peaceful visits to Abiquiu, during which they traded deerskins for guns, horses, flour, and corn.

RELIGIOUS IMPULSE

The serenity of this spectacular red-rock country seemed to tap the spirituality of its residents. Early manifestations took the form of witchcraft and what the Spanish referred to as "idolatrous worship." This wizardry was unacceptable to Fray Juan Jose de Toledo, who was sent from Santa Fe to administer to the village's spiritual needs. He sent soldiers door-to-door to round up anyone engaged in sorcery. Eight perpetrators were flushed out, convicted of witchcraft, and sentenced to be servants of a prominent colonist.

By the turn of the century, another group of religious fanatics had formed. The Penitentes were a confraternity of the Catholic Church that believed in experiencing the suffering of Christ by flagellation. Formed by Spanish men isolated in rural towns without resident priests, this order (also known as the "Brotherhood of Light"), sought forgiveness for its members' sins, as well as for the sins of those who nailed Christ to a cross. Penitentes performed community service, assisting the sick and poor, comforting the bereaved, and counseling those who were troubled. By voting as a block, they wielded much political power. In Abiquiu, the Brotherhood built two *moradas*, or meeting houses—rectangular adobe

Saints and cruicifixes at Martinez Hacienda.

structures that had no windows, one door, and a wooden cross in front. As curiosity spread among outsiders, Penitente gatherings and rituals became secret.

The high point of their year was Holy Week, and its climax was the re-enactment of the Crucifixion of Jesus. A procession of bare-backed men climbed a hillside, followed by a member chosen to be Christ. As they marched, the men whipped themselves until they bled. When they were no longer able to lash themselves, their companions took over the torture. The men screamed in pain, a flute player coaxed wails from his instrument, tin cans and chains rattled, all combining to create a mood of suffering and despair. "Christ" labored under a wooden cross that weighed as much as 100 pounds (46 kg). Once atop the hill, the cross was erected and "Christ," bound tightly, hung there for about an hour. Supposedly, this re-enactment of the Crucifixion is no longer performed in New Mexico.

This rare photograph captures Penitentes flagellating themselves in 1896. (Museum of New Mexico)

Another form of worship takes place atop a piñon-and-juniper-covered mesa in the Chama River Valley at **Dar Al-Islam**, a Muslim community best known for its stark, ivory-colored, adobe mosque. The multi-domed structure with fluid walls was designed in 1980 by Egyptian architect

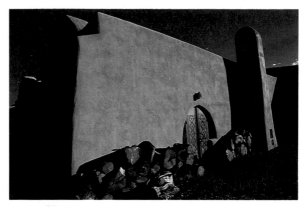

Dar Al-Islam Mosque at Abiquiu is a fine example of modern adobe architecture.

Hassan Fathy. Next door, a series of barrel vaults covers a 10,000-square-foot (3,048-sq-km) Muslim school.

Farther south at Santa Cruz is a sizable Sikh community where white-clothed and turbaned families are a common sight. They work as lawyers and business owners in Española and Santa Fe. Each spring, the Sikhs sponsor a Peace Prayer Day during which they invite their neighbors to share songs and stories. A few miles upriver, at the end of an unpaved road sits **Christ of the Desert Monastery.** Here, Benedictine monks grow their own food, raise bees, weave, make pottery and furniture. They worship in a stunning adobe chapel with a floor-to-ceiling glass wall that seems to bring inside the nearby soft-hued red cliffs. The Presbyterians are also represented in this region of religious fervor at Ghost Ranch. (See "Ghost Ranch," following.)

GHOST RANCH

Ghost Ranch, established in 1766, is a collection of adobe buildings nestled among maroon shales and dusty orange and purple sandstone hillsides. It was named for the *brujas* (witches), who are said to inhabit its numerous canyons. In 1934, Arthur Newton Pack, a wealthy Easterner, turned the working cattle operation into a fancy dude ranch where wild horses, burros, and mountain sheep roamed nearby, and where rattlesnakes hid in the cool shadows of rocks. One of his early customers, who turned out to be his most famous, Georgia O'Keeffe, was one of the most important painters of the twentieth centry. Once she set foot on Ghost Ranch, O'Keeffe never left it behind for long. Eventually, she bought a portion of the ranch and lived in a small U-shaped adobe house with whitewashed walls.

Today, the Presbyterian Church operates an adult study center at Ghost Ranch. Seminars are offered year-round and topics range from archaeology, paleontology, and theology, to pottery and wood carving. Next to the ranch's main buildings are two museums that highlight the area's natural history. The **Florence Hawley Ellis Museum of Anthropology** displays a re-created Spanish ranch house and interpretive exhibits of Indian pottery and crafts from people living in a 60-mile (96-km) radius during the past 12,000 years. The **Ruth Hall Museum of Paleontology** features *Coelophysis,* a 6-foot-long (2-m) dinosaur that was capable of remarkable speed when it came time to catch his dinner. These dinosaurs roamed the Ghost Ranch region 250 million years ago, making them the oldest in the state. In 1981, *Coelophysis* was named the state fossil.

From Ghost Ranch, a trail through fragrant juniper and piñon pines leads to the **Ghost Ranch Living Museum**, which like the Living Desert Museum outside of Carlsbad, is home to a collection of animals native to the area. Black bears, bobcats, mountain lions, Mexican gray wolves, and elk roam about in separate enclosures. All have been injured, orphaned, or are ill and unable to survive in the wild. Take the self-guided tour past golden eagles, red-tail hawks, jet-black ravens, and a beaver pond, and learn about the region's ghostly rock formations and pastel striations in the "Up Through the Ages" exhibit.

■ OJO CALIENTE

The hot mineral waters that bubble to the surface at Ojo Caliente have been attracting travelers for thousands of years. The crumbling remains of three prehistoric Tewa pueblos sit atop a mesa overlooking a more recent chapel and an assortment of simple homes along the meandering Rio Ojo Caliente.

According to Tewa legend, Poseyemu, a mythical hero, sprang to life from piñon nuts gathered by a young virgin at one of Ojo Caliente's five springs. Every year, he returns to visit his grandmother who lives in the curative waters at the spring. Today, at **Ojo Caliente Mineral Springs** a rustic adobe bathhouse separates men and women. The inside pools are open year-round and maintain temperatures ranging from 98 to 113 degrees F (37–45°C). The standard soak in waters that contains arsenic, iron, soda, and lithium is followed by a sweat-inducing wrap in heavy wool blankets. Massages, herbal wraps, and facials also are offered, in addition to overnight accommodations at the resort and in town.

■ NORTH TO CHAMA

North of Abiquiu, US 84 climbs along the side of a red-rock mesa as it heads toward Abiquiu Lake. From this incline, one of the most magnificent views in the state unfolds southward. Slate-blue mountain ranges line the horizon, and the sparkling blue Chama River wends its way among the square plots of tiny farms where horses graze in moss-green meadows and red-tail hawks circle overhead. Purple-yellow-pink cliffs fall away to the east.

Three miles (5 km) north of Ghost Ranch stands a sandstone cliff face rounded by centuries of whipping wind and pounding rain. It's called **Echo Amphitheater** and is a lovely spot to enjoy a cold drink and sandwich at picnic tables maintained by the Forest Service. A 10-minute walk leads to the 200-foot-high (65-m) beige wall. Be careful not to talk behind your companion's back because your conversation will easily be picked up and transmitted throughout the camping and picnic area. And the echo won't wait for you to finish.

Leaving Echo Amphitheater, the road climbs northward toward a stand of ponderosa pines before it drops into the Chama Basin, where the tin roofs of **Tierra Amarilla** homes glint in the sun. Here in the broad valley, churro sheep graze alongside cattle. Tierra Amarilla, named for the yellow-colored soil of the area, began as a land-grant settlement in the mid-1800s. But the village really took hold in 1865 when U.S. soldiers were dispatched to protect settlers from raids by Jicarilla Apaches and Utes. In 1872, both tribes were forced to relocate to reservations.

The town has gained a reputation as a seat of land-grant activism since 1967, when Reies Lopez Tijerina dramatized the plight of land-grant heirs who have lost their claim to the land through sales to outsiders by what he views as trickery or fraudulent means. Tijerina, along with 20 followers, raided the Rio Arriba County Courthouse, wounding two policemen, attacking two others, and holding many more bystanders hostage for hours. When Tijerina's group escaped to the nearby mountains, it took 500 lawmen to flush them out. Although Tijerina faded into the background after serving eight months in prison, the land-grant movement continues to flare up now and then.

The tiny sheep ranching community of **Los Ojos** was struggling to survive in 1981 when residents put their heads together and created Ganados del Valle, a collectively run economic development corporation. Today, the village is home to Tierra Wools, where weavers work on looms in the back and shoppers can browse through clothing, tapestries, pillows, rugs, and piles of hand-spun yarn. Churro sheep produce the wool, and Los Ojos residents spin and weave it. Close by, the historic Parkview grocery store, reopened in 1990, operates as a general store that also sells locally made jams, tortillas, and handcrafts. Its coffee shop is the perfect place to sit and think about which rug to buy at the wool showroom.

Across the valley, the waters of the Rio Brazos tumble through the steep walls of the Brazos Box Canyon. A narrow road follows the river up to the mouth of the dead-end canyon where two lodges nestle among tall ponderosa pines, shimmering aspens, and spruce trees. From Corkins Lodge, the sheer granite face of the 11,000-foot (3,353-m) Brazos Cliffs loom above. This land is private, so it's best to ask permission to prowl around.

■ CHAMA

This small town at the base of 10,000-foot (3,048-m) Cumbres Pass retains an outpost feel, a reminder of its formative days in the mid-nineteenth century when a lace curtain in the front room and windowbox geraniums were signs of status. Residents don't have to store their home-grown vegetables in cool cellars anymore, but a hardy constitution helps to withstand sub-zero winter temperatures and the piles of snow that reach to the rooftops. Homes are still simple, folks still friendly, and the railroad (built in 1878) still runs into town.

Today the **Cumbres and Toltec Scenic Railroad** no longer hauls cattle. Instead, it carries summer tourists aboard one of the nation's few remaining coal-fueled, narrow-gauge trains. From mid-June through mid-October, a jet-black locomotive pulls seven enclosed passenger cars away from the Chama station. Slicing through groves of golden aspens and struggling up the steep mountain pass, it belches charcoal-gray smoke. Golden eagles soar overhead, orange-lichen cover craggy volcanic outcroppings, and backpackers disappear along the banks of the meandering Los

A whisper can be heard from one side of Echo Canyon to the other due to its unusual acoustical configuration.

Piños River. The train picks up speed as it emerges from the steep-sloped Toltec Gorge, sweeping past yellow-tipped chamisa and sweet-smelling sagebrush. The day-long journey ends in Antonito, Colorado, where passengers can either spend the night or return to Chama by van.

River-runners, and those who'd like to be, should consider running the Chama River from just below El Vado Dam to Abiquiu Reservoir. This 33-mile (53-km) stretch of the blue-green Chama winds its way between 1,500-foot (457-m) hills past the dilapidated remains of an old homesteader's ranch and beneath dusty or-ange rock faces and sagebrush meadows. Rounded orange globemallow, red and purple penstemons, bright purple thistles, and brilliant red-orange desert paint-brush blossom from the riverbank. The current virtually disappears at Monastery Lake, a flat stretch that precedes Christ of the Desert Monastery, home to a group of Benedictine Monks. (See Christ of the Desert Monastery, in "Religious Im-pulse" above.)

Once past the monastery, the river picks up speed and heads into a series of rapids with names like Skull Bridge, Gage Station, Screaming Left, and Sidekick. Then, before you know it, you're back on shore.

■ JEMEZ MOUNTAINS

One hundred and fifty million years ago the dinosaur *Seismosaurus,* which, at 120 to 140 feet long (45 m), was probably the longest creature to ever sprout from an egg and grow up, lumbered through the area of the Jemez Mountains. Ten million years ago, camels, elephants, and horses roamed the tall grasses of northern New Mexico. One million years ago, a mighty explosion—far greater than the blast that ripped the side off Mount St. Helens in 1980—changed the landscape forever. Ash and fiery lava oozed from a volcano that scientists estimate was between 14,000 and 27,000 feet (4,267–8,230 m) high and that blew a hole in the ground 12 miles (19 km) across and 3,500 feet (1,067 m) deep. For thousands of years, eruptions poured forth, some ash hurtling up to a thousand miles (1,600 km) away. This violent activity left behind an entire mountain range with its tallest point, Redondo Peak, a mere 11,254 feet (3,421 m).

Long extinct, the volcano also left behind an extensive network of geothermal pockets. Many remain locked in the earth, while others have burst forth in hot springs scattered throughout the Jemez Mountains. Ironically, the volcano's caldera, known as Valle Grande, has turned into a lush green meadow upon which cattle graze contentedly.

Volcanic tuff from the massive explosion blankets the landscape for miles, creating cone-shaped tent rocks and hoodoos (free-standing formations with a pancake-shaped rock on top). Black volcanic glass, called obsidian, covers some of the tuff.

In the late 1100s, ancestors of the Pueblo Indians found tuff-covered cliffs ideal for carving out homes. At **Bandelier National Monument**, these Indians began growing corn, beans, and squash alongside Frijoles Creek, which flowed through a narrow canyon. They wove cotton cloth and painted black geometric designs on their pottery. Eventually, they moved to the base of the cliffs, erecting a communal house called Tyuonyi, a three-story, free-standing masonry pueblo with 400 rooms. Only one entrance led into the community, which was built in a circle around a plaza. *Kivas* were dug into the open courtyard. A combination of famine, drought, soil-eroding flash floods, and disease drove the Indians out, and by A.D. 1550 they had resettled along the Rio Grande.

Today, a 1.5-mile-long (2.4-km) paved loop trail leads past the cliff dwellings and restored ruins. Rough-hewn ladders reach to the carved-out cliff faces where traces of ancient fires can be seen in faint black soot on ceilings. Ceremonial Cave sits 150 feet (46 m) above the canyon floor and can be entered by climbing a series of spindly, but sturdy, ladders. Rather than the site of secret ceremonies, some anthropologists think the cool chamber once held tethered turkeys waiting to be dinner. The monument is named for Adolf Bandelier, a Swiss-born, self-taught historian who documented the history of the Rio Grande Pueblo Indians. Between 1880 and 1886, Bandelier visited pueblos and talked to their residents, balancing their oral histories against written records. He also wrote "The Delight Makers," a fictionalized account of life in Frijoles Canyon when Tyuonyi was inhabited.

More cliff homes are preserved north of Bandelier on the Santa Clara Reservation. A steep staircase of stone steps leads to **Puye Cliff Dwellings,** which was once one of the most extensive cliffside villages. Some were mere caves, others had porches or open rooms attached. Wooden ladders and steps carved into the volcanic tuff were used to get from one dwelling to another and up to the pine-covered mesa above. Puye's residents, who lived there from A.D. 1450 until the latter part of the sixteenth century, constructed *kivas* on the cliff's edge, along its base,

and on a ledge halfway to the top of the mesa. Their glazed red pottery was painted with serpents who were said to guard the springs that provided their lifeblood.
The dwellings, which are closed in the winter, were the prehistoric home of the
Santa Clara Indians, who now live nearby on more than 40,000 acres of rich farmland, rangeland, and forests.

NM 4 crosses the gently sloping Jemez Range, passing by the Valle Grande, meandering clear-blue streams full of brown and rainbow trout, and pine-covered
hillsides. On the mountains' western edge, a sulphur smell greets the nostrils, indicating that the supernatural-looking Soda Dam is right around the corner. Calci-
um carbonate and travertine deposits from a nearby hot spring have oozed into
the river and hardened into a mushroom-shaped dam. Hot rocks near the surface
cause the spring to bubble year-round, even when the rocks are covered with snow.
In the winter, steam rises, adding to an already eerie atmosphere.

Two miles (3 km) downstream is **Jemez Springs**, once the site of sheep wars,
vigilante activities, and gambling enterprises. In the early 1900s, this raucous village attracted swaggering Texas "gunslingers," who were tossed quickly from saloons by local ranchers and bartenders who found their bravado unimpressive.
Today, the sleepy town, squeezed between steep, red, sandstone hills on the banks
of the Jemez River, is home to the Servants of the Paraclete, a residential center for
Catholic priests experiencing personal or professional difficulties, and the **Bodhi
Mandala Zen Center**. This center, which backs up to the clear waters of the shallow Jemez River and contains its own well-maintained hot spring, welcomes
overnight non-Buddhist visitors.

Just north of town, the eight-foot-thick (2.4-m) rock walls of the church of San
Jose de los Jemez and the nearby prehistoric pueblo of Giusewa (a Tewa word that
means "Place at the Boiling Waters") are preserved at **Jemez State Monument**.
The massive church was founded in the early 1620s by Franciscan missionary Fray
Alonso de Lugo. A self-guided tour takes you inside the fortress-like church, built
with small windows for protection from expected invaders. Early twentieth-century excavations revealed one of the few fresco paintings in a New Mexico mission
church, but the fresco is gone and only stone now remains. A dirt path marked
with small arrows leads past priest quarters and the low walls of the adjacent Indian village.

In the early 1630s, the missionary enterprise at Guisewa was abandoned, and
Jemez Pueblo became the center for religious activities. Located 10 miles (16 km)

south of Jemez Springs, the pueblo's low adobe homes hug the brilliant brick-red earth. Coyote fences made with thin sticks form small corrals, and *hornos* the color of the rich earth appear beside nearly every home. Under shady *ramadas* that line NM 4 north of the pueblo, women sell bread they have baked inside these adobe ovens. They also cook up frybread on the spot, and the pleasing smell of baking dough mingles with the sweet piñon scent from the fire. Young Jemez men are famous as cross-country runners and firefighters. Many spend their summers fighting forest fires throughout the United States.

■ Los Alamos

In 1918, Ashley Pond fulfilled a life-long dream by establishing a school where young boys were taught standard book-learning, but could also ride horses, cut wood, and obtain the common-sense values that only ranch living can teach. The Los Alamos Ranch School was centered in a two-story log cabin designed by famed Santa Fe architect John Gaw Meem, hidden among tall pines atop the finger-like mesas of the Pajarito Plateau. A.J. Connell, an active Boy Scout leader from Santa Fe, became administrator and continued following scouting principles. Charted as Troop 22, the ranch school became the first mounted troop of scouts in the country.

During the summer of 1922, a young physics professor from Berkeley, J. Robert Oppenheimer, accompanied a pack trip from Frijoles Canyon into the Valle Grande. During subsequent trips into the Jemez wilderness, Oppenheimer often passed by the growing ranch school, occasionally stopping at Edith Warner's tearoom near Otowi Bridge that crossed the Rio Grande on present-day NM 502.

Twenty years later, when Oppenheimer was asked to help select an isolated site for a laboratory to develop the world's first atomic bomb, he thought of the ranch school. In 1941, it was forced to close to make room for the Manhattan Project. For the next three years, scientists secretly gathered in the ponderosa pine forests, sharing ideas. Prefabricated apartment houses and wooden barracks were erected to house hundreds of scientists and technicians who arrived by train, many not even apprised of their destination. They were issued driver's licenses with only numbers, no names, and all mail was sent to a Santa Fe post office box. People who applied to empty trash were only hired if they were illiterate. Even the scientists' families who accompanied them to the mountain outpost that came to be called "The Hill" didn't know exactly why they were there. But they made the best of it: wives taught in classrooms, shopped in Santa Fe, and attended ceremonies at nearby pueblos. Oppenheimer, Niels Bohr, and other scientists often stopped at Warner's tearoom, never letting on what they were doing up in the mountains. On July 16, 1945, the secret was out. The first atomic bomb was detonated in the pre-dawn desert at Trinity Site, 60 miles (96 km) north of Alamogordo. (Edith Warner's 20 years as a neighbor of the San Ildefonso Indians and the secret community of Los Alamos is chronicled in *The House at Otowi Bridge* by Peggy Pond Church.)

The Atomic Age had begun. After the war, Oppenheimer and his chief assistants moved out. But Los Alamos National Laboratory stayed behind, continuing in nuclear weapons research. The town that grew up to support the laboratory now is home to one of the highest concentrations of Ph.D.s in the country. Makeshift buildings have been replaced by permanent tan-colored concrete structures. The research has branched off into other areas besides nuclear energy. As the Cold War ended, scientists scurried to focus their research on ways to clean up hazardous-waste sites and develop alternative energy sources.

Although the laboratory maintains high security, the public **Bradbury Science Museum** is open to the public. It documents the early days of Project Y, the code name given to the Manhattan Project. Replicas of the bombs dropped on Japan are on display, along with hands-on laser exhibits, and examples of current research into the nature of nuclei, atoms, and molecules. The **Los Alamos Historical Museum** also traces the history of the secret city, but houses in addition Anasazi artifacts and a bookstore well stocked with titles on Los Alamos and the Southwest.

■ PECOS NATIONAL MONUMENT

By A.D. 1450, Indians in the Pecos River Valley were living in a multi-story village on a rocky ridge overlooking the river and pine-studded mesas beyond. Dwellings rose five stories high and were divided into 600 rooms and 22 *kivas*. These Towa-speaking Indians cultivated corn, squash, beans, and cotton in the fertile valley and foraged for wild berries and nuts in the foothills of the Sangre de Cristo Mountains. They were a small people; most women standing under five-feet (1.5

m). Men draped themselves in animal skins, and women wore one-shouldered dresses and turkey feather robes.

When Franciscan friars arrived at the pueblo in the 1620s, they ordered the Indians to build the 170-foot-long, 90-foot-wide (52-by-27-m) Mission de Nuestra Señora de los Angeles de Porciuncula. In addition to introducing Catholicism to the Indians, the friars taught them the Spanish way of life. They organized weaving rooms, tanneries, classrooms, and a carpentry shop, planted gardens of flowers and vegetables and fruit orchards, and brought in small bands of goats, sheep, cattle, and horses. In exchange, the Indians submitted to baptism and provided labor to maintain the community. That the Indians didn't much appreciate the new lifestyle became evident when they enthusiastically participated in the 1680 Pueblo Revolt, burning the church and joining in the attack on Santa Fe. When they were reconquered 12 years later, the Indians built a smaller church. By this time, repeated attacks by Comanches on the pueblo village, coupled with smallpox outbreaks, had severely reduced the population. Eventually, Pecos residents moved into nearby villages or joined their brethren at Jemez Pueblo, the only remaining Towa-speaking community. In the mid-1800s, when travelers passed by on the Santa Fe Trail, all that remained were the crumbling ruins of the once-proud pueblo.

Famed potter Maria Martinez applies slip on a bowl at San Ildefonso Pueblo in 1941. (Museum of New Mexico)

The partial walls of the massive church still stand, testament to long hours of Indian labor. To the north are the ruins of the extensive pueblo. At a restored *kiva,* a ladder leads into a musty chamber that holds memories of many secret ceremonies. Push a button on one of the vertical support beams, and drumbeats and chanting voices fill the dank room, much as they might have hundreds of years ago. The **Fogelson Visitor Center,** named after the area's large landowner (actress Greer Garson's husband) provides both an excellent introduction and in-depth look at the Indian and Spanish eras.

Pecos National Monument is situated four miles (6.4 km) north of I-25 on NM 63. Two miles (3 km) past it, the tiny village of Pecos supplies campers and fishermen heading into the Pecos Wilderness. NM 63 follows the narrow, slow-moving Pecos River, penetrating the tall pines of the forest until ending at the hunting and fishing resort of Cowles. A few dude ranches and camps are spread out along the river, which is stocked with rainbow and brown trout.

■ ENCHANTED CIRCLE

An 86-mile (138-km) loop strikes out from Taos, heading north between the craggy rim of the Rio Grande Gorge and the western edge of the Sangre de Cristo Mountains. It then cuts through the tall ponderosa pines and douglas fir trees of the rugged range, and drops into the serene, spacious, ridge-rimmed Moreno Valley before returning to Taos along the meandering Rio Fernando de Taos. The Enchanted Circle winds around the state's tallest peaks: at 13,000 feet (3,962 m), Wheeler Peak is the highest.

Arroyo Hondo, the remains of an 1815 land grant, straddles the rushing Rio Hondo, a runoff stream from the nearby mountains. The first Hispanic settlers put in vegetable gardens along the fertile river plain and grazed cattle and sheep in tall grass meadows. A number of Penitente *moradas,* marked by wooden crosses in front, are an indication of the strength this religious confraternity maintained here during the mid-1800s.

It didn't take long for an enterprising Anglo to disrupt the tranquil lives of the settlers. In 1830, Simeon Turley established a prosperous cattle and sheep ranch in Arroyo Hondo. He also planted acres of corn and wheat. Turley dammed the Rio Hondo, built a grist mill, and hired Hispanic settlers and Taos Pueblo Indians to

Cemetery and old mission, Taos.

work for him. He was probably best known for the "Taos Lightning" that he distilled. This moonshine often was the cause of disruption at fiestas in northern New Mexico.

During the uprising of 1847 (see "SANTA FE/TAOS" chapter), Turley escaped after a two-day battle at his ranch, during which his mill was burned. He sought refuge at a neighboring ranch, only to be killed there by his pursuers.

In the 1960s, canvas tepees appeared in the village at the New Buffalo commune, which sprung up near the earthen adobe homes. Part of the back-to-the-land movement, commune members dreamed of leaving behind modern urban life and returning to a more cohesive existence unencumbered by social mores with which they disagreed. Today, only a few members remain. A dirt road leads to the Rio Grande, passing by small gardens, barking dogs, and disinterested sheep. During the spring, trucks hauling hypalon rafts share the bumpy road with residents. At the John Dunn Bridge, which crosses the river where the Rio Hondo flows into it, boaters put in to run the Lower Taos Box, a 17-mile (27-km) stretch of the Rio Grande that passes underneath the 600-foot-tall (183-m) Rio Grande Gorge Bridge and through exhilarating boulder-choked rapids. Once beyond the gorge bridge, no roads enter the steep volcanic canyon until the end of the trip.

The remoteness and challenging whitewater combine to make this the premier one-day river trip in the state.

North of Arroyo Hondo, atop a gravel ridge, **Questa** has changed from a farming and trade center to a community focused on mining. Molybdenum (a major ingredient in lightbulbs, television tubes, and missile systems) is removed from an ancient volcanic caldera on the steep banks of the blue-green Red River. The only trading Questa shares in anymore is at its few gas stations, restaurants, and motels. The tiny village also markets honey, which can be purchased from the beekeepers themselves at their homes north of town.

NM 38 passes alongside slopes scarred by the mining operation as it follows the Red River to a town named for the blue-green waterway that runs red after rainstorms. Surrounded by hillsides blanketed in tall pines, **Red River** was platted in the late 1800s by the Mallette brothers, who sought to take advantage of a mining boom in the area. By 1905, the town supported 15 saloons, four hotels, two newspapers, a barbershop, hospital, and thriving red-light district. The failure of any big strikes spelled the end of Red River's mining era. But prosperity arrived in the 1920s when flatland vacationers came looking for relief from their homes among the dusty plains of Oklahoma and Texas. They found it in cool, clear streams, radiant aspen groves, and stately pine forests—not to mention dust-free air. Fishing, hiking, bicycling, and pack trips have since lured vacationers to the cool slopes in the summer. Construction of the Red River Ski Area in 1958 turned the town into a year-round resort. Shops, restaurants, and motels line the main street, making Red River a pleasant place to walk around and browse.

A few stone walls and cemetery grave markers are all that remain of **Elizabethtown,** the scene of an 1866–1875 gold rush during which thousands of prospectors feverishly scoured the flanks of 12,500-foot (3,810-m) Baldy Mountain. The rowdy mining town was named after the daughter of Capt. William Moore. A Union soldier stationed at Fort Union, Moore opened up the town's first store in 1867. Two hotels, four more mercantiles, and seven saloons quickly followed. Gold worth millions of dollars was removed from claims staked in the pine-studded hills before the ore played out. In 1903, a fire destroyed much of the dying town's business district. Baldy Mountain endures, of course: a rounded bare knob that still stands like a beacon overlooking the tall grasses of the Moreno Valley.

In 1919, Charles Springer, a prominent cattleman, banker, and engineer, decided it was time to provide a stable water source for the vast fields of the Moreno

Valley. He designed and built Eagle Nest Dam at the head of Cimarron Canyon. Today, a five-mile-long (8-km) lake, named after the dam, is tapped for irrigation. The lake holds some of the biggest rainbow trout and kokanee salmon in the state, which anglers go after even in winter through holes in the ice. A year after the dam went up, a village followed. The abundance of soaring golden eagles in the mountains that surround the lush Moreno Valley inspired residents of Thermal to rename their town **Eagle Nest.** For years, Eagle Nest was the largest town in the valley, but today has been relegated to the status of a stock-up and overnight stop because of newer developments nearby.

The **Vietnam Veterans National Memorial** sweeps upward from a hillside at the south end of Eagle Nest Lake. The solemn white structure, with 50-foot-high (15-m) front walls was raised piece-by-piece by the family of Dr. Victor Westphall, whose son was killed in a 1968 enemy ambush in Vietnam. The chapel, the first memorial to Vietnam vets built in the United States, was completed in 1971. It is open 24 hours a day, and is now recognized as a major national Vietnam veterans memorial.

After a shaky start in the mid-1970s as a ski area, **Angel Fire** has blossomed into a year-round resort that offers golf, fishing, tennis, hiking, and horseback riding. From the ski area's 34 miles (54 km) of trails, the vast Moreno Valley unfolds below with snowcapped Wheeler Peak visible in the distance.

GEORGIA O'KEEFFE

That first summer I spent in New Mexico I was a little surprised that there were so few flowers. There was no rain so the flowers didn't come. Bones were easy to find so I began collecting bones. When I was returning East I was bothered about my work—the country had been so wonderful that by comparison what I had done with it looked very poor to me—although I knew it had been one of my best painting years. I had to go home—what could I take with me of the country to keep me working on it? I had collected many bones and finally decided that the best thing I could do was to take with me a barrel of bones—so I took a barrel of bones.

On a warm May day in 1930, Georgia O'Keeffe stepped off a train at the small station in Lamy, New Mexico, and beheld a pale-green landscape covered in bushy piñon and juniper trees, gray-green in the brilliant New Mexico sunshine. She was 41 years old and had ventured west without her husband, Alfred Stieglitz, to spend the summer painting whatever the dry, dusty desert offered as a subject. By then an established painter, O'Keeffe instantly was enamored with the radiant light and the sharp edges of mountains, trees, and flowers caused by the thin, dry air. "No one told me it was like this!" she told her host, Mabel Dodge Luhan, a wealthy art patron who owned a sprawling compound in Taos.

After one of her paintings sold in New York for $6,000, O'Keeffe bought a black Model A Ford, which she used to explore the countryside. One day, motoring with Luhan's husband, Tony, a Taos Indian, O'Keeffe reached the lavender, dusty orange cliffs of Abiquiu, about 60 miles (96 km) west of Taos. O'Keeffe and Luhan were searching for Ghost Ranch, a place Luhan thought the painter would enjoy, but they never found an entrance. "This is my world, but how to get into it?" O'Keeffe remembered thinking at the time.

A few years later, she found the ranch, a cluster of low adobe buildings set in the shadows of a sandstone mesa speckled with piñons and junipers. Owner Arthur Newton Pack had just purchased the working cattle ranch and was turning it into a fancy dude ranch. O'Keeffe moved into a cottage and returned there every summer until 1940, when she purchased Rancho de los Burros, a U-shaped adobe house Pack had built for himself three miles (5 km) from the main house. Whitewashed rooms surrounded a patio, and a huge bedroom window overlooked a flat-top mesa called the Pedernal, which lay 10 miles (16 km) to the south. Behind the house to the north, rosy red, pale yellow, and coral cliffs rose to meet an azure sky. The colors of these corrugated cliffs shifted as the sun moved across the sky. The artist replaced adobe walls with huge panes of glass, and while the interior remained sparsely furnished, it overflowed with bones, rocks, shells, pine cones, driftwood, and feathers she collected on daily walks through sandstone canyons and piñon-juniper forests.

> The unexplainable thing in nature that makes me feel the world is big far beyond my understanding—to understand maybe by trying to put it into form. To find the feeling of infinity on the horizon line or just over the next hill.

In 1945, O'Keeffe purchased a dilapidated hacienda that overlooked the Chama River in the nearby village of Abiquiu. She had the place rebuilt to her specifications—once again, glass walls replaced older adobe ones, fireplaces were installed in every room, and village women plastered mud on the rounded inside walls.

The following year, Stieglitz died in New York, and shortly thereafter, O'Keeffe moved to New Mexico for good. She continued to paint the soft curves of Abiquiu's hills and flowers, casting many in ethereal poses. "Two walls of my room in the Abiquiu house are glass and from one window I see the road toward Española, Santa Fe, and the world. The road fascinates me with its ups and downs and finally its wide sweep as it speeds toward the wall of my hilltop to go past me," she said to describe two 1964 paintings of US 84.

In 1972, a young impoverished potter came asking for work. After a few rebuffs, the aging artist hired him to do odd jobs at her Abiquiu home. Juan Hamilton subsequently became her constant companion, and as her eyesight failed, he managed her affairs. Their relationship, one based on friendship, lasted until O'Keeffe's death in 1986. She was 98.

*Georgia O'Keeffe near the "Pink House," Taos, 1929.
(Museum of New Mexico)*

SANTA FE AND TAOS

BROWN ADOBE HOUSES, SOME NEARLY 200 YEARS OLD, line narrow dirt streets as reminders of a past that doesn't feel too far away in the town of **Santa Fe**. Laid out in the protective foothills of the Sangre de Cristo Mountains, Santa Fe's crooked streets follow the contours of the uneven earth. Most buildings are one story high, and painted in all shades of brown—from tawny to ginger to coffee. Even though many are of frame construction, nearly all reflect the flat-roofed, box-shaped, adobe building style that dominated the city's early architecture. Yards are often small, and shabby exteriors frequently belie elaborate interiors with pine *vigas,* corner *kiva* fireplaces, polished brick and tile floors, and fluid, curving walls and doorways. Due to this indigenous architectural style, taken from Indian pueblos, the town blends in with the landscape of piñon and juniper. At odd moments in the spare desert light it seems to have sprouted from the earth.

The town of **Taos,** 70 miles (112 km) north of Santa Fe, was built on a high plateau between a deep chasm carved by the Rio Grande and the majestic peaks of the Sangre de Cristos. This smaller version of Santa Fe maintains the tradition of low-slung homes along winding dirt streets, which are rarely identified by signs. With its small population (4,500) and its isolated location, the village tends to be less fashionable and "hip" than Santa Fe. People choose lifestyles that meet basic needs and activities revolve around the Rio Grande and nearby mountains. Recycling takes on new meaning in homes built of old tires and empty aluminum cans. It's easy to be yourself in Taos, no matter how unusual you might be.

Both Santa Fe and Taos attract artists, writers, natural healers, psychics, and other creative minds from around the world whose spirits respond to the soft golden light of early morning and the dusty red of evening. The hustle-bustle of modern life is tempered, as people linger over cappuccinos or spend a day chopping and hauling piñon wood from the nearby mountains. Blue jeans and cowboy boots are de rigueur.

Both towns boast an inordinate number of lodgings, galleries, museums, gift shops, bookstores, and restaurants. Taos attracts individualists with a keen appreciation of its outpost character, while Santa Fe is more for the idiosyncratic cosmopolitan and gourmet.

St. Francis of Assisi Mission, Taos.

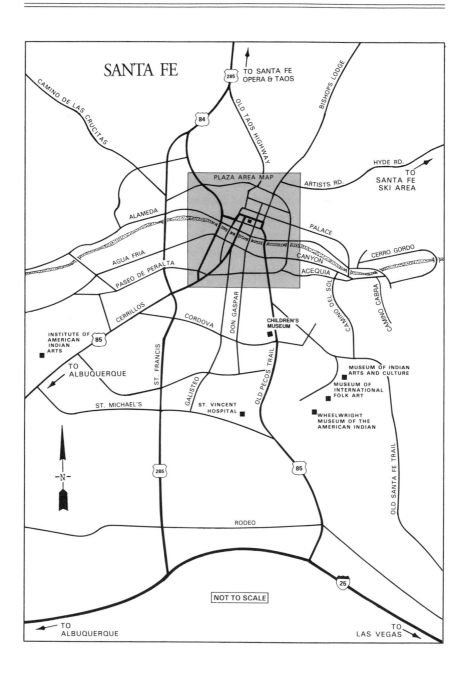

Both towns, however, are in danger of losing what makes them so appealing: their tri-cultural mixture of Indians, Hispanics, and Anglos. As urban outsiders descend upon the two communities, seeking clean air, simpler lifestyles, and aesthetic sophistication, many long-time residents have been forced to leave, taking traditions with them. But those traditions—of roasting and freezing chile, slapping out fresh tortillas, and sharing in the springtime ritual of clearing out irrigation ditches—continue to thrive in the small communities that dot the roads between Santa Fe and Taos.

■ HISTORY

Ancestors of today's Taos Pueblo residents lived nearly 1,000 years ago in small villages throughout northern New Mexico. By 1350, they had settled along the shallow waters of the Rio Pueblo where they erected, tier by tier, the stepped walls of Taos Pueblo. Nearby they grew squash and beans, and corn that women ground between two rocks and then cooked into flat corncakes. Men hunted deer, rabbits, and squirrels in the nearby mountains. Due to the isolation of this northernmost pueblo, Taos was a major target of raiding Comanche and Ute Indians who scoured the northern plains. But this same seclusion also kept away Spanish missionaries. Even though a mission church was built there in 1617 and the Pueblo Revolt of 1680 was plotted at Taos, few Spanish moved into the area until the eighteenth century.

Rather, missionaries concentrated on pueblos closer to Santa Fe, established in 1610 as the capital of the new Spanish colony. During its formative years, Santa Fe was maintained primarily for the purpose of bringing the Catholic faith to New Mexico's Pueblo Indians. In 1680, however, the Indians rebelled against the Spanish and their religion. Colonists who escaped from their homes fled to the Palace of the Governors, an enclosed one-story compound that housed the governor, the town's chief political officers and their offices, a military chapel, shops, and work rooms. As the surviving colonists huddled together inside the governor's palace, the Indians outside set fire to a church and other prominent buildings around the plaza, dancing and shouting victory chants. Once the Spanish were cornered and sufficiently frightened, the Indians allowed them to depart, and they marched in good order for 300 miles (480 km) until they reached El Paso, where they remained for the next 12 years.

Diego de Vargas, a member of one of Spain's leading families, was assigned the task of restoring Spanish rule to New Mexico. In 1692, he led a squad of soldiers and Indians up El Camino Real to Santa Fe. There he surprised a group of Indians who had turned the governor's palace into a pueblo. After minor resistance, the Indians surrendered peacefully, returning the battered capital to the Spanish. Every September since 1712, this reconquest has been celebrated as Las Fiestas de Santa Fe.

After securing the capital, De Vargas returned to El Paso, where he gathered colonists to resettle the territory. In October 1693, he ushered northward a ponderous entourage that included 70 families, 18 friars, 100 soldiers, 2,000 horses, 1,000 mules, and 900 head of cattle. Eighteen carts hauled heavy supplies, including three cannons. A small wooden statuette of the Virgin, known as La Conquistadora, accompanied this excursion. La Conquistadora originally had been brought to the capital in 1625, but was carried down to El Paso by the retreating Spaniards in 1680.

Upon arrival, De Vargas discovered the Indians had, in his absence, changed their minds and decided to keep Santa Fe and resist the Spanish.

La Conquistadora, who accompanied Spanish colonists in their reconquest of New Mexico from the Indians. (Museum of New Mexico)

Well-armed and organized, De Vargas's men succeeded in taking back the capital by force. Tradition has it that De Vargas attributed his success to the Virgin Mary through La Conquistadora, and today she stands on a gilded altar in the north chapel of St. Francis Cathedral. Every June, La Conquistadora is paraded through town to Rosario Chapel, the site of De Vargas's camp during the reconquest. A novena of masses is said before a procession returns her to the cathedral.

After a few more Indian uprisings were quickly quashed, the conquering Spanish moved in by droves, settling the protective hills near the new capital and the high Taos Plateau where they grew vegetables, wheat, and barley alongside streams that flowed from the nearby mountains. In 1617, Fray Pedro de Miranda built a mission near Taos Pueblo. An important landowner in the region was Fernando de Chavez, whose family was slain during the Pueblo Revolt. Chavez didn't return after the reconquest, but his name was attached to the land; and in 1710, when Cristóbal de la Serna petitioned for a land grant, he identified Chavez as the previous owner. Thus, the Spanish settlement became known as Fernando de Taos. In 1716, a second community was established a few miles south and is known today as Ranchos de Taos.

Typically, homes were joined together by a solid rear wall that provided protection from raiding Comanches, who continually threatened settlers. During 1759, for example, 50 Spanish women and children were abducted by Indians. The following year, Spanish soldiers bent on revenge fought and killed 400 Comanches among the tall grasses of the high plains.

A tradition that persisted during these unsettled times was the annual Taos Trade Fair, at which Ute, Apache, and Comanche Indians, laden with buffalo hides, jerky, and buckskins, pitched tepees outside of town, and traded for Spanish guns, knives, and ammunition, as well as vegetables and grains cultivated at the pueblos. Ill feelings were set aside during this boisterous occasion, and large amounts of local moonshine, called Taos Lightning, were consumed. By evening, everyone had joined together at an all-night fandango.

Sign language was used to secure deals. Goods were bartered—no money changed hands. Spanish or Indian captives often accompanied the Indian traders who sought to trade goods for their release. Sometimes the Spanish governor led a retinue from Santa Fe to oversee the noisy gathering. As soon as the fair ended and parties departed, however, tribes began plotting upcoming raids. During the nineteenth century, the trade fair brought mountain men of French descent with beaver pelts, and Missouri merchants freshly arrived on the Santa Fe Trail with calico, jewelry, handkerchiefs, furniture, glassware, paper and ink, spices, and medicine. Today, the fair is reenacted in late September at the Martinez Hacienda, followed a week later by the feast of San Geronimo at Taos Pueblo, which commemorates a pueblo trade fair that dates to prehistoric times.

By 1821, Mexico had declared its independence from Spain, and Santa Fe became a far-flung outpost (nearly 1,400 miles [2,400 km] north of Mexico City) of the struggling new nation. In the mid-1800s, the United States' doctrine of Manifest Destiny brought Gen. Stephen Kearny and his troops to the Southwest to claim the territory for the United States. While most of New Mexico rolled over and let him fly the Stars and Stripes, a group of headstrong Taoseños loyal to Mexico mounted a resistance effort. On a wintry January night in 1847, Hispanic settlers and Taos Indians converged on the Taos residence of Charles Bent, governor of the new U.S. territory of New Mexico, killed him, and paraded his scalp on a board through the streets. A week later, soldiers arrived from Santa Fe and defeated the insurgents who had barricaded themselves inside the Taos Pueblo mission church.

Independence from Spain also opened doors to trade with the United States. Under Spanish rule, the northern province could trade only with Mexico, but Mexican leaders relaxed that edict and encouraged a business relationship with the United States. The Santa Fe Trail was quickly established as a major trade route between Santa Fe and Independence, Missouri. Caravans rolled across the prairie, bringing cloth, tools, furniture, and dishes, along with adventurous American settlers.

The 1848 Treaty of Guadalupe Hidalgo ceded New Mexico to the United States, which immediately began wielding its influence. Lawyers, newspapermen, and shopkeepers flocked to the newly opened frontier. In Santa Fe, Archbishop Jean Baptiste Lamy arrived in 1851 and promptly began molding New Mexico's laid-back clergy into disciplined church leaders. He also designed a cathedral in the Romanesque style of his native Auvergne, France. Begun in 1869, it took 17 years to complete St. Francis Cathedral, which today dominates the end of San Francisco Street in downtown Santa Fe. Built of light-tan volcanic stone quarried in hills south of town, the cathedral stands as a monument to Lamy, who went on to build 45 more churches and bring a handful of parochial schools to the wild New Mexico Territory.

Outside of Santa Fe, however, New Mexico continued to be ruled by the smoking gun. In 1878, President Rutherford B. Hayes appointed Lew Wallace as governor to enforce law and order. In between trying to negotiate the capture of Billy the Kid and administer the state, Wallace penned *Ben Hur* in 1880 while living at the Palace of the Governors.

SANTA FE TRAIL

William Becknell knew a good deal when he saw one. Part of a carefree fivesome trapping and hunting horses in the Southwest in 1821, the veteran Indian fighter paid close attention to the dizzying profits his group reaped when they were invited to Santa Fe that September to celebrate Mexico's newly won independence from Spain.

Under Spanish rule, New Mexicans were forbidden to trade with anyone other than Mexico. Traders loaded *carretas* and pack mules with bearskins, piñon nuts, tallow candles, and wool and slowly made their way along the Chihuahua Trail, traveling 550 miles (880 km) to Chihuahua City or another 900 miles (1,440 km) on El Camino Real to Mexico City. There they exchanged their frontier goods for spices, chocolate, shoes, writing paper, and ink. Large caravans usually made the rough trip twice a year.

Because of this isolation, Santa Fe's residents rarely saw new wares. But once word reached the frontier capital of Mexico's independence, New Mexico's borders were flung open to traders. In no time, Becknell and his party sold their supply of brightly colored blankets, knives, kettles, and looking glasses brought along to trade with Indians. And their profits were three-fold!

Soon thereafter, Becknell hightailed it back home to Franklin, Missouri, where he restocked and headed west again. This time, instead of following the Arkansas River into southeastern Colorado and then into New Mexico along the steep slopes of Raton Pass, Becknell veered south across the Arkansas River about 20 miles (32 km) west of Fort Dodge, Kansas, crossing the Oklahoma panhandle and the Cimarron River in a straight shot that led to Santa Fe.

For the next 59 years, Becknell's Cimarron Cutoff was the principal trade route to the Southwest. The main arm of the Santa Fe Trail continued into Colorado, where Bent's Fort became the largest trading post of the West. This mountain branch was longer, but wood and water were plentiful, compared to the Cimarron Cutoff, which cut 10 days off the trip but entailed crossing the 60 miles (96 km) of bone-dry desert and hostile Indian country between the two rivers.

The Santa Fe Trail was the first major Western trade route and preceded by two decades the more northern Oregon and California trails. By 1831, oxen were replacing mules as the preferred beasts of burden on the trail. Eight of the slow but steady animals could pull 2-plus tons of cooking pots, calico cloth, knives, and tools in a wagon with iron-rimmed wheels as tall as a man's head. Each spring, 100 of these wagons gathered in Missouri for the 900-mile (1,440-km) trek across the plains of Kansas and the tall-grass prairies of northeastern New Mexico. The lumbering caravans averaged 15 to 20 miles (24 to 32 km) a day and in New Mexico passed by Rabbit Ears Mountain, Starvation Peak, the abandoned Pecos Mission (now Pecos National Monument), and Pigeon's Ranch. At the end of the trail in Santa Fe, tired oxen were traded or sold for fresh ones and the Conestoga wagons were loaded with gold, silver, wood, and furs.

This opening up of the West was not without its hazards. Pawnee, Apache, Comanche, and Ute Indians, unhappy with these intrusive caravans, often killed traders they encountered. In mid-July 1828, just inside what was to become the state of New Mexico, two scouts riding ahead of a caravan curled up for a nap on a bank of the North Canadian River as they waited for the wagons. A raiding party of Pawnees spotted the sleeping men, and creeping silently, seized their rifles and shot Capt. Daniel Munroe and Samuel McNees, just as the wagon train rolled down the opposite bank. As the men were being buried, six Comanche Indians rode up. No questions were asked and all but one was killed. The spot became known as McNees's Crossing. Today the crossing is only a dry river bed in the middle of a cow pasture.

In 1849, when Dr. J.M. White, his family, a servant, and four men left a wagon train near Point of Rocks, a rugged 150-foot-tall (46-m) promontory near Farley, New Mexico, to push on by themselves, a group of Apaches approached the group asking for gifts. Dr. White refused. The Indians shot all of the men and took the women captive. Led by legendary Indian fighter Col. Kit Carson, a group of men chased the band. (Carson himself had made the western trip 23 years earlier as a 16-year-old.) Just as they were closing in on the Apaches, the Indians shot Mrs. White to death with arrows. The servant was never found.

Yet another battle ensued near the Point of Rocks when some 200 Comanches set upon a wagon train on January 1, 1833. After slaughtering all of the party's mules and horses and wounding most of the 12 traders in the caravan during a 32-hour period, the Indians let them go.

After the New Mexico territory had won its independence from Mexico in 1848, forts were erected to protect traders from the bitter Indians. The Civil War delayed the coming of the Santa Fe Railroad, but in 1880 the iron horse began inching its way across the Mountain Branch of the Santa Fe Trail, tunneling through mountains in Raton Pass and chugging across northern grasslands before it reached Lamy, outside of Santa Fe.

Today, tall grass covers deep indentations carved into the soft earth from years of wagon wheels creaking across the now-silent prairie. These ruts that stretch to the eastern horizon and ghosts in the wind are all that remain of the first major trade route that connected New Mexico to the eastern United States.

Recently, Congress honored the Santa Fe by designating it a National Trail and providing funds to preserve and mark the vestiges of this once-vital lifeline.

In 1879, the Santa Fe Railroad reached Lamy, 18 miles (29 km) south of Santa Fe (the closest passenger trains ever·came to Santa Fe itself). With this comfortable and efficient mode of travel, ever more immigrants from the U.S. arrived, bringing with them their own ideas and traditions. Red-brick Victorian houses with double-hung windows were soon being built alongside brown adobes with rough-hewn panes.

Seventy years later, in 1949, Ernie Blake arrived in Santa Fe to help build the Santa Fe Ski Basin on the western slopes of 12,409-foot (3,782-m) Lake Peak. The Swiss-born mountaineer managed the small ski area for five years, until he discovered the perfect location for his dream ski resort at the abandoned copper mining camp of Twining, north of Taos. Against the advice of friends who warned him the slope was too steep and would scare off skiers, Blake installed the first lift in January 1956 and went on to mold Taos Ski Valley into one of the world's most popular resorts. Today, the mountain offers skiers some of the most challenging terrain in the West.

■ ARTISTS ARRIVE

In 1848, two Philadelphians, Edward and Richard Kern, arrived at Taos, and if their stay was brief, the brothers earned the distinction of being the first artists to visit the town. Fifty years later, a broken wagon wheel detoured painters Bert Phillips and Ernest Blumenschein, who were on their way to Mexico, into the dusty town. Once there, they found themselves enthralled with the handsome, chiseled faces of the Taos Indians, the deep-dark eyes of Hispanic farmers, and the layers of pine-covered mountain ridges. They stayed to establish what came to be known as the Taos School—a group of painters who displayed throughout the world spiritual canvases of Indians and mountains, awash with the ethereal New Mexico light.

Taos became firmly established as an art colony in 1915 when the Taos Society of Artists was formed. In addition to Phillips and Blumenschein, members were J.H. Sharp, Oscar Berninghaus, E. Irving Couse, Victor Higgins, Walter Ufer, and Kenneth Adams. The following year, a bored wealthy Easterner by the name of Mabel Dodge Sterne moved to Taos. In 1923, she married a Taos Indian, Tony Luhan. To her wide circle of friends back East she wrote of sunsets transforming the high plateau and pine-clad mountains into a rose-red tableau, and of Indian people living a simple life of survival in multi-level adobe structures with no electricity or plumbing.

Artists who came at her invitation included Ansel Adams, Andrew Dasburg, Georgia O'Keeffe, Marsden Hartley, and John Marin. Perhaps her greatest visitor arrived in 1922. D.H Lawrence and his wife Frieda spent that fall and winter and the spring of 1924 at Kiowa Ranch north of Taos, a gift of the generous Mabel Dodge Luhan. Even though his time in New Mexico was short, Lawrence wrote that the state changed him forever.

> All those mornings when I went with a hoe along the ditch to the Cañon, at the ranch, and stood, in the fierce, proud silence of the Rockies, on their foothills, to look far over the desert to the blue mountains away in Arizona, blue as chalcedony, with the sage-brush desert sweeping grey-blue in between, dotted with tiny cube-crystals of houses, the vast amphitheatre of lofty, indomitable desert, sweeping round to the ponderous Sangre de Cristo mountains on the east, and coming up flush at the pine-dotted foot-hills of the Rockies! What splendor! Only the tawny eagle could really sail out into the splendor of it all.

Lawrence left behind half a dozen paintings—stylized figures displaying an amateurish quality unlike the sophisticated prose of his novels and essays. The paintings now hang on the walls of the manager's office at La Fonda, a hotel on the plaza in the town of Taos. For $1, you can view the bare breasts of plump women with piercing eyes. Just as interesting are photographs, many signed, of Taos' famous residents, including film actor and director Dennis Hopper, Frieda Lawrence, and Cubist painter Andrew Dasburg.

In 1930, Lawrence died in France from tuberculosis. A few years later, his wife Frieda returned to Taos with his ashes and her new lover, Angelo Ravagli. Today, the ashes are housed in a small chapel at the ranch that Frieda bequeathed to the University of New Mexico. Her own grave is nearby.

Most artists and writers who came to the state arrived by train and many of them preferred the juniper foothills of **Santa Fe** to the plateau outpost of Taos. They included Willa Cather, Mary Austin, and Oliver La Farge, who won a 1929 Pulitzer Prize for a Navajo love story called "Laughing Boy."

One group of Santa Fe artists—who met while painting the high desert country-side and the people of Santa Fe—formed Los Cinco Pintores (The Five Painters). Their goal was to "bring art to the people," and members were Jozef Bakos, Walter Mruk, Will Shuster, Willard Nash, and Fremont Ellis. The group's first exhibition was in 1921 at the Museum of Fine Arts. All built homes on Camino del Monte Sol and worked in studios along and near Canyon Road, today the most concentrated art district in the city. They were dubbed "the five nuts in five mud huts." Ellis's works are for sale at his Canyon Road studio, which is open by appointment.

Will Shuster briefly broke away from painting in 1926 to help create Zozobra, a menacing 40-foot-tall (12-m) wooden puppet that has come to symbolize Las Fiestas de Santa Fe. The weekend celebration, which commemorates the 1692 re-occupation of Santa Fe by Diego de Vargas, begins at dusk on the Friday following Labor Day. Zozobra, also known as Old Man Gloom, eyes gleaming with anger, waves his arms and groans in anguish at Fort Marcy Park, trying to dissuade the Fire God from igniting his papier-maché body with a flaming torch. The effigy always loses and goes up in a burst of flame to the cheers of 40,000 spectators, gleeful to see gloom disappear for another year.

Many others followed these early artists to northern New Mexico, including woodcutter Gustave Baumann, Russians Leon Gaspard and Nicolai Fechin, and painter Robert Henri.

The growth of the Santa Fe and Taos art colonies fostered a new respect for Indian artists, such as Allan Houser, Dan Namingha, Michael Naranjo, and Pablita Velarde, whose works hang in museums and galleries.

Blumenschein House in Taos is a fine example of "Santa Fe style."

D.H. LAWRENCE IN TAOS

D.H. Lawrence and his wife Frieda spent the fall/winter of 1922–23 and the summer of 1924 at a ranch outside Taos.

*W*e leave the ranch quite wild—only there's abundant feed for the five horses. And if we wanted to take the trouble, we could bring the water here as McClure did, and have a little farm.—There's quite a lot of land, really—I'd say 180 acres, but it takes a terrible long time to go around the fence, through the wild forest.—We got lots of wild strawberries—and we still get gallons of wild raspberries, up our own little canyon, where no soul ever goes. If we ride two miles, we can get no farther. Beyond, all savage, unbroken mountain.

We get our things from Taos—17 miles—either by wagon or when someone is coming in a car. Our road is no road—a breaking through the forest—but people come to see us. Every evening, just after tea, we saddle up and ride down to Del Monte Ranch for the milk, butter, eggs, and letters. The old trail passes their gate, and the mailman, on horseback, leaves all the mail in a box nailed on a tree. Usually we get back just at dusk. Yesterday we rode down to San Cristobal, where there is a cross-roads, a blacksmith, and a tiny village with no shop, no anything, save the blacksmith—only a handful of Mexicans who speak Spanish—we went to get Frieda's grey horse—the Azul—shod. They call him in Spanish *el Azul*—the Blue. During the day there's always plenty to do—chopping wood, carrying water—and our own work: sometimes we all paint pictures. Next week the Indian Geronimo is coming up to help me mend the corral, and build a porch over my door, and fix the spring for winter, with a big trough where horse can drink. I want a Mexican to come and live here while we are away, to keep the place from going wild, squirrels and bushy-tailed pack-rats from coming in, and to see the water doesn't freeze for the horses. It gets very cold, and snow often knee deep. Sometimes, for a day or two, no getting away from the ranch.

There, I hope that's all you want to know.

—D.H. Lawrence in a letter to his niece, 1924

■ SANTA FE SITES AND ATTRACTIONS

In the early days, their isolation caused Santa Feans to remain a part of three worlds: that of the spiritual Indians, the sensuous Spanish, and Anglo adventurers. For example, they adopted the earthen building styles of their neighbors, the Pueblo Indians in order to deal with an intense summer sun, spring winds that whipped up the sandy soil, and a white winter carpet that turned streets into mud bogs when it melted away. But they steadfastly retained the colorful dress of their forefathers to the south in Mexico or across the Atlantic Ocean in Spain.

Unwittingly, these hardy and ingenious people derived a unique and indigenous fashion statement known as "Santa Fe Style" that today can be found in all corners of the United States. While dirt-and-straw adobe bricks survive only in dry climates, *vigas* and *latilla* ceilings and red-brown clay tiled floors go anywhere, most notably, perhaps, in the restaurants of Los Angeles and New York.

But it's in New Mexico where they seem to belong. Cozy corner *kiva* fireplaces warm cold nights, flat roofs become gardens during summer months, and doorways curve into adobe benches underneath cobalt-blue wood-trimmed windows. Navajo and Chimayo textiles adorn walls and floors. Chairs, tables, and cupboards are intricately carved in the old Spanish Colonial style. Tin light fixtures and frames hang on white plaster walls.

In the early 1900s, a group of Santa Fe painters, writers, architects, businessmen, and politicians began a movement to preserve this Spanish-Pueblo architectural style, with its flat-roofed adobe buildings. The movement resulted in important new buildings that celebrated their vision: the Museum of Fine Arts, La Fonda Hotel, the New Mexico School for the Deaf—all sporting *vigas,* deliberately uneven walls, and *kiva* fireplaces.

But as Santa Fe Style has gained in popularity, so have its travesties multiplied. One newcomer to Santa Fe, an apartment manager, wanted to erect a 15-foot-high (45-m), turquoise-colored coyote outside the apartment complex because she thought it was the town's symbol. After all, coyotes howling at the moon are everywhere in the "City Different," one of Santa Fe's labels. These wooden sculptures come in a multitude of colors, from fire-engine red to seafoam green, and often wear a contrasting bandana around their necks. Another cliché is brightly painted wooden snakes, writhing as if to escape their cuteness. Add to these new arrivals a 20-pound (9-kg) squash blossom necklace with enough turquoise to fill a small safe, finely worked silver concha belts, and cow and ram skulls with horns, and you've got what many people refer to as "Santa Fe Tacky."

Tacky or stylish, Santa Fe is different and unlike "the deadly monotony of 10,000 American towns," as Santa Fe painter Carlos Vierra described the rest of the United States in 1917.

GALLERIES AND SHOPS

More than 200 galleries line the plazas and winding streets of Santa Fe. They are stocked with items ranging from the sublime to the ridiculous, including Western

landscape paintings, cowboy portraits, acrylic abstracts, old and new pottery, ban-
dana-bedecked howling coyotes, bronze buffaloes, and the works of a few European masters. Roy Rogers floor lamps stand next to glass cases stuffed with
exquisite Hopi silver bracelets and earrings. Ancient Mimbres pottery and yucca
water baskets are for sale next door to a shop that displays silver spurs and leather
saddles. In many galleries and shops, a friendly hound or gray cat extends the initial greetings.

A stroll up the winding **Canyon Road,** an old Indian trail that leads into the
piñon foothills, is an immersion into the town's eclectic art world. Nearly 100 galleries, shops, and restaurants line the narrow road. Even Los Alamos National Laboratory is represented in the metal sculptures of Tony Price, who gathers all of his
materials at the laboratory's junk yard. An African Nuclear Shaman, Rockette Nuclear Kachina, and Hopi Mudhead are represented in his science-fiction sculptures
at the non-profit **TenGam Exhibit Gallery.**

The sweet smell of piñon smoke wafts from *kiva* fireplaces, which provide
welcome warmth on a chilly winter day. The stark white walls and bleached
wood floors of **Janus Gallery** and its abstract mixed-medias contrast with a
homey feeling at **Kania-Ferrin Gallery,** where you walk through the kitchen to
check out a Fiji war club. Two horse-chestnut trees and a turquoise picket fence

Shopping and strolling are favorite pastimes in Santa Fe.

mark **El Zaguan,** a nineteenth-century hacienda that has been turned into private apartments. The west garden of this rambling adobe with its three-foot-thick (1-m) walls was designed by Adolf Bandelier in the late 1800s, and its peony bushes were imported more than 100 years ago from China. The garden's wrought-iron benches are a pleasant place to rest and listen to the songs of birds and the hum of traffic along the road. On Christmas Eve, votive candles are set in dirt inside paper bags and line walls, rooftops, and the narrow streets of the area. These flickering lights are called *farolitos.* Those who share in the tradition of strolling among the twinkling lights may stop to warm their hands at small bonfires of stacked piñon wood, called *luminarias.* Neighbors play guitars and share hot apple cider and *biscochitos*—small anise-flavored sugar cookies.

During a springtime stroll, the white and pink blooms of cosmos mix with other wildflowers along narrow Canyon Road, leaving barely a sidewalk for folks on foot. Coyote fences (wooden posts strung together with wire) and stone walls ensure privacy for the few residents along this scenic thoroughfare. Where Canyon Road joins Camino Cabra, **Cristo Rey Catholic Church** stands as a memorial to Francisco Vasquez de Coronado. Dedicated in 1940 to commemorate the 400th anniversary of the Spanish explorer's travels in the Southwest, the massive adobe structure was built primarily to house a magnificent stone *reredos* (altar screen)—the most famous piece of ecclesiastical art created in New Mexico during Spanish colonial times. Clearly the focal point of the otherwise austere sanctuary, the faded colors and weathered white stone elicit a feeling of reverence. This screen, commissioned in 1760, served as the prototype for the numerous wooden altar screens found in churches throughout the state. A total of 180,000 adobe bricks were used in construction, all molded from the soil on which the building stands.

Farther into the foothills, on Upper Canyon Road, artist Randall Davey's home has been turned into regional headquarters for the **Audubon Society,** and nature trails wind through its grounds at the mouth of **Santa Fe Canyon.**

Additional shops and galleries are scattered throughout the blocks surrounding the plaza and along Guadalupe Street.

MUSEUMS

Four state-run museums are located in Santa Fe, including the nearly 400-year-old **Palace of the Governors,** which specializes in New Mexico history. The block-long adobe palace was built around a courtyard, and its rooms attach to each other, beckoning exploration from one to the next. Exhibits follow a chronological order and feature ancient Indian pottery, a rebuilt two-wheeled *carreta,* maps of eighteenth-century Spanish America and a nineteenth-century chuck wagon. Outside the restored government building, Indian artists sit patiently on the brick sidewalk beside blankets spread with their crafts and art work. Rain or shine, warm or cold, these artisans display their handmade jewelry every day of the year. Prices are reasonable and the artists enjoy talking about their work.

Across the street from the palace, the **Museum of Fine Arts** houses a permanent collection of more than 8,000 works, including seven paintings by Georgia O'Keeffe and other regional pieces by Gustave Baumann, Will Schuster, John Marin, Marsden Hartley, and painters from the Taos School. Completed in 1917, this massive structure was the first example of the Pueblo Revival style to be built in Santa Fe and acted as a stimulus to the development of the city's emerging art colony. Changing shows display works from the permanent collection, along with contemporary local and regional painting, sculpture, and photography.

The **Museum of International Folk Art,** located southeast of downtown among juniper and yellow-tipped chamisa, is a whimsical, fascinating world of toys, textiles, and crafts collected from 100 countries. A walk through the wonderful Girard Wing takes you past a mesmerizing fantasy world of African puppets, antique dolls from around the world, Russian icons, and table settings complete with plastic vegetables and rubber hamburgers. Tiny figurines depicting people of all ages shop and work in a detailed miniature Mexican village that includes green shrubbery. Doll houses line the streets of a typical American town, and an array of intricately carved boats, mostly Oriental, line up in a busy harbor ready to unload their wares. This wing was built in 1983 to house the one-of-a-kind Girard Collection, 106,000 items of folk art gathered by architect Alexander Girard and his wife, Susan, during a lifetime of travels. The museum also concentrates on Hispanic folk arts in the Hispanic Heritage Wing, opened in 1989. Changing exhibits display tinwork, Spanish colonial furniture making, folk costumes, and textiles. The museum houses the largest collection of Spanish colonial folk art in the United States. *Bultos* and *santos* reveal an evolution of style through nearly three centuries.

The **New Mexico Museum of Indian Arts and Culture,** opened in 1987 across the parking lot from the Museum of Folk Art, details the history and contemporary lives of Pueblo, Apache, and Navajo Indians. Their story is told through displays of Clovis points, ancient cookware, clothing, and diagrams. Exhibits draw from collections of the 60-year-old Laboratory of Anthropology, located next door, including the first black-on-black pot fired by famed potter Maria Martinez of San Ildefonso Pueblo, a bridle that belonged to Apache leader Cochise, a 151-foot-long (46-m) hunting net made of human hair and fiber dating to 1100, and more than 50,000 baskets, items of pottery, jewelry, weaving, and carving. In addition, modern Indian artists demonstrate their craftsmanship, weaving on looms and molding pottery.

Walking into the **Wheelwright Museum,** located next door to the Museum of Folk Art, is like walking into a giant Navajo hogan, a circular one-story structure used for ceremonies and residences. As in all Navajo dwellings, the entrance faces east, to best achieve a sense of harmony with the sun streaming in every morning. This private museum is dedicated to preserving and furthering the traditions of Native Americans and contains textiles, baskets, pottery, jewelry, folk arts, fine arts, and clothing, mostly of Navajo origin. In addition, the Wheelwright's collection of 600 Navajo sandpainting reproductions is the largest in the world. Pueblo, Plains, and Apache Indians also are represented in the exhibits, which include the Case Trading Post, a replica of an early twentieth-century reservation store. During early July, special dances, demonstrations, markets, ceremonies, and storytelling go on for a week.

SANTA FE WALK

The winding streets of Santa Fe, which often seem too narrow for cars, are perfect for a leisurely stroll. Following is a suggested walk that starts at the St. Francis Cathedral. This taste of old Santa Fe represents only a partial look into the romantic city's past. Nearly every street surrounding the Plaza contains its own treasures and is worth exploring.

Built of sandstone and a lightweight volcanic rock, the towering Romanesque **St. Francis Cathedral** looms at the end of East San Francisco Street, in stark contrast to nearby low earthen-colored adobe buildings. Originally, plans included building a 160-foot (99-m) steeple on each of the two towers, but today the only visual evidence of such intentions are supports that jut from the left tower.

As you enter the grounds, you'll see the statue of Archbishop Jean Baptiste Lamy, the driving force behind this mammoth undertaking. Inside, 55-foot-tall (17-m) taupe walls are decorated with intricate geometric designs painted on the many sweeping arches that reach up to support the vaulted ceiling. The brightly colored stained-glass windows are finely crafted and exquisitely detailed. The serene La Conquistadora, who accompanied Spanish colonists to Santa Fe in the early 1600s, stands proudly on her own altar in her own chapel. She wears a delicate lace veil and a billowing gown that is changed with the season or holiday: at Christmas it is kelly green.

The nearby **Loretto Chapel** at 219 Old Santa Fe Trail was another of Archbishop Lamy's projects, designed to meet the spiritual needs of Loretto Academy, founded in 1853 by New Mexico's first six nuns. The small Gothic chapel, fashioned after Sainte Chappelle in Paris, offers a lot for its size: European-made stained-glass windows, Italian statues depicting the stations of the cross, and a faux-marble wooden altar.

But most impressive is a 33-step wooden staircase that twists in a double helix and was built without a nail, screw, or any support. Known today as the "miraculous staircase," this wondrous feat of carpentry contains no imprint of its master builder, a mysterious man equipped with a hammer, saw, and a T-square. His only request was for two tubs of water. He accepted no payment and disappeared after completing the project. Some say he was St. Joseph, the carpenter saint. Others say he was Yohon Hadwiger, a carpenter visiting from Vienna, Austria.

Heading south, Old Santa Fe Trail crosses the Santa Fe River, which rushes with water in the spring, but becomes a dry ditch by fall due to dams and reservoirs high up in the mountains.

Across the river is **Barrio de Analco**, Santa Fe's oldest neighborhood, originally settled in the 1600s by Tlaxcalan Indian servants from Mexico who accompanied early Franciscan missionaries and Spanish officials to the new territory. Narrow brick sidewalks buckle and porch roofs slant, showing their age. The **Chapel of San Miguel** stands in the center of this historic district. A finely crafted stone wall protects the simple adobe chapel from the busy street. Inside, an animated gilded statue of St. Michael, the church's patron saint, stands centered on an ornate wooden altar.

Cottonwoods provide shade, and a cloyingly sweet fragrance emanates from purple wisteria blossoms as the ancient narrow De Vargas Street leads west to the **Santuario de Guadalupe** at the corner of Agua Fria and Guadalupe streets. Built sometime between 1776 and 1795, this adobe shrine to Our Lady of Guadalupe, patron saint of Mexico, displays one of the finest and most unique *reredos* in the Southwest. Painted in 1783 in Mexico, this oil-on-canvas altar screen was created expressly for the Santa Fe chapel and was hauled up the Chihuahua Trail in an oxcart. Carved *vigas* and corbels adorn the high ceiling, and the windows are stained glass. Today, the small chapel is still in use and is often the site of theatrical and musical performances.

Crossing back over the Santa Fe River, Guadalupe Street intersects with San Francisco Street, which leads back to the Plaza.

RESTAURANTS
Finding a great place to eat in Santa Fe is never a problem, but during the summer, getting a seat in a restaurant can be a different story. About 200 restaurants with menus offering everything from sushi to chicken-fried steak line major thoroughfares or are tucked into back-alley adobe buildings. The cuisine represents the city's varied cultures, especially the newly transplanted ones.

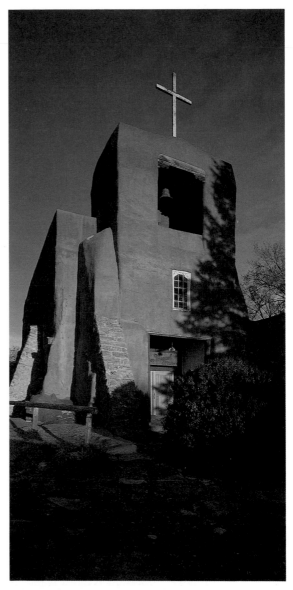

San Miguel Chapel, Santa Fe.

(For more specific information, see "Restaurants" in "PRACTICAL INFORMATION.")

The **Natural Cafe** caters to vegetarian palates, while the tony **Coyote Cafe** is beyond the pocketbooks of most Santa Feans. *Tapas* (Spanish hors d'oeuvres) are served in the cozy confines of **El Farol,** and the mocha cake at **The Shed** and **La Choza,** with the same owners, is worth saving room for. Despite the town's twentieth-century influences, breakfast burritos, chile rellenos, tamales, and enchiladas remain the food of choice. At **Old Mexico Grill,** a comfortable eatery with tiled floors and a copper-covered grill, Mexican paella and shrimp marinated in tequila bring to mind balmy ocean breezes and the stone streets of Puerto Vallarta.

To entice its trendy visitors, the **Zia Diner** replaces mundane pinto beans with sleeker black ones, and blue corn tortillas have nearly run the traditional yellow variety out of town. British visitors and anyone else just needing a rest from shopping may enjoy high tea, which is served daily in the lobby of the St. Francis Hotel. In Santa Fe, you can expect to pay a few dollars more than anywhere else in the state, but after all, location is everything.

Because of the overwhelming number of offerings, it's wise to gather recommendations rather than waste time finding out that many restaurants don't live up to their decor.

■ THE HIGH ROAD

Most of the small Hispanic farming villages that line what has become known as the "high road," linking Santa Fe and Taos, were settled in the eighteenth century. Remarkably, these picturesque hamlets—with their weathered log barns, thick, adobe-walled homes, and tin roofs that reflect the shimmering sunlight—appear much as they did 200 years ago. Most people speak Spanish as easily as English. Every spring, members of community *acequia* associations gather: armed with shovels, rakes, and pitchforks, they clear debris from irrigation ditches and ensure an uninterrupted flow of mountain runoff throughout the summer. Fall brings a harvest of beans and apples, followed by day-long wood-cutting expeditions to the nearby mountains.

Heading north out of Santa Fe, this scenic route starts out by passing **Tesuque, Pojoaque,** and **Nambé** pueblos. At Nambé, hikers can walk to a series of three waterfalls five miles (8 km) up Nambé Creek and listen to a ranger tell of a time long ago when a pueblo maiden was courted by two rivals—a warrior and a hunter. When the jealous warrior killed the hunter, both were swallowed up by the earth. The falls were formed by the girl's tears as she wandered and wept in mourning.

Winding among rolling hills dotted with piñon pines and junipers, the high road drops into the village of **Chimayo**, which is tucked into a cottonwood-shaded valley. Here, Hispanic weavers craft brightly colored clothing and blankets, characterized by bold stripes. Originally, Spanish colonial artisans wove these beautiful textiles for their own use. Interest in the craft flagged and in the early 1800s, Santa Fe residents sent to Spain for expert weavers to revive the art and teach their children. Two of these artisans, Juan and Ignacio Balzan, rejected the capital city for the sheltered hamlet of Chimayo. There, they taught the craft to Chimayo residents who continue the tradition today. Ortega's Weaving Shop is now headed by David Ortega, a member of the sixth generation to live and work in this spot. His two sons are also weavers.

This peaceful town is also known for **El Santuario de Chimayo,** which attracts thousands of pilgrims every year during Holy Week. Some worshipers walk along the shoulders of freeways and two-lane highways from as far away as Albuquerque, 80 miles (128 km) south. They come to express their faith at the adobe chapel whose bell towers rise above ancient cottonwoods. Inside a small, candlelit anteroom built onto the structure, they collect from a tiny hole in the ground a sample of the *tierra bendita* (sacred earth) that many believe has healing powers. According to ancient legend, fire and smoke erupted near where the sanctuary stands today, leaving a pool of mud. Pueblo Indians used the soil for medicinal purposes, eating it or smearing it on their bodies.

The family chapel was built between 1813 and 1816 by Bernardo Abeyta who, legend has it, was deathly ill when a vision led him to a spot where immediately he was cured. He erected the small church atop the spot to give thanks. Testaments of healing, such as discarded crutches, hang from the adobe walls of a small room that attaches to the main chapel.

Before leaving town, a perfect rest stop is **Rancho de Chimayo,** the restored 1880 home of the Jaramillo family, now a restaurant. A strain of chile grown only in the fields of this area is featured in the New Mexico cuisine here. Diners can bask in the warmth of a *kiva* fireplace in one of the wooden-floored dining rooms, or sip on a margarita in cool shade on the outside patio. Another Jaramillo family home has been turned into a quaint bed and breakfast. The operations are run by descendants of the Jaramillo family, who were early Chimayo settlers.

Cordova, a tiny enclave that hugs nearby hillsides, boasts a longstanding tradition of woodcarvers. Look for signs that mark their workshops.

With the stunning 13,000-foot (3,962-m) Truchas Peaks as a backdrop and the Rio Grande Valley in the distance, the tin roofs of **Truchas** (Trouts) rise from fertile vegetable and bean fields. Wild herbs, scrub oak, and cattails prosper in back yards. It's easy to see why, in the mid-1980s, Robert Redford filmed *The Milagro Beanfield War* in this bucolic setting. Many trails branch out of town into the piñon and ponderosa pine hills of the Carson National Forest.

One of the finest eighteenth-century Spanish Pueblo-style churches survives at **Las Trampas,** on high ground next to the road. In contrast to the more refined restoration at the Chimayo sanctuary, San Jose de Gracia at Las Trampas retains a rustic simplicity. The Las Trampas church initially was known as the Church of the Twelve Apostles, and it has been said that only 12 men at a time were permitted to erect its four-foot-thick (1-m) adobe walls. The church, which stands 34 feet (10 m) tall, was built with an outside choir loft so the chorus could move outside to sing during religious processions. Inside, plain wooden benches rest on uneven wood-planked floors. Painted *vigas* and corbels, along with elaborate paintings, add decoration to the stark interior. If the church should be locked, visitors need only ask a neighbor to open the heavy wooden doors that lead to its cool interior.

Picuris Pueblo is a small, yet growing, pueblo situated in an open valley along the Rio Pueblo. A tribal museum tells the story of the isolated pueblo, which today has 150 residents. Guides take visitors past the remains of its prehistoric village that stands near modern-day residences.

Abandoned movie theaters and car dealerships attest to the long-lost commercial prosperity once enjoyed by the village of **Peñasco.** Originally established in 1796 as three settlements along the Rio Santa Barbara, Peñasco still stretches along the waterway. But as its younger residents move away in search of better jobs, the small farms and ranches that gave the village its identity are disappearing. Many historic adobe homes, dance halls, and restaurants remain, but some are no longer occupied.

A dirt road follows the shallow, tree-shaded Rio Santa Barbara into the **Pecos Wilderness** to campgrounds surrounded by fields of wildflowers and trails that lead to mountain lakes and the high peaks that protect the valley settlements.

This family chapel built by Bernardo Abeyta between 1813 and 1816
at Chimayo has become a local pilgrimage site.

The paved road that leads to Taos, NM 518, climbs steeply, leaving behind the fertile valleys and entering into tall pine forests and mountain meadows of the Taos Plateau. **Fort Burgwin Research Center** straddles the road. Restored and run by Southern Methodist University, the fort was built in 1852 to protect Taos from raiding Comanche and Ute Indians. Research focuses on the ruins of Anasazi dwellings on the site that date to A.D. 1100. During summer months, music and theater presentations, along with seminars, are offered.

The road ends at **Ranchos de Taos,** a few miles south of the village of Taos. This small village was established in 1716 by Spanish homesteaders. Comanche raids made life unpredictable for settlers until the end of the nineteenth century. Many fine adobe buildings have been restored in this hamlet, and it is home to one of the most photographed and painted eighteenth-century missions, the Church of St. Francis of Assisi, built in 1730 to convert Taos Indians. Burros hauled huge adobe bricks up earthen ramps. A fortress-like church, its walls are 13 feet (4 m) thick at the base and are supported on the outside by heavy adobe buttresses. Like most churches of its day, the Ranchos Church supports two bell towers. Unlike many, however, the left tower is slightly taller than the right, a testament to New Mexico's disregard for symmetry. One artist attracted to the irregular lines of the church's walls was Georgia O'Keeffe. "Most artists who spend any time in Taos have to paint it, I suppose, just as they have to paint a self-portrait. I had to paint it—the back of it several times, the front once."

Inside, enormous *vigas* and corbels support a high ceiling. Most notable among a collection of European and New Mexican artwork is a painting that is said to glow in the dark.

■ TAOS SITES AND ATTRACTIONS

GALLERIES, MUSEUMS, AND HISTORIC HOMES

Easy to inspect on foot, most Taos galleries hug the narrow streets and historic sites surrounding the central plaza. Occasionally a crow calls from the treetops above the **Charles Bent home** where New Mexico's first American governor was killed and scalped during the Taos Rebellion. Pink plaster is peeled away where his wife and two other women dug into the thick adobe wall in their attempt to escape Bent's killers. The women were spared. A black-cloth Penitente mask and leather whip are protected in a glass case as a reminder of the days when that self-torturing Catholic confraternity flourished in northern New Mexico. A broad-backed Bent family wooden chair with leather seat sits in a room next to a marble-topped dresser.

Offices and a courtroom at the old two-story **Taos County Courthouse,** which faces the plaza, have been turned into galleries and shops. **Burke Armstrong Fine Arts** takes up what must have been the courtroom. Modern soapstone sculptures by Taos Pueblo artist John Suazo and landscape paintings of the Southwest now share the space with a series of frescoes painted on the walls in 1934 by Emil Bisttram, Bert Phillips, and Victor Higgins. Classical animated scenes represent virtues and vices such as Reconciliation and Transgression, which are written in both English and Spanish on each panel.

Friendly shopkeepers encourage browsers interested in custom women's clothing, deep purple cellophane-looking duffel bags, or seventeenth-century maps. More than 50 galleries are scattered throughout the town's dusty streets. Mixed medias by Larry Bell hang at **New Directions** on the plaza, and R.C. Gorman's pastel Indian women line the walls at his **Navajo Gallery** on Ledoux Street. Gorman, a Navajo artist, has lived outside of Taos since 1968.

At the **Taos Book Shop,** one of the nine book shops in Taos, Barbara Chavez, the owner's mother, invites you to pick out a book and curl up with it in a comfortable overstuffed chair in front of a warm fire.

Kit Carson, who at age 16 signed on with a wagon train heading across the Santa Fe Trail, made his home in Taos. Even though the famous trapper and Indian fighter spent most of his time on the road, in 1843 he presented to his new bride, Josefa Jaramillo, a 12-room adobe home near the central plaza. Seven of the Carson's eight children were born inside the 30-inch-thick (76-cm) adobe walls of the U-shaped building, occupied by the family for 25 years. Today, the **Kit Carson Home,** built in 1825, is one of three historic museums operated by the Kit Carson Foundation. A walk through the meandering dirt- and wood-floored rooms provides a glimpse of life in the Carson household where the couple's children played and helped their mother prepare meals, and where Carson met with traders, dignitaries, and military men who passed through New Mexico. You'll see shotguns that probably accompanied the Kentucky-born scout on his many missions into the wilderness. You'll also see one of Josefa's narrow-waisted tan and brown silk dresses and a fringed beige shawl on display inside a glass case. The living room, with

Carson's black wooden desk in a corner and wooden organ along a wall, seems to be awaiting the return of its inhabitants.

The fortress-like adobe walls of the **Martinez Hacienda,** two miles (3 km) outside of Taos, alongside the Rio Pueblo, were built to provide protection from Indian attacks. Construction of the home, begun in 1804, was often interrupted by

Kit Carson and his wife Josefa fed their eight children out of this kitchen.

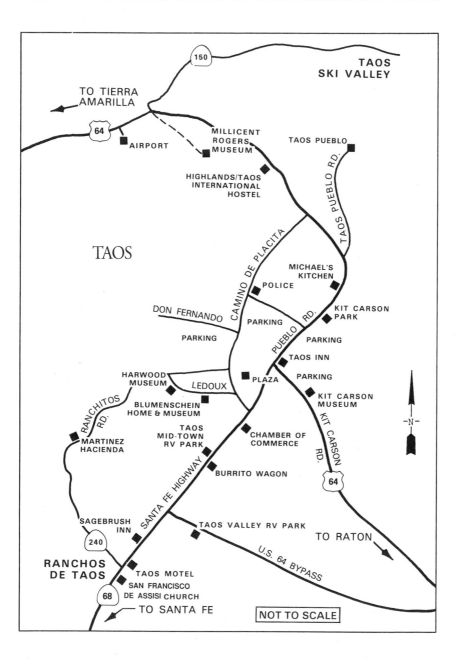

NOT TO SCALE

Comanche and Apache raids. Even after completion, tending sheep outside its protective walls was hazardous. Antonio Severino Martinez, one of the area's chief traders, hauled over the Chihuahua Trail to Mexico tallow candles, piñon nuts, jerky, beaver pelts, wool, and woven belts in two-wheeled *carretas* and atop pack mules, bringing back cloth, nails, tools, sugar, and chocolate. Martinez, who also served as mayor of Taos, turned his home into a showpiece, with 21 rooms surrounding two courtyards. Each room reveals a different *latilla* construction of split pine, juniper, or aspen pole, all hauled from the nearby mountains. A shepherd's fireplace, set deep enough into the adobe wall so that large pots could fit inside, takes up one corner of the kitchen. A *carreta*, with wooden wheels worn smooth from its travels, is sheltered under a covered *zaguan* (entry way). Today, local weavers and quilters spin wool, work on wooden looms, and sew quilts in rooms off the rear courtyard, much as they might have done 150 years ago.

From 1919 until his death in 1960, artist Ernest Blumenschein, along with his wife Mary, lived and worked in a 12-room, eighteenth-century adobe home in downtown Taos. Today, the **Ernest Blumenschein Home** appears much as it did when the painter lived there. Wooden armoires shipped from France stand against adobe walls, and a cedar table and matching sideboard, made by a Taos craftsman, fill the dining room. Paintings by Blumenschein, his wife, their daughter Helen, and other Taos artists line the walls.

Millicent Rogers, a Standard Oil heiress, came to New Mexico in 1948 for a short visit and, caught by its spell, built a home in Taos. For the next five years, until her death in 1953, Rogers amassed an extensive collection of ancient Indian pottery, nineteenth-century Navajo blankets, *kachinas,* jewelry, and Spanish Colonial *bultos,* pressed tin light fixtures, and frames. In 1956, her son, Paul Peralta Ramos, established the **Millicent Rogers Museum,** which includes one of the largest collections of black-on-black pottery created by San Ildefonso potter Maria Martinez. One large deer-motif pot dates to 1919, the year Maria and her husband, Julian, devised the technique. One room is dedicated to Maria and her family, some of whom are also potters. Photographs depict the precise, time-consuming process of coiling the clay and achieving the shiny black glaze over an outdoor fire covered with metal and cow manure.

RESTAURANTS

Taos restaurants are less interesting than those in Santa Fe. Apart from innovative pastas and seafood at the **Apple Tree,** shrimp burritos and steak picante at **Doc Martin's,** and the lightness of fresh fish topped with vegetable relishes at **Lambert's,** the choices are traditional New Mexican. In keeping with its Pueblo-Spanish decor, even the fast-food outlets boast stuccoed mud-colored exteriors. No golden arches reach for the sky. (For specifics see "Restaurants" in "PRACTICAL INFORMATION.")

JEWISH TRADITION IN NEW MEXICO

In 1492, when Columbus set sail to discover America, Ferdinand and Isabella of Spain issued the infamous Edict of 1492, which forced Spanish Jews to choose between exile or conversion. Some Jews became "new Christians," many only pretending to convert, and in the early years of the Conquest, emigrated to Mexico. When the Inquisition reached the New World, the "new Christians" found themselves once again under suspicion, and many began moving to the farthest reaches of the empire, into what is now New Mexico.

Ostensibly practicing Catholics, these Jewish families clung in private to their traditions: lighting candles on Fridays, baking unleavened bread, and keeping the Sabbath. Recently, Jewish families searching for their roots have found hundreds of gravestones with Hebrew inscriptions in isolated cemeteries across the state.

Although the oldest synagogue in the United States was founded in New York in 1645, it may be that its first *minyan* was held in New Mexico.

NORTHWESTERN
N E W   M E X I C O

SANDSTONE BLUFFS AND MESAS RIMMED IN MUTED SHADES of red and gray rise above the box canyons and grama grass meadows of northwestern New Mexico. Parched riverbeds that swell with muddy water after a summer cloudburst and then dry up again meander throughout rangeland dotted with chamisa and salt-bush. This gentle landscape is interrupted by the rugged El Malpais lava flow, with its chilly ice caves and hardened tubes of lava. In the Bisti Badlands, the fossils of horned dinosaurs lay strewn among eerie mushroom-shaped spires, and Shiprock, a basaltic core that once filled the center of a volcano, now stands like a beacon in the desert. Nearby flows the blue-green water of the San Juan River as it wends its way toward Utah.

Among these strung-out mesas, abrupt rock cliffs, and buttes is a treasure trove of Native American dwellings, old and new. Ragged remains of ancient Indian villages lay scattered throughout broken mesas and cliffsides. Some have been excavated and preserved, others are covered with mounds of windswept soil. Indian influence, past and present, is greater here than anywhere else in the state, and much of the land belongs to New Mexico's three major Indian groups: the Navajo, Apache, and Pueblo.

The Anasazi, ancestors of the Pueblo Indians, lived alongside riverbeds that once flowed year-round, where they cultivated beans and corn and erected rock buildings held together with mortar. The excavation of 11 of these sites has revealed the most extensive ancient Indian ruins in the country. Little evidence, on the other hand, remains of the ancestors of the Apache and Navajo, nomadic hunters and gatherers, who moved about in search of food.

Northwestern New Mexico is still largely rural, with many modern-day Indians living in small communities or on isolated ranchos spread across their reservations. Of the few sizable towns, Gallup, at the southern end of the Navajo Reservation, is the major trading center for Indian wares, and Farmington at its northern border serves as a business hub.

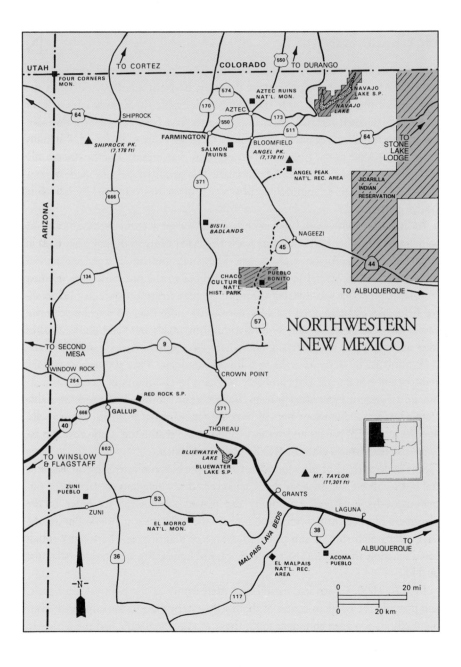

■ CHACO CANYON

Today, most of the state's 19 pueblos hug the Rio Grande, clustered in north-central New Mexico. But it wasn't always that way. Between A.D. 900 and 1200, the ancestors of these Indians made their homes alongside the flowing Chaco River and atop high desert mesas. More than 2,000 sites have been documented throughout the northwestern region, and it is likely there are more to be found. We know these early people as the Anasazi, a Navajo term that means "Enemy Ancestors." We also know that during the Chaco years, this primitive culture made a giant evolutionary leap in its approach to life, which never was surpassed by following Native generations.

As many as 5,000 small, brown-skinned Indians grew corn, beans, and squash in irrigated fields beneath sandstone walls in Chaco Canyon during what has become known as the Anasazi Golden Age. They built multi-story stone and mortar homes with rooms several times larger than those in the previous stages of their culture. River water was diverted through complex irrigation systems into ditch-fed fields. An elaborate road network connected more than 75 pueblos scattered throughout the region. These 30-foot-wide (9-m) roads were laid out in straight lines unimpeded by rough terrain, and where they passed over bare rock the roads were bordered by masonry walls or a line of boulders. This 400-mile (640-km) transportation and trade route probably was used by communities spread throughout northwestern New Mexico to exchange crops, pottery, and clothing made from deer, elk, and antelope hunted in nearby mountains. Seashells, copper bells, and the remains of parrots and macaws found in the crumbling ruins prove the Indians also had contact with tribes as far south as Mexico.

The large number of *kivas* found in Chaco's pueblos indicates religion was central to the culture and suggests that Chaco served as a religious center for the numerous outlying villages. Astronomy also played a major role as shown by the placement of small corner windows built into the thick walls at Pueblo Bonito, the largest excavated ruin. A sun priest in charge of planting and harvesting rituals could schedule those events based on the play of light along an interior wall at the pueblo.

By A.D. 1000, Chaco had established itself firmly as the political, economic, and possibly the religious center of the northwestern plateau. As improved farming methods provided abundant food, these productive people had the leisure to develop their artistic abilities. They etched petroglyphs of snakes and spirals into the soft sandstone, wove baskets and sandals from desert grasses, and fashioned clay bowls, pitchers, water jars, and mugs with detailed black-on-white geometric designs.

The Anasazi mysteriously disappeared from the canyon by the fourteenth century. Theories abound as to why they abandoned their pueblos at the height of their culture. Archaeologists attribute the exodus to drought, to disease, to roving bands of Indians who continually threatened these people, or to outbreaks of fighting among the Anasazi themselves. One thing is certain. A drought struck the region in 1276 and lasted 25 years. They may have traveled south to build new homes near more reliable sources of water, such as the Rio Grande.

When the Navajo entered the area in the 1770s, they found the broad basin unoccupied. The once-flowing river was dry and ran only after summer rainstorms. The fields of corn and beans had been overtaken by desert grasses and sagebrush, and the voices of a vibrant culture were silent.

Today, the wind whistles through the canyon and carries new voices, those of visitors at **Chaco Culture National Historical Park.** Extensive rock ruins blend with towering sandstone cliff faces that provided the ancient masons with their building materials. Along the banks of the bone-dry riverbed, partial walls appear rust red against an azure sky, steel gray under a blanket of clouds, or dull umber when covered with snow.

At Pueblo Bonito, Anasazi masons shaped thousands of rocks of all sizes with crude stone hammers and axes in the construction of more than 600 rooms and 40 *kivas.* The varying construction techniques reflect the order in which these carefully crafted walls were built. For example, the oldest walls were one-stone thick with generous applications of mud mortar. Later walls had thick inner cores of rubble topped off by a veneer of stonework so precisely fitted that little mortar was needed. Stone bases remain that once steadied masonry pillars supporting heavily beamed four-story roofs.

Across the dry wash from Pueblo Bonito is the giant *kiva* of Casa Rinconada, which was built apart from other communities, indicating that it was possibly used as some sort of community center. A smooth stone bench that traces the outer wall is a perfect place to rest and listen to the silence, broken only by occasional gusts of wind. The musty smell of sandstone mingles with imagined memories of the many ceremonies that must have taken place here at one of the largest "great *kivas*" in the Southwest.

Behind Pueblo Bonito, Pueblo Alto sits atop a mesa. Its location at the junction of several prehistoric roads suggests it served as a trade and distribution center.

Today, a few gravel roads lead to the park—from I-40 to the south and NM 44 to the northwest—where the only accommodation is a campground. Tours are offered daily, and pamphlets for the self-initiated also are available at each of eight restored ruins that stretch for a few miles alongside Chaco Wash. Well-marked hiking trails lead from the now-silent riverbed to additional ruins such as Pueblo Alto, Penasco Blanco, and the symmetrical village of Wijiji.

Consisting of more than 600 rooms, Pueblo Bonito is considered one of the most sophisticated examples of Anasazi architecture. (Paul Chesley)

CHACO OUTLIERS

While most of the prehistoric villages served by the Chaco road network have remained unexcavated, two outlying sites are preserved and partially reconstructed at **Aztec Ruins National Monument** and **Salmon Ruin.**

The communal dwellings of Aztec were built on a rise overlooking the blue-green Animas River, and they reveal construction methods similar to those used at Chaco Canyon. (The crumbling walls and rectangular rooms were named by nineteenth-century settlers who mistakenly assumed the pueblo was built by the Aztec Indians of Mexico.) A walk through the largest pueblo, a U-shaped village that covered two acres and contained 500 rooms in three stories, allows you to look across the decaying walls into a maze of square and rectangular adjoining rooms and to crawl through tiny doorways. You can peer into subterranean *kivas,* built with thousands of soft taupe sandstone slabs. Anchoring the pueblo is the Great Kiva, constructed in the twelfth century and reconstructed in 1934. The grand underground space was broken only by massive columns that supported a roof estimated at 90 tons. This is the only reconstructed great *kiva* in the Southwest. As you descend into the flat-top, underground sanctuary, push a button to hear recorded Native American music, take a seat on the mud-brown rock bench, and try to recapture the solemnity that must have pervaded Anasazi religious ceremonies.

Much of this site remains unexcavated under sandy mounds scattered in the shade of cottonwood trees. No one knows if the mounds cover dwellings or trash heaps.

Salmon Ruin sits atop a bluff overlooking the farmland of the San Juan River valley two miles (3 km) west of Bloomfield. A well-traveled Chacoan road leads directly north from Chaco Canyon for 50 miles (80 km) through dusty arroyos and across desert mesas to the C-shaped, 250-room pueblo. Most building materials here were imported: sandstone was quarried at sites 30 miles (48 km) distant, and timbers used for the *vigas* (roof beams) were hauled from southern Colorado. Nearby petroglyphs depict ears of corn on a stalk, and some archaeologists speculate that the small community was developed as an agricultural center to serve the main Chaco Canyon villages.

Salmon Ruin was named for George Salmon, an 1880s homesteader who protected the site from vandals and thieves in search of ancient pottery. His home still stands nearby.

The pueblos of Aztec and Salmon were abandoned by the mid-twelfth century, only to be reoccupied in the early thirteenth century by Indians from the nearby Mesa Verde culture of southwestern Colorado. But they, too, left later that century, never to return.

■ ACOMA PUEBLO

At the same time the Anasazi were at the peak of their civilization, residents at Acoma were building adobe and rock homes high atop the 357-foot (109-m) Rock of Acuco. This multi-colored sandstone mesa rises from a sandy plain dotted with chamisa and juniper trees southeast of present-day Grants. Some historians estimate Acoma Pueblo has been occupied since A.D. 1075, making it the oldest continuously inhabited city in the country.

The Acomas say their ancestors arrived in A.D. 600 from Mesa Verde in what today is southern Colorado. According to legend, the Indians were told by Iatiku, mother of all Indians, to seek a mesa resembling the tip of an ear of corn. They found Enchanted Mesa and built a rock-walled village atop the majestic mountain. Only one route led up the precipitous 430-foot (131-m) cliffs of the desert monolith, and another legend has it that one day, when most of the tribe was tending fields on the plains, a violent storm moved in, wiping out the path to the top. A young girl and her grandmother were stranded on top. Rather than starve, they leaped to their deaths. The tribe moved to the nearby Acuco Mesa.

Some historians believe the early dwellers chose to build atop Acuco for its protection from marauding tribes. The solitary citadel served the tribe well in 1540 when Spaniards came searching for the Seven Cities of Cibola and mistakenly thought they saw those riches reflected in the pueblo's mica window panes. Though their attempt to scale the mountain was unsuccessful, the soldiers killed 100 Acoma men.

At one time, several thousand Indians lived in multi-story rock-walled dwellings crowded onto the 70-acre mesa. They must have wakened to a dawn in which a brilliant sun illuminated a distant snowcapped peak (now called Mount Taylor) and fields below of corn, beans, and squash—much the same view as today. Descending a steep staircase carved from the soft rock, they would have set about their various occupations—gathering wood from nearby woodlands and tending to their fields. Every night they would have climbed the steep mountain to the village.

Acoma residents successfully held off intruders until 1598, when the pueblo voluntarily submitted to the Spanish. This peaceful acquiescence was short-lived, however; the Indians killed Juan de Zaldivar and 12 soldiers who were seeking cornmeal. Unfortunately for the Indians, Zaldivar was a nephew of Juan de Oñate, Spanish governor of New Mexico. Seventy men quickly avenged Zaldivar's death, killing at least 100 Acoma men and kidnapping 60 young Indian girls to sell in Mexico as slaves. They also severed a foot from each of the remaining Indian men.

With the Indians securely subdued, the Spanish soon were overseeing construction of the San Esteban del Rey Mission, completed in 1640. Forty-foot-long (12-m) roof beams were cut in the Cebolleta Mountains, 30 miles (48 km) south, and carried on men's backs up the rugged slopes of the mesa.

Today, you can walk inside the mission where stark, white-washed walls contrast with a wooden altar painted in bright reds, blues, yellows, and greens. Each year, prior to San Esteban's feast day, which honors the patron saint, the walls are freshly painted with traditional yucca and sheepskin brushes. The paint is ground from pink and white sandstones quarried at nearby mesas.

About 13 Acoma families reside at the pueblo, which has never had running water or electricity. All of life's essentials, even dirt for the pueblo's cemetery, must be hauled up from below. An occasional antenna attached to a generator-driven television rises above the ancient dwellings and keeps the inhabitants up to date on world events. Most of the tribal members have opted to live in the nearby villages of Acomita, McCartys, Laguna, or Paraje, where they can bathe in hot water from a spigot and are closer to schools and work.

The only way outsiders can see the mesa-top village is on a guided walking tour, which departs regularly from a visitor center at the base of the mountain. A tribal member acts as a guide, leading guests into the mission church and its cemetery, then through the narrow streets that wind among the multi-storied rock and adobe buildings. Ladders reach to upper stories and ceremonial *kivas*. Around every corner, artisans display for sale the tribe's precise thin-shelled pottery painted with orange and black pigments taken from sandstone and rich alpine soil. An occasional truck rattles by, ascending the mountain on a narrow road financed in 1941 by a movie company so that parts of the film *Sundown* could be shot at the pueblo. Fake trees and real ostriches were imported as set designers turned the dusty pueblo into a jungle city in the film that starred Gene Tierney.

Mission Church, Acoma.

Each guide embellishes the tribe's legends as her mood dictates. As you stand at the edge of the mesa, wondering which tale to believe, a breath-taking panoramic view spreads out before you. Below, a carpet of yellow-tipped chamisa periodically gives way to red-tinted sandstone buttes and boulders. An occasional raven soars nearby, uttering a hoarse, lonely call. Peering over the sheer cliff face that surrounds the mesa, it's easy to see why Acoma Pueblo for so long kept outsiders away.

After the hour-long tour, you can take the path of the original inhabitants back to the visitor center. An ancient rock stairway used for thousands of years by the Indians leads you along narrow, often steep, passages through the soft sandstone. Natural steps have been worn smooth, along with handholds carved into the weathered sandstone walls.

■ ZUNI PUEBLO

The radiant desert sunsets that have been attracting people to New Mexico for years proved to be the undoing of sixteenth-century Zuni Indians living at Hawi-kuh, a settlement 12 miles (19 km) south of the present-day pueblo. It was here that in 1539 Fray Marcos de Niza, searching for the fabled Seven Cities of Cibola, caught a glimpse at sunset of the walls of the pueblo's dwellings, turning gold in the waning light. Gifted with an excitable imagination, the man of God thought he saw gold-plated walls and envisioned treasure-laden streets. Returning to Mexico, he passed on his account to Antonio de Mendoza, viceroy of New Spain. Mendoza enlisted the financial assistance and energetic support of Francisco Vasquez de Coronado, the young governor of a New Spain province. The next year, Coronado arrived at Hawikuh to find flat-roofed mud huts and angry Indians who tried to resist his troops. The "cities" turned out to be Zuni villages.

The Zunis had something much more valuable than gold: they had an integrated and sophisticated civilization, a sacred land, their religion, and ancient traditions. They grew corn, beans, and squash alongside the Zuni River in the slate-blue shadows of surrounding mesas; they raised turkeys and kept eagles in captivity for their feathers. They traded turquoise and salt to Plains Indians for buffalo hides and to Mexican tribes for parrot plumes; they thought nothing of running 20 miles (32 km) round-trip to carry messages.

Although the Zunis grudgingly accepted the Spanish presence, allowing them to build churches and erect crosses, they never fully embraced the Christianity that was forced upon them. Occasionally they burned mission churches and killed priests who wouldn't stop harassing them. Even today, Christianity takes a back seat to their own ancient religion, and the Zunis maintain an elaborate ceremonial organization. Because they believe the sun is the source of life, the most revered man in the tribe is the Sun Priest, who oversees solstice ceremonies. Other esoteric cults include the rainmaker, ancestor, *katsina*, beast, and war gods. Sacred Zuni fetishes, which include quartz crystals, turtle-shell rattles, and seashells were used by the priest in charge of each cult to carry out his duty.

The Zunis took part in the Pueblo Revolt of 1680, killing a friar and burning the mission church, but feared the certain retaliation of the Spanish. After the rebellion, they took refuge on Towayalane, or Corn Mountain, a majestic mile-long (2-km) multi-colored sandstone mesa that stands three miles (5 km) southeast of the present-day pueblo. They built three-story rock houses alongside a shallow wash where the mesa makes a slight dip. The Indians remained here, continuing to farm the lowlands, for 12 years, until Diego de Vargas reclaimed the territory for Spain. Then the Zunis came off the mountain and settled at the site of the present-day pueblo.

As time went on, Zuni craftsmen became famous for making extraordinarily beautiful jewelry, in particular silver pieces inlaid with turquoise, shell, and jet. They have also made a craft of animal fetishes fashioned out of carved minerals, glass, and stones, embellished with gemstones. In addition, Zuni "needlepoint" is the placement of tiny gemstones (most often turquoise) close together in intricate patterns set in silver.

Zuni Pueblo has 8,000 members, making it the largest in New Mexico. It appears much like any other small New Mexican town, with a maze of low, flat-roofed houses, small vegetable patches, and dusty unpaved streets. A few craft shops are mixed in among stores and businesses. If in the morning you notice the delicious smell of baking bread, follow your nose and you'll find yourself standing beside a *horno,* a beehive-shaped clay oven of ancient design built at the side of nearly every home.

Tribal permission is required if you wish to visit two nearby places of interest— the crumbling ruins at Hawikuh and the unexcavated Village of the Great Kivas, three ancient pueblos located 18 miles (29 km) north of Zuni.

Shalako dancers at Zuni Pueblo in 1897. (Museum of New Mexico)

SHALAKO DANCE AT ZUNI PUEBLO

As the short winter day gives way to evening, residents at Zuni Pueblo excitedly anticipate the final celebration of their ceremonial year. Huddled in doorways, wrapped snugly in wool blankets against the chill of the fading light, the Zunis occasionally glance to the south, listening for a loud clacking sound that comes from a wooden beak. They are waiting for the arrival of the Shalakos, six 10-foot-tall (3-m) gods who will spend the night blessing six houses built in their honor during the previous year and offering prayers so that the tribe may enjoy fertility, long life, prosperity, and happiness.

The Shalako ceremony is a reenactment of the creation and migration of the Zuni people to Heptina, or the "Middle Place," which was destined to be their home. This is the most elaborate and unique of any pueblo ritual, beginning at dusk and lasting throughout the night. The date, in late November or early December, is determined in the fall. Outsiders are invited to witness the symbolic night-long dances only if they agree not to take photographs, or make sketches or tape recordings of the event.

Serious organization for the ceremonies begins shortly after the Zuni New Year in the first part of January, almost a full year earlier. Tribal ceremonial leaders select impersonators of the dance characters, and families accept responsibility for building or remodeling houses that will be used to entertain the gods. In addition to the six Shalako houses, two more are built each year: one for the Council of the Gods—the Longhorn House—and one for the Mudheads, or Koyemshi, a group of 10 dancers who wear knobby, adobe-colored masks and paint their bodies with pinkish clay, creating the effect of distorted creatures. During the year, religious and house-building activities of the Mudheads take up so much of their time that they do not take other jobs.

Shalako Day begins with women baking bread in beehive-shaped *hornos* and stirring great pots of chile and beans that will serve the visiting gods and guests. These women also grind corn into sacred meal that the gods will use to bless shrines and the Shalako houses. In addition, six shrine sites throughout the pueblo must be readied for the various performers who will visit them later in the day.

In mid-afternoon the Fire God makes his appearance, accompanied by his ceremonial Godfather. A 10- to 14-year-old boy is chosen as Fire God and is identified by a black mask painted with yellow, blue, red, and white dots and by numerous turquoise necklaces. Fire God and his Godfather visit sacred shrines in the pueblo and then retire to the Longhorn House where they wait for the four-member Council of Gods. These gods follow the Fire God to the shrines, performing prayers and rituals at each one. Each of the gods wears a distinct mask and costume that identifies him as either the Rain Priest, the Hututu, or one of the two Yamuhaktos, each representing one of the four directions of the compass.

At dusk the Shalakos slowly walk over the top of a hill on the south side of the Zuni River. Two horns and wooden eyes jut from the spectacular turquoise mask that is adorned with a profusion of feathers: eagle feathers for the headpiece and downy feathers that run from the ends of the horns down the back. These imposing bird-like creatures are robed in white embroidered ceremonial clothing, and a massive ruff fashioned from glossy raven feathers.

They proceed to their sacred shrine, located southwest of the laundromat. Occasional clacks can be heard from their wooden beaks snapping together. As the skies darken, red firefly-like lights flicker from cigarettes smoked by the gods and their assistants. Well after dark and after cold temperatures have numbed onlookers' feet, the Shalako follow a special footpath to the river and then pick their way across. They never use a nearby bridge. Members of the crowd fall in behind one of the Shalako, following the dancer to the house that has been prepared for him.

Solemnly, the Shalako plants prayer plumes and seeds inside the threshold and deposits seeds in baskets in front of an altar at the west end of the room. An excavation below this altar signifies the fourth womb in the world, through which the Zuni people emerged in their creation. Then the Shalako mask is placed in front of the altar where it remains until the dancing begins shortly after midnight. Numerous rituals follow, including a feast for invited Indians, during which the Shalako impersonator takes a little food from each bowl passed to him and wraps it in *piki* —a paper-thin bread made from blue corn. He also walks to the river where he makes sacrificial offerings to tribal ancestors.

Shortly after midnight, a group of men gathered about a large drum in a corner of the room begin a rhythmic pounding that continues until sunrise. Others shake rattles and begin chanting. The Shalako dancer dons the awkward mask and begins moving in time to the drumbeat. He gracefully dips and sways, and swoops from one end of the room to the other, often clacking his protruding beak. The dance is interrupted only when the Shalako's understudy assumes the beat, giving the main dancer a break.

During the night-long ceremony, the Mudheads travel in pairs to each Shalako house, singing and providing comic relief, often taunting the towering Shalako dancers.

In the morning, the Shalakos leave their houses and proceed back across the river, returning to their ancestral homes, leaving behind enough blessings and good will to sustain the Zunis for another year.

■ THE WAY TO GRANTS

Indians from Zuni and Acoma pueblos knew their way through pine and juniper forests and across a massive lava flow, the remains of five major eruptions from nearby volcanoes, that sprawls between the two pueblos south of the present-day town of Grants. (As recently as 700 years ago, rivers of molten rock and flying cinders oozed across the sandstone and limestone valley. Indian legends tell of rivers of "fire rock.") Carrying precious loads of salt and turquoise, the natives walked the jagged landscape—warm black rocks under an intensely blue sky. They filled wide gaps in the hardened lava with boulders to create bridges and erected cairns from the sharp rock so they wouldn't lose their way across the unrelenting terrain.

Early Spanish and American travelers rarely ventured across the hardened lava. Leading their horses around it, they called the 114,000-acre lava-rock valley El Malpais (The Badlands). In 1988, the federal government recognized the unique geological features of the area and established **El Malpais National Monument and Conservation Area** and opened up a visitor center in Grants, 10 miles (16 km) to the north.

The valley's violent past can be seen along a portion of the trade route marked by the Indians. Aptly called the Zuni-Acoma Trail, the 7.5-mile (12-km) path crosses all five of the major lava flows that blanket the broad valley, giving hikers a chance to walk on chunky lava called AA and ropey lava known as pahoehoe. A network of four-by-four wooden posts connects the ancient rock cairns, providing easily spotted trail markers—the undulating lava flow looks the same in every direction, so it's easy to lose the trail. Before striking out from one marker, be sure to have the next one in sight.

The volcanoes that once spewed blistering hot lava still brood above the scene. The crater of one of them, Bandera Crater, can be seen at the end of a one-half-mile-long (1-km) trail carpeted in soft cinder. Peering down 800 feet (244-m) into the extinct volcano, it's reassuring to know that the last time it erupted was about a million years ago. All that remains are rust-colored scree walls with an occasional ponderosa pine stretching for the sun. A ghostly silence is disturbed only by a dislodged basalt pebble tumbling toward the crater's center. Nearby, a sturdy wooden staircase leads 75 feet (23 m) below the jagged surface of broken basalt to the opening of an ice cave. The cave was formed when molten lava, within a crust of cooling and hardening lava, flowed through. Afterward, moisture seeped through the cracked and porous basalt and froze in the cold cave. A blast of chilly air emanates from the opening, which is coated with thick layers of mossy green ice. Icicles dangle from the ceiling, and steady droplets of water drip from them into a blue-green pool. This brisk, 31-degree F (0° C) air prevents lengthy visits. Heading upward toward the warm 80-degree F (27° C) sunshine, the staircase passes by brilliant orange, yellow, and brown lichen draped across volcanic boulders.

At the eastern edge of the flow and visible from NM 117 is a magnificent natural arch aptly called La Ventana (The Window). Years of wind pounding against the soft sandstone and water seeping into cracks have left a 125-foot-high (38-m) opening in the rock. Black and red striations of color called desert varnish play on the underside of the 165-foot (50-m) span. A short walk to the giant window is well worth the effort.

The ancient Indian trade route, which NM 53 roughly follows, also passes by a massive 200-foot-high (61-m) sandstone mesa visible for miles, atop which sit two unexcavated Zuni pueblos. It's been preserved as **El Morro (The Bluff) National Monument.**

At the base of the pale cliff is a natural basin filled with water, replenished by summer rains and winter snows. A natural rest stop for nearly a thousand years, travelers couldn't resist leaving their marks on the nearby smooth sandstone surface. Indian petroglyphs were first, followed by signatures and messages written by Spanish explorers and later Anglo settlers. Two years before Jamestown, Virginia, was founded in 1607, Juan de Oñate left an inscription: "Passed by here the Governor Don Juan de Oñate, from the discovery of the Sea of the South on the 16th of April 1605." The "Sea of the South" was the Gulf of California. When Diego de Vargas was on his way to reclaim Zuni after the Pueblo Revolt, he too left his mark: "Here was the General Don Diego de Vargas who conquered for our Holy Faith, and for the Royal Crown, all of New Mexico at his own expense, year of 1692." Through the centuries, explorers, traders, soldiers, surveyors, and settlers carved messages as they passed by. Thus the name Inscription Rock seems most appropriate.

El Morro National Monument's fine visitors center, with a museum featuring tools and pottery from the pueblo, is open year-round.

Ancient Indians and Spanish explorers left drawings and messages at El Morro. (Paul Chesley)

■ GRANTS

Set on a flat plain in the protective shadows of the towering Mount Taylor, an 11,300-foot (3,444-m) ancient volcano, Grants is once again a busted mining town trying to revive itself. One main street pretty much takes care of the sights in this dusty community, named after the three Grant brothers, Angus, Lewis, and John—who won a contract to build the section of the Atlantic and Pacific Railroad between Isleta Pueblo and Needles, California. Grants's entire economic history, in fact, has been one of boom and bust. First it boomed in 1881 as a camp for railroad workers, when 4,000 men and 2,000 mules hauled ties for the tracks. With the completion of the railroad, the town's population dwindled; by the late 1920s it was 350. Revitalized by the construction of Bluewater Dam on the nearby Rio San Jose, Grants bloomed as an agricultural community. The town went crazy for carrots—lush-topped ones, the kind Easterners craved. By 1941, the water from the dam had helped to produce about 2,000 train carloads of carrots a year, valued at $2.5 million. When their competitors began encasing carrots in colorful cellophane wrapping, the Grants farmers didn't follow suit and demand dropped.

The town's next wave of prosperity began in 1950 when Paddy Martinez, a Navajo sheep rancher, found an unusual-looking yellow rock at the base of Haystack Mountain, adjacent to one of his pastures. The first time he'd seen such a rock was in 1937, when three men informed him the government would pay $10,000 to anybody who found the ore. Martinez rode his horse into Grants where he showed his rock to a merchant friend, who scoffed at the idea it was uranium. Martinez staked a mining claim anyway. Within a month, word had spread and hundreds of prospectors were scouring the area. Martinez's claim finally put the town of Grants on the map, and helped complete the demise of the carrot industry. Grants was incorporated in 1960, and the uranium industry attracted hordes of residents.

Paddy Martinez, by the way, never mined the uranium. He only rented the land around Haystack Mountain from the Santa Fe Railroad, which paid him a monthly sum for his discovery. With his monthly check, Martinez moved to a bare bones circular Navajo dwelling called a hogan on the shores of Bluewater Lake and continued to graze sheep.

By the early 1980s, the demand for uranium had dropped. The last Grants-area mine closed in January 1990. Just so people won't forget the golden days of uranium, the **New Mexico Mining Museum** at Grants was opened in 1986. There, a simulated uranium mine complete with elevator simulates a 900-foot-descent (274-m) into the earth.

About 27 miles (43 km) east of Grants, **Laguna Pueblo** is visible along I-40 near exit 114. Laguna, named for a nearby lake that has since become a meadow, was established in 1699 by the Spanish governor Pedro Rodriguez Cubero. Later that year, the San Jose de Laguna Church was completed, making it the last of the early mission churches to be established in New Mexico.

Today, the church still stands on a hill overlooking simple pueblo dwellings. Its plain, if imposing, exterior belies the rich decorations within. The ornate and colorfully painted pine altar carved by Indian craftsmen is flanked by paintings of St. Barbara and St. John Nepomucene, and an animal hide attached to the ceiling is colored with Indian symbols of the rainbow, sun, moon, and stars. Despite the fact that it's uncomfortably close to the freeway, Pueblo-traditions have been well preserved.

■ GALLUP

Gallup isn't quite sure what it is. As one of the nation's foremost trading centers for Native American arts and crafts, Gallup calls itself the Heart of Indian Country. And for good reason: the town is 25 miles (40 km) southeast of Window Rock, Arizona, capital of the Navajo Nation; 98 miles (157 km) southwest of Chaco Canyon, home of the ancient Anasazi; and 38 miles (61 km) north of Zuni Pueblo. Most of the Indians you see along the streets of Gallup have come in from the nearby Navajo Reservation to shop, sell their wares, and sometimes to have a few drinks. Liquor sales are prohibited on the reservation.

At one time, this gritty little town was the epitome of the Wild West. Its first building was the Blue Goose Saloon, constructed in the 1860s near a stagecoach stop. After coal was discovered north of Gallup in the late 1870s, miners from across Europe, including Slavs, Czechs, Austrians, and Italians, converged on the town. The immigrants worked hard in the sooty mines, digging out jet-black lumps of carbon. After railroad tracks reached the community in 1881, pint-sized steam engines hauled low-slung cars overflowing with coal to loading points where commercial trains picked it up. Outside of town, mining camps sprung up, appearing much like today's suburbs. Some homes were built of stone, and some camps had schools and saloons for miners who didn't want to make the few-mile trip to Gallup. One camp, Clarkdale, even had a library with a pool table. The coal mines were closed in 1950, but many descendants of these miners continue to live in Gallup.

Within two years after the Santa Fe Railroad arrived in Gallup, 22 saloons (including the Bucket of Blood) and two dance halls were competing with the Blue Goose for business. David Gallup was paymaster of the railroad, which ended at the western outpost. Come payday, workers would say they were going to Gallup's to collect their wages. The name stuck.

During those early years, prostitution and gambling were in an exuberant state of availability, if illegal. Soldiers, lumberjacks, cowboys, railroad workers, and miners were regular customers. On the other hand, in 1895, a bevy of respectable East Coast women arrived at Gallup to work for a Harvey House restaurant and according to some, improved the town's reputation from that of a rowdy rest stop to a credible community. Many of these women married and settled in Gallup, turning the wild outpost into a quiet family town.

Beginning in the 1930s, Hollywood directors began gathering in Gallup to use its unspoiled red-rock canyons and majestic piñon-covered mesas as backdrops for Westerns. These included the *Big Carnival,* starring Kirk Douglas; *Four Faces West,* with Joel McCrea; and the *Bad Man,* starring Wallace Beery, Lionel Barrymore, and Ronald Reagan. To house the stars in style, R.E. Griffith, brother of director D.W. Griffith, built the El Rancho Hotel in 1937. The two-story oversized ranch house still boasts its original motto: "Charm of Yesterday, Convenience of Tomorrow," but has added a new theme: "Home of the Movie Stars." The entrance opens onto a brick-floored lobby where guests can share a bench with a wooden Indian and marvel at the deer heads, Navajo rugs, and loads of Indian and Western art tacked to the walls. A gallery of autographed photographs of the stars lines a second-floor balcony. Rooms are named after the Hollywood stars who slept in them: Lee Marvin, Betty Grable, and Burt Lancaster, to name a few.

Route 66, America's mythic highway connecting the orderly Midwestern corn fields with the turbulent waters of the Pacific Ocean, bisected Gallup in 1926, and many of the shops and tourist courts that sprang up to entice a new world of motorists are still in business.

Gallup's most popular annual event is the **Inter-Tribal Indian Ceremonial.** Begun in 1922 when a contingent of Gallup businessmen invited a group of local Indians to dance and display their crafts at the McKinley County Fair, the show

Navajo weaver Nellie Mae Davis cradles her grandson. (Paul Chesley)

now attracts Native American dancers, craftsmen, and cowboys from throughout North America. When they get a break from competing in the professional All-Indian Rodeo, these weathered Indian cowboys in worn jeans and scuffed boots walk through the streets of Gallup. For a Saturday parade that weaves through downtown, different tribes bring out their finery. Members wear ornate turquoise necklaces, feathered headdresses, and buffalo masks, and they pause often to dance a few steps to the rhythmic beat of drums. East of town at **Red Rock State Park,** professional rodeo cowboys from across the country try to stay atop bucking horses in the saddle bronc competition, or bind together the legs of squeamish calves in the calf roping contest. Nearby, there's lots for sale: Indian frybread topped with plenty of sugar and honey, or Navajo tacos—frybread covered with mutton, cheese, lettuce, and tomatoes. Indian crafts range from traditional Navajo blankets, silver jewelry, and beadwork to modern sculpture and painting. During the fair, the town's population of 20,000 doubles, and lodging is virtually unobtainable without reservations months in advance.

A marvelous way to travel to Gallup is on the **Southwest Chief,** the AMTRAK train that travels daily between Los Angeles and Chicago. A Navajo tour guide

Branding cattle, San Gabriel Ranch, 1927. (Museum of New Mexico)

boards the train in Gallup and spends the next two and a half hours imparting some of the tribe's lore and legends to interested passengers. As the silver train painted with red, white, and blue stripes rumbles past vermilion mesas, stands of gray-green piñons and junipers, and isolated communities, the guide may point to a traditional Navajo hogan and explain why it is built facing east. "The philosophical reason is because we believe that all good things in life come from the east when the sun rises in the morning. But it also has practical purposes. Obviously, if you've got the sun shining at your door in the morning, it's going to warm your house up a little faster."

■ THE FARMINGTON AREA

To the Navajos, the area of present-day Farmington was known as "To-tah," which means "Among the Waters." Three of the region's major waterways meet three miles (5 km) apart: the gently flowing Animas River skirts Farmington's eastern edge, then empties into the wide San Juan River south of town. The smaller La Plata enters the San Juan west of town after irrigating fields of hay and corn.

When local residents think of the Farmington area, they think of an outdoorsman's paradise: great skiing, fishing, and hiking. When a businessman thinks of Farmington, he may be considering the large deposits of oil, natural gas, and coal that lie in the San Juan Basin, beneath some of the most unusual land formations found in the state. The main thoroughfares of Farmington are crowded with small businesses, restaurants, and shops, and are fine places to stock up coolers and tackle boxes.

World-class downhill skiing, backpacking, and hiking are accessible an hour's drive north in the southern Rocky Mountains at Durango, Colorado. Three marinas with boat docks service boaters at Navajo Lake State Park 34 miles (54 km) east of town. Just downstream from Navajo Dam is the finest trophy stream fishing in New Mexico in the clear, cold, blue-green waters of the San Juan River. A nearly four-mile (6-km) stretch, called the Quality Waters, harbors big, fat trout that would rather fight than be served as dinner. Strict restrictions apply. Fishermen must use barbless hooks and may not take home more than one 20-inch (51-cm) lunker. The locals say once you've fished these waters, no other New Mexico stream will ever satisfy you.

AZTEC

If you're driving back to Farmington thinking about the number of huge fish that got away, you might wish to take a 19-mile (30-km) detour north along NM 173 to hike the Indian ruin inappropriately named Aztec (it was built by the Anasazi). The town of Aztec seems misnamed as well. Nothing about its hilly, tree-shaded streets filled with Victorian brick buildings recalls the ancient Aztec Indians of Mexico. Shops and businesses along Main Street have retained an early twentieth-century Midwestern appearance, and the only modern touches are a few pastel-painted storefronts.

Aztec boasts two claims to fame: first, it's home to "6,000 friendly people and six old soreheads." No doubt there are 6,000 friendly people, so where did the soreheads come from? The sorehead tradition began in 1969 when a good-natured Chamber of Commerce erected the first welcoming sign that listed 4,000 residents and six old soreheads. Townsfolk loved the idea, and many clamored to become designated a sorehead. Secret ballots were sent to the town's clubs and organizations seeking nominations. The winners posed for the local newspaper with bags over their heads and their backs to the camera. Their identities never were revealed, although many residents claim to be one of the originals. Since 1987, the

Earlier settlers mistakenly thought these Anasazi ruins were Aztec in origin, thus: Aztec Ruins.

honor has been spread around as ballots are sent out every year to add six new soreheads to the roster. Only now they remove the bags.

Aztec's second claim to fame is as an All America City, an award it received in 1963 after the town's citizens built NM 173, a two-lane road that connects Aztec with the San Juan River just below Navajo Dam. No government funds were used in construction: businesses donated supplies, men and women volunteered labor, and children held fundraisers to help cover expenses.

SHIPROCK

Along the wide, placid San Juan River heading back to Farmington and beyond toward Shiprock, fertile fields fed by the river suggest the origins of Farmington's name. Today, small farms and orchards of apple, pear, and peach trees flourish, but it's the vast deposits of coal, oil, and natural gas that have come to dominate the area's economy. Farmington sits at the edge of the Navajo Reservation with the dusty town of Shiprock set squarely within it. Both are more interested in serving their residents than attracting tourists.

To the southwest of the town of Shiprock, a 7,178-foot (2,188-m) jagged rock monolith dominates the semi-desert landscape. **Shiprock** begins as an apparition,

Known to the Navajo as Tse Bida'hi *(Winged Rock), Shiprock rises 1,500 feet (457 m) from the desert floor. (Paul Chesley)*

NAVAJO GIRL

Some of the men of Jemez rode out to meet the Navajos. John Cajero was one of them. He was then a man in his prime, a Tanoan man, agile and strong in his mind and body, and he was a first-rate horseman. He was mounted on a good-looking gray quarter horse, which he handled closely and well, and he cut a fine figure upon it in his blue shirt and red headband, his manner easy and confident. He singled out old friends among the Navajos, and soon there was a cluster of riders holding up on the side of the road, convened in a high mood of fellowship and good humor—and a certain rivalry. Then John Cajero was holding the coils of rope in his hands, shaking out a loop. Suddenly he leaned forward and his horse bolted into the road between two of the wagons, nearly trampling over a dog; the dog lunged away with a yelp and ran at full speed, but the horse was right upon it, bunched in motion, and the rope flashed down and caught the dog up around its hips and set it rolling and twisting in the sand, jerking it up then into the air and slamming it down hard, as the horse squatted, jamming its hooves in the earth, its whole weight cracking against the bit. And John Cajero played out a little of the rope from his saddle, and the dog slithered out of the noose and ran ahead, its tail between its legs, and went crouching and wary under its wagon. John Cajero laughed, and the others, too, though their laughter was brittle, I thought, and the Navajos watched evenly the performance, the enactment of a hard joke, and considered precisely what it was worth. There was a kind of trade in this, a bartering of nerve and arrogance and skill, of elemental pride. Then, getting down from his horse, John Cajero drew a dollar bill from his pocket, folded it once lengthwise, and stuck it down in the sand. He gestured to the others; it was a beckoning, an invitation, but I did not understand at first what he meant them to do. He swung himself up into the saddle and gestured again, pointing down to the money on the ground. No one moved; only they were watchful, and he urged his horse away, prancing, a little distance. Then he turned the horse around and set it running—or loping, rather, not fast, but easily, evenly—and reached down from the saddle for the dollar bill. It seemed that his fingers brushed it, but he could not take hold of it, for the stride of the horse was broken slightly at the crucial moment. It was the barest miss—and a beautiful, thrilling thing to see—and he was upright in the saddle again, his motion and the motion of the horse all of a piece. I was watching him so intently that I did not at first see the girl. She came from nowhere, a lithe, lovely Navajo girl on a black horse. She was coming up fast in John Cajero's dust, faster than he had come, and her horse was holding steady in a long, loping stride, level and low. When I saw her she was already hanging down nearly the whole length of her arm from the saddle horn, her knee cocked and her long back curved like a bow, her shoulders close against the deep chest of the horse; she swung her left arm down like a scythe, and up, holding the dollar bill with the tips of her fingers until it was high over her head, and she was standing straight in the stirrups, and her horse did not break stride. And in that way she rode on, past John Cajero, along the wagon train and into the village, having stolen the show and the money, too, going in beauty, trailing laughter. Later I looked for her among the camps, but I did not find her. I imagined that her name was Desbah Yazzie and that she looked out for me from the shadows.

—N. Scott Momaday
The Names, a Memoir, 1976

fuzzily coming into view. But once you've spotted it, this volcanic core of an extinct volcano commands your attention. You can't take your eyes off the massive form that rises from a dusty plain. Navajos call the mystical rock Tse Bida'hi (the Rock with Wings) and many tribal legends surround it. Numerous rock climbers have scaled it, and two have died trying. Shiprock has been closed to climbers since 1970.

Nearby is yet another natural marvel, the **Bisti Badlands**, 3,968 acres of giant mushroom-shaped spires surrounded by red, green, and bone-white cliffs located 32 miles (51 km) south of Farmington in the San Juan Basin. The eerie desolation of this wild moonscape is all that remains of what once was a shallow sea bordered by swamps and forests and inhabited by dinosaurs. Eons of wind and water have carved the sandstone and shale formations. The Bisti, along with the nearby 19,922-acre De-na-zin area, are rich in fossils, left behind from the days 75 million years ago when duckbill and horned dinosaurs sloshed along the seashore. Huge conifers towered above a jungle of ferns and palms. Salamanders, snails, worms, sharks, and crocodiles choked the waterways.

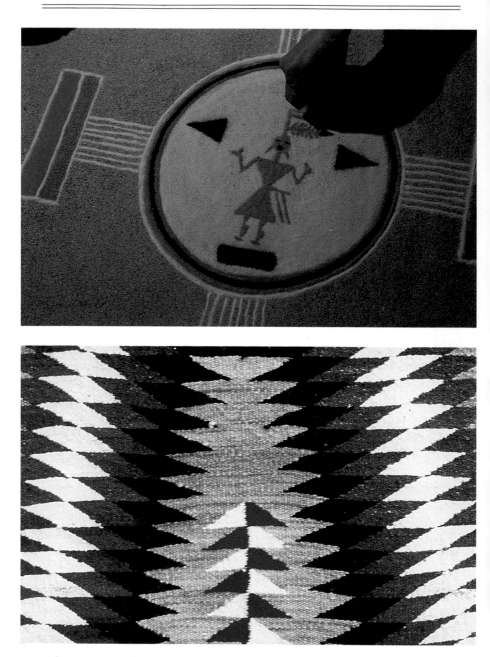

(above) Navajo sand mandala. (Paul Chesley); (below) Navajo rugs represent nature's patterns. (opposite) Minnie Martine, a famed weaver at the Ramah Navajo reservation. (Paul Chesley)

Today, snakes and lizards scurry across the hard rocks, which are absent of any vegetation, a reminder of the days when their ancestors dominated this barren sandstone wilderness. Unfortunately, billions of tons of coal lie near the surface underneath the Bisti, posing the constant threat that this magical, unspoiled land could be destroyed by open-pit mining.

■ JICARILLA APACHES

Jicarilla is a Spanish name meaning "Little Basketmaker." The colonials were impressed by the beautiful baskets, especially two-handled vessels coiled and stitched with sumac twigs and small woven drinking cups (*jicara* means "small cup"),

Navajo weavers outside a hogan on Navajo tribal lands. (Museum of New Mexico)

fashioned by this band of Apache, which roamed the forests and canyons of northwestern New Mexico.

When the federal government, a century ago, placed the Jicarillas on 722,000 acres of land that included deserts and forests along the Continental Divide, it was clear to everyone that the Indians had received a bad deal. First of all, they were accustomed to a nomadic existence—hunting deer and gathering nuts and berries (later pillaging wagon trains) for their survival. Accustomed to roaming freely, the Apaches had a difficult time settling down to an assigned spot and, having little experience in farming, their attempts at cultivating the sandy soil they'd been given were not always successful. But at least their new home had variety, with its pine-covered mountains, tall grass meadows, canyons, mesas, and sagebrush prairies. As it turned out, the land also was rich in fossil fuels, namely oil and natural gas. The sale of leases has made the Jicarilla the richest tribe in the state.

The Jicarilla have also capitalized on their dynamic landscape. At Stone Lake Lodge they cater to fishermen and especially to hunters who flock like geese to the reservation for its prize deer, elk, turkey, cougar, and waterfowl. North of the lodge at the capital of Dulce, most of the tribe's 2,000 members make their homes. At the tribal gift shop, few of the Jicarilla's namesake baskets are for sale, but oil paintings, leather craft, and intricate bead work are plentiful.

■ CUBA

This gas-stop town between Albuquerque and Farmington was established in 1769 when 35 families received the San Joaquin del Nacimiento Land Grant to ranch and farm at the western edge of the San Pedro Mountains near the headwaters of the Rio Puerco. Today, the small community pierced by NM 44 continues as a ranching and farming center, as well as the gateway to the Santa Fe National Forest for backpackers, hunters, and fishermen.

SOUTHWESTERN
NEW MEXICO

FROM THE AQUAMARINE WATERS OF ELEPHANT BUTTE LAKE and the cactus prairie near Lordsburg to the pine-clad mountains of Silver City, southwestern New Mexico offers a vibrant diversity of landscape. The bone-dry desert is relieved by the Rio Grande, which wends its way through the region, creating wetlands for migratory birds and providing sustenance to fields of onion, cotton, and chile. Pale-green hillsides dotted with piñon and juniper rise to the dense woods of the Gila National Forest, once home to the Mimbres Indians and still home to mountain lions and black bears. You can drive for miles without seeing another car and if you do, it'll probably be a pickup truck with a gun rack in the cab.

Like a hazy mirage, rugged mountain ranges soar upward from the flat, desolate landscape where wide expanses of desert grasses mix with the crooked branches of mesquite trees. Vast stretches of cracked earth covered with clumps of grass are marked by isolated ranches and barbed-wire fences that extend in long lines against the hills.

Along NM 9, which dips close to the Mexico border, immigrants illegally slip across the open range in the dark of night. Water flows steadily in irrigation ditches along US 85, which passes cotton fields displaying their unmistakable white bolls. Just across the road, a dark-green carpet of chile fields provides a stunning contrast. In the fall, the chile's pungent odor assaults your olfactory nerves and is a reminder that winter is just around the corner.

The past, too, is never far away. Here you'll find the remains of ancient Indian cliff dwellings, the crumbling ruins of nineteenth-century forts, and the tattered shacks of once-thriving mining camps.

In recent years, the quiet, slower-paced lifestyles of ranching and farming, along with a mild climate have been attracting retirees. Nowhere else in the state are motorists more apt to lift a hand across a steering wheel as a greeting in passing, or a sales clerk to inquire where you are heading. Many towns are so small, every stranger who stops is noticed.

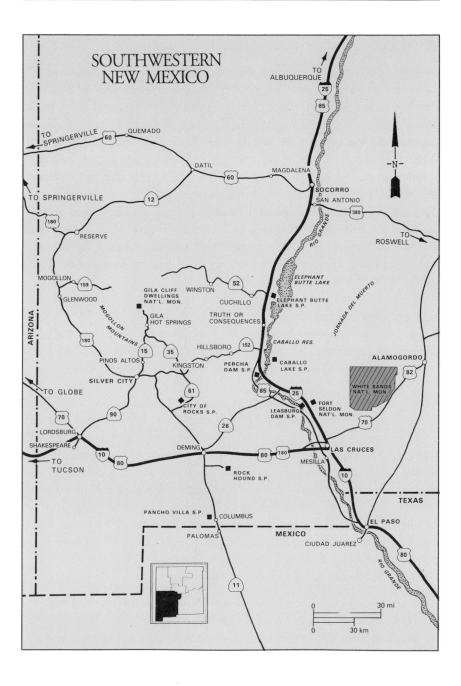

SOUTHWESTERN NEW MEXICO

TO ALBUQUERQUE

TO SPRINGERVILLE
QUEMADO
60
TO SPRINGERVILLE
DATIL
60
MAGDALENA
SOCORRO
SAN ANTONIO
12
380
180
RESERVE
TO ROSWELL
RIO GRANDE
MOGOLLON
159
WINSTON
52
GILA CLIFF DWELLINGS NAT'L. MON.
ELEPHANT BUTTE LAKE
GLENWOOD
CUCHILLO
GILA HOT SPRINGS
ELEPHANT BUTTE LAKE S.P.
MOGOLLON MOUNTAINS
TRUTH OR CONSEQUENCES
JORNADA DEL MUERTO
ARIZONA
15
35
HILLSBORO
152
CABALLO RES.
ALAMOGORDO
180
KINGSTON
PERCHA DAM S.P.
CABALLO LAKE S.P.
82
PINOS ALTOS
SILVER CITY
85
25
WHITE SANDS NAT'L. MON.
TO GLOBE
61
FORT SELDON NAT'L. MON.
CITY OF ROCKS S.P.
LEASBURG DAM S.P.
70
70
90
26
180
LORDSBURG
SHAKESPEARE
DEMING
80
LAS CRUCES
10
80
MESILLA
TO TUCSON
ROCK HOUND S.P.
10
TEXAS
PANCHO VILLA S.P.
COLUMBUS
EL PASO
PALOMAS
MEXICO
CIUDAD JUAREZ
80
11
RIO GRANDE
-N-

0   30 mi
0   30 km

■ HISTORY

As early as 3000 B.C., the ancestors of the Mogollon Indians learned how to cultivate corn and squash from their southern neighbors in Mexico. By 300 B.C., they had added red kidney beans and were shaping pottery and living in pit houses dug four feet (1.2 m) underground and covered with timber and dirt. In the first centuries of A.D., the Indians moved into large caves along the Gila River where they continued to grow corn, beans, and squash. Others built freestanding masonry dwellings deep in the mountains. One branch of Mogollons, the Mimbres, developed exquisite black-on-white pottery and created designs that ranged from geometric patterns to stylized reptiles. These fragile pots are usually found with a hole punctured in the bottom at grave sites. Through this hole, the pot's spirit, thought to be part of its maker, is released. An extensive permanent exhibit of this prehistoric pottery can be seen at Western New Mexico University Museum in Silver City.

By A.D. 500, the Mogollon culture had peaked. But the Indians continued to hunt and farm in the mountains and valleys of southwestern New Mexico until the early 1300s, when they left the Gila to resettle along the Rio Grande and other drainages of the region. One of their cave settlements has been preserved at the Gila Cliff Dwellings National Monument, 44 miles (70 km) north of Silver City.

APACHES AND GERONIMO

By the early 1300s, bands of Apaches had entered the region to hunt deer and bison. Women supplemented their diet by gathering berries, roots, and seeds as they moved about. Historians tend to lump the southern Apaches into two main groups: the Mescaleros, who lived in animal-skin tepees, and the Chiricahuas, who erected grass and brush huts called *wickiups.* Young girls wound their hair around two willow hoops, worn over their ears, while some older women adopted the style of Plains Indians and braided their hair in long plaits. The women sewed deer-skin robes and animal-skin moccasins, which could be pulled up to the knee for warmth, or folded down to protect against thorns and rocks.

Of the Mescaleros, the late C. L. Sonnichsen wrote:

> They owned nothing and everything. They did as they pleased and bowed to no man. Their women were chaste. Their leaders kept their promises. They were mighty warriors who depended on success in raiding

for wealth and honor. To their families they were kind and gentle, but they could be unbelievably cruel to their enemies—fierce and revengeful when they felt that they had been betrayed.

In the sixteenth century, Spanish explorers investigating New Mexico passed through the southwest on their way north. At that time, several groups of Pueblo Indians were living in earthen homes along the southern Rio Grande. They were probably both alarmed and amused by the cumbersome entourages led by armored conquistadors that traipsed by looking for gold. After giving up on this fruitless venture, the Spanish concentrated on colonizing what today is northern New Mexico. As a result, southwestern New Mexico was well-traveled but rarely settled. Towns such as Socorro and Mesilla served as stations on El Camino Real, "the King's Highway," a 1,500-mile (2,400-km) trade route that connected Mexico City with the provincial capital of Santa Fe. The northern part of this trail, from Chihuahua to Santa Fe, became known as the Chihuahua Trail.

Entire families made this arduous journey, carrying household goods and chickens in *carretas* and herding cattle and churro sheep. Accompanied by soldiers and priests, these caravans inched along a dirt path that hardly could be called a road. Clouds of dust and the loud creaking of the two-wheeled *carretas* marked their progress. As more people made the grueling journey to Santa Fe, they began to notice the fertile fields of the Mesilla Valley.

The noisy caravans drew the attention of the roaming Apaches, who resisted the Spaniards from the outset. The Indians attacked the travelers, stealing water, food, and animals, and sometimes taking captives.

One Apache warrior in particular carried with him his entire life a hatred for the intrusive Spanish. Born a member of the Bedonkohe Apache band sometime in the late 1820s, his given name was Goyahkla, but later he became known as Geronimo. As a child, before he even saw a Spaniard, Geronimo heard stories of campaigns in which they acquired the Apaches as slaves or killed them outright. When the Apaches retaliated, the Spanish turned other tribes against them.

When he was 17, Geronimo was designated a warrior, which gave him the right to accompany his tribe into battle. He spent 60 years traversing the wooded canyons outside Silver City and the desolate cactus plains that spilled into Arizona and Mexico, alternately living peacefully and fighting for his people. By the mid-1850s, he had lost two wives and four children to the Spanish.

As early as 1855, the United States government was coercing Indians to sign treaties giving away their land, but Geronimo didn't trust the white man's word, nor did he like the idea of living on a reservation. As U.S. soldiers gradually reduced his domain, capturing Indians and sending them to reservations, however, Geronimo realized his days of freedom were numbered and he began negotiating with the American officers. During this time he tried unsuccessfully to live on the San Carlos Reservation in Arizona. Finally, on September 5, 1886, the aging warrior, his conditions met, surrendered for the last time to Brig. Gen. Nelson Miles at Skeleton Canyon, on a rugged raiding route between Mexico and the Arizona mountains. "We placed a large stone on the blanket before us. Our treaty was made by this stone and it was to last until the stone should crumble to dust; so we made the treaty and bound each other with an oath," Geronimo said.

General Miles promised the great warrior cattle, horses, mules, and farming tools, along with a house and a large tract of land covered with timber, water, and grass. Geronimo was also guaranteed a reunion with members of his tribe already in the government's custody.

Instead, Geronimo and a few other warriors were sent by train to Florida. They spent the next eight years either incarcerated or working for the federal government in Florida and Alabama. Many died of tuberculosis. Finally, in 1894, they were reunited with their families and relocated to Fort Sill, Oklahoma, where they were given houses, land, and animals. During the following years, Geronimo became a celebrity, making appearances at regional conventions and fairs. At the Louisiana Purchase Exposition at St. Louis in 1904, he was a main attraction, selling his photograph for 25 cents and signing autographs. "I often made as much as two dollars a day, and when I

The great Apache warrior, Geronimo, in 1885. (Museum of New Mexico)

returned I had plenty of money, more than I had ever owned before," he said. The beaten warrior died in 1909 after falling off a horse.

SETTLEMENT AND THE RAILROAD

Settlement came to the region in the nineteenth century after the Treaty of Guadalupe-Hidalgo was signed in 1848, ending the Mexican-American War and designating the Rio Grande as the boundary between the two countries. As the town of Mesilla sat on the west side of the river, it was relegated overnight to the status of a Mexican border town. The burgeoning community swelled further as Mexicans flocked north to the area's lush cropland. In 1854, the U.S. signed the Gadsden Purchase and for $10 million bought from Mexico all land west of the Rio Grande. Mesilla now flew the U.S. flag and the town boomed: mule trains, stagecoaches, and miners en route to the silver and copper mines of the Gila Mountains stopped for supplies and horses at what now was a safe haven. Mesilla was also an important way station on the Butterfield Trail, a stagecoach route established in 1850 to transport passengers and the mail twice a week 2,800 miles (4,480 km) from Tipton, Missouri, to San Francisco. In 1863, the river changed its course after a flood, and Mesilla found itself on the eastern side of the Rio Grande where it sits today.

After the Mexican-American War, the U.S. government concentrated its energies on the Apaches, who continued to attack stagecoaches and wagon trains. Uncertainty as to what the Indians might do added a sharp edge of fear to all journeys through this wild territory. Sometimes the warriors killed their victims, but most often they took firearms, food, supplies, livestock, and horses. One stagecoach driver, Bigfoot Wallace, was once forced to walk 80 miles (128 km) to town after the Apaches purloined his mules. On another occasion, he came limping into El Paso with his stage stuck full of arrows.

In an effort to calm travelers' nerves, the federal government erected numerous forts in the region during the 1860s and 1870s. The remains of one of these, Fort Selden, built 12 miles (19 km) north of Las Cruces in 1865, has been preserved as a state monument. During its 25 years of service, the fort's soldiers saw little action with the Apaches. Its claim to fame was that Gen. Douglas MacArthur learned to ride and shoot there before he learned how to read and write. His father, Capt. Arthur MacArthur, served as commander at the military post.

In the 1880s, the Southern Pacific Railroad began wending its way east across the Southwest into New Mexico, and the towns of Lordsburg and Deming sprang up as railroad camps. In 1881, the Atchison, Topeka & Santa Fe Railroad, which made its way southward through New Mexico, joined its competitor the Southern Pacific at Deming to form the second transcontinental railroad route in the country.

Mesilla, which had been the largest city of the region, began to decline when the railroad bypassed it, choosing instead to locate a depot at the county seat of Las Cruces. There, Victorian homes with screened-in porches were built alongside traditional single-story adobes for tuberculosis patients who came for the clear dry air of the Southwest. They came in far greater numbers once they could ride in the comfort and safety of railroad cars. Many of these "lungers" enjoyed the mild climate and rural valley so much that they stayed on after their recuperation.

The discovery of silver, gold, copper, iron, lead, and zinc in the mountains southwest of Socorro already had attracted miners who set up rudimentary camps near their claims. In 1871, Silver City was established and soon became a place where rowdy miners swapped stories, ordered supplies, and enjoyed an occasional home-cooked meal. With the arrival of a spur that linked the mining camp to the Deming station, miners no longer had to travel as far to haul in supplies and ship valuable ores. Speculators and businessmen of a type not inclined to endure dusty, bumpy stagecoach rides now began crowding onto trains headed to the fledgling mining towns. Farmers and ranchers took a new look at the arable land along the Rio Grande, which became appealing once the threat of Apache attacks was removed. Now that passengers were protected inside rail cars, the forts were no longer needed, and they were all abandoned by the end of the century.

OUTLAWS AND LAWMEN

During this era, legends were born. Billy the Kid, known as Henry McCarty to his Silver City classmates, lived in the mining district with his mother, brother, and stepfather in the early 1870s. One legend has it that he killed his first man in a barroom brawl when he was 12 years old. According to historical accounts, however, the famous outlaw had his first brush with the law at 15, when he was arrested for robbing a Chinese laundry and subsequently escaped from the Silver City jail. As a youth, McCarty was supposedly bold, daring, and reckless, but also generous, frank, and ready to offer his assistance to the town's elderly residents.

BILLY THE KID

Barefoot and bareheaded, Billy the Kid thought he was among friends in the darkened bedroom of Pete Maxwell when he asked who was sitting at the foot of his friend's bed. That hesitation, on a summer evening in 1881, cost him his life. Sheriff Pat Garrett answered the question with two bullets, the first entering just above the outlaw's heart.

The violent death of Henry Antrim, aka Henry McCarty, aka William Bonney, failed to put an end to a legend that germinated during the Lincoln County War, which broke out in 1878. The Kid's early death at 21 in a Fort Sumner bedroom merely elevated the outlaw's status to a mythical one that would continue to blossom as the years passed.

Henry McCarty, as the Kid was first known, was born in the Irish slums of Brooklyn in 1859. He made his way west with his older brother Joe and his mother, Catherine McCarty, who suffered from tuberculosis. In 1873, she married William Antrim at the First Presbyterian Church in Santa Fe, and they moved the family to Silver City where Antrim went about seeking his elusive fortune in the silver mines.

One of Henry's school teachers there recalled him as "a scrawny little fellow with delicate hands (he supposedly loved to play the piano) and an artistic nature, always willing to help with the chores around the schoolhouse."

Catherine Antrim died when Henry was 14, and he started hanging out with George Shaffer, a young friend who liked to drink and steal. One night they made off with a bundle of clothing from a local Chinese laundry, for which Henry was caught. While in jail, he wriggled his wiry body up a chimney to freedom. At 15, he headed for Arizona where he shot his first man on record and didn't stick around to plead self-defense.

Back in New Mexico, Henry, now a seasoned outlaw, changed his name to William Bonney. His baby face and beanpole body secured him the nickname "the Kid." Wavy brown hair accented his 5-foot 7-inch, 135-pound (61-kg) frame. Innumerable books have been written about Billy, and while these mountains of words paint a picture of a half-crazed, ruthless, bratty teenage killer, in reality, Bonney was charming, cheerful, loyal, and generous. He didn't smoke or drink, refused to consort with prostitutes, and dressed neatly in dark colors—except for an occasional Mexican sombrero. His downfall was a hair-trigger temper that could be set off without warning.

Shortly before the outbreak of the Lincoln County War, Bonney was hired to work on a ranch owned by John Tunstall, a young Englishman who sought to undermine the economic stronghold of Lincoln's James Dolan and Lawrence Murphy.

After the murder of Tunstall set off the war, the young Bonney vowed, "I'll get some of them before I die." As a member of the Regulators, a group of men that formed to avenge Tunstall's death, he did just that. Bonney played a role in the killing of three men he believed were Tunstall's murderers, and he was blamed for shooting Sheriff William Brady, who previously had mistreated some of the outlaw's friends. It was for Brady's murder that Bonney was convicted in a rundown adobe Mesilla courtroom in April 1881, and returned to Lincoln for his hanging.

Shackled and handcuffed, Bonney awaited his fate in an upstairs room adjacent to the sheriff's office in the Lincoln County Courthouse, guarded closely by deputies Bob Olinger and James Bell. One evening while Olinger took five other prisoners across the street to eat at the Wortley Hotel, the Kid found himself alone with Bell. He asked Bell to escort him to the privy. As they returned, Bell carelessly lagged behind, which gave Bonney a chance to beat the deputy to the top of the stairs, shackles and all. Hiding behind a corner, Bonney quickly twisted his skinny hands from the handcuffs. When Bell topped the staircase, Bonney viciously swung the loose cuff across the deputy's head, cutting open two gashes across his scalp. Bleeding and slightly stunned, Bell was no match for the agile outlaw who wrestled away the deputy's holstered revolver. As Bell retreated down the stairs, Bonney shot him dead.

Next, the outlaw grabbed Olinger's loaded shotgun from his office and ran to a corner window. Olinger rushed across the street and after opening the outside gate to the courthouse looked up into the barrel of his own shotgun pointing at him from an upstairs window. Bonney didn't hesitate to fire, shredding Olinger's upper body with a heavy load of buckshot the lawman had loaded earlier in the day.

The town was terror stricken. No one moved to approach Bonney as a friend saddled up a horse for him. According to an account from *Billy the Kid, a Short and Violent Life*, by Robert Utley, Bonney smashed Olinger's shotgun across the railing of the courthouse porch and hurled its pieces at the dead lawman who had despised and verbally abused the desperado.

His bold and fearless flight from Lincoln solidified Bonney's standing as the territory's leading fugitive. The *Las Vegas Optic*, a daily newspaper editorialized, "With a heart untouched to pity by misfortune and with a character possessing the attributes of the damned, he has reveled in brutal murder and gloried in his shame."

After his escape, Bonney was taken in by his many friends throughout the region, who fed and sheltered him. One of these was Pete Maxwell, son of Lucien Maxwell, previous owner of the Maxwell Land Grant, who had renovated the barracks of Fort Sumner as his home. Spending the night at the old fort, Bonney was heading to Maxwell's house to cut a slab of meat for a midnight snack when he entered his friend's bedroom asking about a couple of strangers outside.

Inside was a third visitor, Sheriff Pat Garrett, who had come to inquire about the Kid's whereabouts and by chance found his prey.

William H. Bonney, otherwise known as Billy the Kid. (Museum of New Mexico)

The arrival of the railroad didn't eliminate the need for lawmen, and Socorro had one of the flashiest in Elfego Baca. In 1884 at the age of 19, Baca traveled 137 miles (219 km) from his home in Socorro to Frisco (now Reserve) to stump for a sheriff's candidate. While Baca was trying to win votes for his friend, an inebriated Texas cowboy began shooting up the town and harassing residents. Since Baca was the closest thing to a lawman the town had at that moment, he appointed himself deputy sheriff. His first act was to arrest the perpetrator. Baca quickly found himself surrounded by 80 agitated cowboys who demanded he release their friend. He refused and barricaded himself inside a low-slung *jacal,* a small hut constructed of poles spaced at least two inches (5 cm) apart and connected by mud plaster. During the next 36 hours, more than 4,000 shots were fired at the *jacal.* A total of 367 bullets riddled the small front door, hitting nearly everything inside, including silverware and a plaster-of-paris reproduction of a saint, known as Nuestra Señora Santa Ana, which Baca slyly used as a decoy. The self-appointed sheriff was untouched, though he killed four of the Texans. Baca gave up the fight when a deputy arrived from Socorro. He was subsequently tried and acquitted.

Baca eventually served as mayor of Socorro, deputy U.S. marshal, county clerk, and school superintendent. He earned a law degree and in 1919 became the nononsense sheriff of Socorro County. Once, instead of having his deputies arrest suspects indicted by a grand jury, he sent the suspects a letter that read, "I have a warrant here for your arrest. Please come in by March 15 and give yourself up. If you don't I'll know that you intend to resist arrest, and I will feel justified in shooting you on sight when I come after you." The Socorro native's life has been immortalized on screen by Walt Disney in a 1958 movie entitled, *The Nine Lives of Elfego Baca.* His survival skills are also remembered every June on the final day of the Hilton Open, a Socorro pro-am golf tournament. The Elfego Baca Shoot challenges golfers to tee off atop 7,500-foot (2,286-m) Socorro Peak, then scramble down the mountain after their balls, until they arrive at the golf course at the New Mexico Institute of Mining and Technology. About 15 shots usually win the hole.

DAMS AND ONIONS

By the early 1900s, farmers along the Rio Grande were beginning to tire of the muddy waterway's irregular behavior. One year, the river would flood its banks, only to dry up the next. Wanting reliability, they actively encouraged construction of a dam that would store water from the wet years and release it during the dry ones. Surveys started in 1903, followed by construction in 1911; Elephant Butte Dam was completed in 1916. The lake that formed behind it would be an oasis for recreational boaters, fishermen, and anyone else seeking relief from the relentless summer sun. A second lake was formed when Caballo Dam was completed in 1938 as a secondary storage reservoir 11 miles (17 km) south.

The already fertile farmland downstream became even more abundant, its fields soon brimming with white cotton bolls, green and red chile peppers, and shady pecan orchards. Today, US 85 passes through the hamlets of Arrey, Hatch, and Radium Springs, beside which neat rows of crops spread to the river and nearby hills. You can tell the season by the smell that greets your nostrils: if it's the sharp aroma of ripe onions, it must be summer. The unmistakable strong odor of chiles means it's fall, and when tufts of wayward cotton bolls stick to roadside signs and litter the highway, winter is nigh.

■ SOCORRO

Socorro, which means help or aid in Spanish, was named by Juan de Oñate, New Mexico's first governor, in appreciation for the food and water Indians provided his entourage there one desperate afternoon in 1598. He had just led the first expedition across the Jornada del Muerto, or Journey of Death, a 90-mile (144-km) expanse of near waterless desert.

The best way to see this quiet town is on foot. To guide walkers through the small historic district, the Socorro County Historical Society has published a map. The self-guided tour begins at the tree-shaded plaza, unromantically named **Kittrel Park** in memory of the dentist who first planted trees and grass there in the 1880s. There is a gazebo in the center of this peaceful park, and black wrought iron benches where you can relax and listen to the songs of robins and finches. The tour takes you past the brick-solid **Hilton Block,** anchored by the Hilton Drugstore, founded by a relative of Conrad Hilton. (Nobody seems to know which one.) Also on the route is the **Val Verde Hotel,** built in 1919 to serve passengers on the Santa Fe Railroad. Abandoned in the 1960s, the hotel reopened in the late 1980s, its rooms rented exclusively to students at the New Mexico Institute of Mining and Technology. The main floor is open to the public and contains the Val Verde Steak House and the Dana Bookstore (which has a respectable collection of Southwest titles). No operas ever have been performed at the J.N. Garcia Opera House a few blocks away. But the recently renovated 1886 building has been the site of concerts, masked balls, school programs, and college basketball games.

Unlike most Spanish communities in New Mexico, Socorro's church was not built on the plaza. Rather, San Miguel Mission was erected three blocks north on the site of the original seventeenth-century mission, which was destroyed during the Pueblo Revolt of 1680. Underneath the present church, built between 1819 and 1821, are four sub-floors beneath which lie the remains of once prominent residents, including Gen. Manuel Armijo, the last Mexican governor of the state.

The walking tour still proves there is more to this dusty town than California Avenue, where businesses, motels, and restaurants line up in a mass of concrete.

Tall trees shade the green lawns on the campus of the New Mexico Institute of Mining and Technology, founded in 1946 to train mining engineers. The school has since branched out to include research projects in petroleum mining and explosives technology. Its mountain-top laboratory is the only one in the country dedicated to studying the physical dynamics of thunderclouds.

Rockhounds might enjoy a stop at the institute's Mineral Museum, which boasts a collection of more than 10,000 specimens, including bison vertebrae, giant ground sloth fossils, turquoise, quartz, and lesser-known gems such as yellow zippeite and charcoal gray goethite. Although the exhibit is mostly geared toward aficionados, giant mammoth fossils and a case of fluorescent minerals from around the world are interesting even to regular folk. Some specimens are for sale.

VICINITY OF SOCORRO

West of Socorro, US 60 traverses the windswept Plains of San Agustin. Past the old shipping center of Magdalena, giant white satellite dishes mysteriously sprout from the horizon, part of a 27-antenna network that makes up the Very Large Array, the world's most powerful radio telescope. Each 94-foot (29-m) antenna weighs 235 tons and moves about on railroad tracks. A visitor center is open daily, displaying photos of Neptune taken by Voyager 2 in August 1989. A self-guided tour also takes visitors past exhibits that illustrate how radios and the telescope work, and how they came to be. If you continue the tour outside, you can walk past one of the giant dishes.

South of Socorro, the sleepy community of **San Antonio** sits on a drainage ditch along the Rio Grande. Historians know it as the birthplace of Conrad Hilton, but travelers know it for the Owl Bar, reputed to serve the finest green chile cheeseburger hereabouts. Sandhill cranes, pure white snow geese, and ducks fly overhead along NM 1 (old US 85), which winds south past fields of wheat, corn, and millet—a lavish dinner table for these birds who spend their winters at the nearby **Bosque del Apache National Wildlife Refuge.** The refuge was established in 1939 to provide a winter home for the graceful whooping crane, then threatened with extinction. A handful of the rare white birds winter at the refuge. While bird watching is best during evening hours from October to February, in the summer, more than 3,000 ducks, hundreds of Canada geese, and scores of wading birds such as herons and egrets take over the wetlands.

The dish-shaped antennas which make up Very Large Array are laid out in the shape of a Y and are connected to form a radio telescope. (Paul Chesley)

■ TRUTH OR CONSEQUENCES

In 1950, when Ralph Edwards put out the word he was looking for a town willing to name itself after his off-beat radio show, cattleman Burton Roach took up the challenge. As a state senator and president of the Hot Springs Chamber of Commerce, Roach thought this might be a way to distinguish his hot springs from all the other hot springs and get some free advertising in the bargain.

The town's citizens voted on the idea, and Hot Springs was transformed into Truth or Consequences, the name of a variety show that reunited long-lost relatives or flew servicemen overseas to see their mothers. Sometimes questions were asked of audience members who were penalized in silly ways if they failed to respond with the correct answer. As promised, Edwards brought his Hollywood production staff and show crew to New Mexico for the first live, coast-to-coast broadcast from its new namesake. It was no joke that the show was aired on April 1, 1950. In fact, since that first year, Edwards has returned every May to emcee the Ralph Edwards Fiesta, accompanied by a handful of his Hollywood cronies. During the first fiesta, 10,000 people lined a two-mile (3-km) parade route, and Edwards honored the occasion by breaking a bottle of mineral water over the head of Roach.

Perhaps it was this brilliant marketing strategy, or maybe it's the attraction of the nearby liquid oases of Elephant Butte and Caballo reservoirs, but T or C, as the town is called, has become a haven for retirees. Some call themselves "snow birds" because they return every winter for the mild days, for trophy fishing at the nearby reservoirs, and for the soothing waters of nine mineral baths that line up on or near Broadway Street at the southern end of town. Downtown sits atop a supply of steaming underground mineral water. Long before the town was established, Indians soaked aching muscles in the soothing waters after a long days' ride. Most of the bathhouses that survive were built in the 1930s to go along with tourist court motels. Each retains a rustic charm and personality of its own.

In the early 1980s it occurred to entrepreneurial landowners outside T or C that the moderate, dry climate might be perfect for wine grapes. They weren't the first to think of the idea. In 1662, a century before the first grapes were planted in California, Franciscan priests were producing naturally fermenting wine for their masses from mission grapes grown in southern New Mexico. If you want to sample local chardonnays, rieslings, and sauvignon blancs, stop by the tasting room at

Alamosa Cellars on NM 195 near Elephant Butte Lake. Or if your preference is sparkling wine, try **Domaine Cheurlin** champagne, along with its pinot noir at the intersection of Warm Springs Boulevard and NM 195.

NEARBY GHOST TOWNS
Several once-thriving mining and commercial centers are scattered in the vicinity of Truth or Consequences, their busy streets now deserted, their bustling mercantile stores now reduced to wooden skeletons. Northwest of town, NM 52 passes through **Cuchillo,** a Hispanic hamlet tucked into an abrupt outcropping. During the 1860 gold rush days, prospectors and suppliers changed horses here, and stagecoaches let their passengers off to stretch their legs. Cans of soup and small jars of spices line the walls of the general store, which has doubled as a bar since opening its doors in 1850.

Gently rising hillsides dotted with piñon pines give way to a broad meadow of pale-green and yellow grasses amid which the mining district of **Winston** sits. Silver was the lure in the 1880s, attracting prospectors to try their luck in the nearby hills. Today, cattle graze in the valley, and tall weeds and grass are what prosper,

Stagecoach leaving Silver City for Georgetown, 1885. (Museum of New Mexico)

jutting up between the false-fronted and mostly abandoned wooden buildings. Beyond this almost non-existent town, the road turns gravel, ending two miles (3 km) closer to the looming mountains at **Chloride**. In 1879, Henry Pye, a mule-skinner and prospector, discovered veins of silver chloride in a nearby rock outcropping. He established a claim, but a few months later, before he could enjoy the wealth he had envisioned, he was killed in an Apache raid. The boom that followed attracted hundreds of miners who built a picturesque settlement of adobe and wooden homes in the range's wrinkled foothills. Today, many original buildings remain, most of them abandoned. A few hardy residents have restored some of the structures and built new ones. Even though they live at the end of a gravel road, 42 miles (67 km) from T or C they hold yard sales.

At the southern end of the Black Range and southwest of T or C, NM 152 crosses rugged mountains, winding among steep, pine-covered slopes. But first, it bisects the old mining district of **Hillsboro,** its tin roofs hidden underneath giant cottonwoods. Once a gold and silver-mining boom town and Sierra County seat, Hillsboro turned into a ranching center after the minerals were depleted. Today, a collection of novelty shops, art galleries, and antique stores line the main street.

(above) Pioneer home near Mora.

(opposite) Rita Hill and daughter, Janaloo, at their ghost town of Shakespeare, two miles south of Lordsburg. (Paul Chesley)

Eccentric artists, solitary writers, and slow-moving retirees share star-filled evenings and quiet days with rough-riding ranchers and diehard miners.

Every Labor Day weekend, the village comes alive during the Hillsboro Apple Festival. People gather in the streets and along sidewalks lined with arts and crafts booths, food stalls, and apples harvested from nearby orchards.

Nine miles (14 km) farther into the mountains, **Kingston** is the last stop before NM 152 climbs over 8,228-foot (2,508-m) Emory Pass on its way to the Mimbres Valley. In its heyday that began in 1880, 7,500 fortune hunters flocked to Kingston's pine-covered slopes, which surrendered more than $10 million worth of silver in less than 15 years. For a short time the town boomed. Twenty-two saloons lined the broad sidewalk on the main street, and Lillian Russell performed at the town's theater. Kingston had no church until a hat was passed in the saloons one night to raise money for one. Today, 30 resourceful people live in this mountain town, writers and retirees joining long-time residents who continue to hold regular meetings of the Spit and Whittle Club. They say they love the clean air and sweet smell of burning piñon on cold days.

■ LAS CRUCES

Framed by the lush banks of the Rio Grande and the dry, rugged Organ Mountains (named for their resemblance to pipe organs), Las Cruces sits in the heart of the Mesilla Valley. When New Mexico was being settled, the wagons of Spanish colonists that passed this way were frequently ambushed by Apaches. In 1787, the bodies of several oxcart caravan drivers were found and crosses were erected atop their graves. Forty-three years later, a party of 30 travelers from Taos met the same fate and more crosses were raised. What began as an eerie graveyard known as La Placita de las Cruces, "The Place of the Crosses," has grown to become the second largest city in New Mexico.

In the mid-1800s, colonists began putting down roots, cultivating corn, beans, and pumpkins along the banks of the Rio Grande. They lived in *jacales,* created by placing poles vertically in a ground trench. The poles were lashed together and coated with mud plaster, forming walls that could be whitewashed. *Vigas* and *latillas* supported dirt roofs. Adobe bricks were used in later homes, brick copings topped parapets, and square wooden columns supported porches. Many of these houses are still visible in the **Mesquite Street** area, east of downtown, Las Cruces's

DRIPPING SPRINGS

At first glance, the jagged Organ Mountains outside Las Cruces appear as dry as the desert around them. And for the most part, they are, except at Dripping Springs. There, a trickle of water seeps from the volcanic rock, forming a few refreshing pools. During and after a rainstorm, the drip becomes a waterfall, sending a roaring river through nearby Ice Canyon.

Until 1988, this desert oasis was known primarily by Las Cruces residents who enjoyed hiking in the mountain foothills, poking around the ruins of an abandoned resort, and soaking in the cool pools. The spring itself was part of a cattle ranch owned by the A.B. Cox family, which generously permitted public use of the property.

In late 1988, the family sold the 2,852-acre spread of cactus-laden foothills and rugged rock outcroppings to the Nature Conservancy, which then transferred title to the Bureau of Land Management. In exchange, the Nature Conservancy, an international non-profit organization committed to protecting significant natural areas, received other BLM lands that it could still sell to cover the cost of purchase.

Now that it's in the public domain, the main ranch house has been turned into a visitor center, and maintained trails wend through ocotillo, cholla, and prickly-pear cactus. A 1.5-mile (2-km) uphill path leads to the spring and ruins of past resorts, the original one built in the 1870s by Col. Eugene Van Patten, who called the place Van Patten's Mountain Camp. At that time, the retreat consisted of a 16-room building that included a dining hall and large ballroom. By the turn of the century, it was known as Dripping Springs Resort and attracted such notables as Pat Garrett and Pancho Villa. Van Patten was married to a local Indian woman, and as a result, a number of Indians lived and worked at the resort, hand-carrying water from the nearby spring to the rooms.

In 1917, Van Patten went bankrupt, and Dripping Springs was sold to Dr. Nathan Boyd, who had homesteaded on a tract of land adjacent to the resort. Dr. Boyd's wife had contracted tuberculosis, which prompted him to turn the resort into a sanatorium. New buildings were constructed in the canyon, including a cabin for the Boyds, and a stilt house used as a dining hall. Dr. Boyd eventually sold the place to another physician, Dr. Sexton of Las Cruces, who continued to operate it as a sanatorium until the early 1940s. In the following years, the buildings deteriorated after local citizens rejected attempts to purchase and preserve the resort. Today, all that remains are two rooms of the main lodge, the tin-roofed stilt house, and Dr. Boyd's stone cabin.

The present-day visitor center was built by the next owner, Franklin Hayner, who operated a Las Cruces lumber yard and traveled the bumpy 10-mile (16-km) gravel road to the former resort only on weekends. In 1958, the Cox family bought the place and turned it into a cattle ranch.

In addition to the spring and ruins, a second trail leads from the visitor center to La Cueva, a volcanic rock outcropping named for a 10-foot-tall (3-m) cave at its southeastern end. Excavations of La Cueva have revealed that it was inhabited as long ago as 5000 B.C., probably as a shelter for early hunters in pursuit of rabbit, antelope, deer, and bighorn sheep. Later, members of the Jornada branch of the Mogollon culture sought the protection of the cave during storms.

In the late 1860s, an eccentric hermit, Giovanni Maria Agostini, moved into the cave. As the story goes, Agostini had been born of noble parents in Italy, but chose to spend most of his life traipsing around Europe and South and North America. Before arriving at La Cueva, he spent four years living atop a mountain near Las Vegas, New Mexico. The mountain retains the name honoring him, Hermit's Peak. In 1869, the 66-year-old man announced his plans to live in the Organ Mountains, despite warnings that Indians were roaming the area. His body was found in the cave later that year, apparently the victim of Apaches.

Today, a picnic area has been installed near La Cueva, along with a few tables near the resort ruins. But even though the ranch is now open to the public Friday

Short-horned lizard, common to the deserts of the Southwest. (Paul Chesley)

through Monday, preservation of the fragile environment remains of primary concern to the Bureau of Land Management.

Of nine threatened and endangered plant species located on the ranch, five are endemic to the Organ Mountains. In addition, seven endangered birds and two mammals live on the ranch along with two extremely rare mollusks, the earred terrestrial snail and Organ Mountain snail. BLM employees are adamant that visitors take care not to disturb the ecosystem. Employees will lead interpretive tours with advance notice They also request that groups of more than 10 people take guided tours.

To reach the ranch, take University Boulevard east off I-25, heading toward the mountains. When the pavement ends, you are on Dripping Springs Road. Most of the 10-mile (16-km) trip is on gravel, and it takes about 30 minutes.

The yucca is New Mexico's state flower. (Paul Chesley)

oldest neighborhood. Homes are stuccoed in pastel pink, green, blue, and shades of brown that range from tawny to deep-chocolate. An occasional shrine graces a front yard.

After the Santa Fe Railroad reached Las Cruces in 1881, farmlands between the Mesquite district and the depot were transformed into homes that reflected the styles of the town's new residents who came from the East Coast. Architectural designs include Hip Box, Queen Anne, and Bungalow, along with some patterned after the traditional adobe style. A few pre-railroad farm houses survive in the **Alameda-Depot Historic District,** which is worth exploring on foot.

South of town, the College of Las Cruces opened in 1880 and within a decade had grown into the New Mexico College of Agriculture and Mechanic Arts, which later would become **New Mexico State University.** The second largest university in the state, it is noted for its agricultural research, especially the cultivation of chile. Thirty of the 200 known varieties of chile peppers are grown and studied in fields irrigated by the Rio Grande. Researchers continually work to develop milder hybrids so people with sensitive palates, most of whom seem to reside east of the Mississippi River, can enjoy its unique spiciness. The grassy campus, with its red-tiled roofs atop tan stucco buildings, stretches across 6,250 acres that include grazing pastures, one of the largest computer centers in the Southwest, and one of three full-time planetary observatories in the country. Clyde Tombaugh, discoverer of the planet Pluto, is professor emeritus at NMSU.

The city's major employer is **White Sands Missile Range,** a 4,000-square-mile (10,360 sq-km) expanse of lonely desert that follows the eastern edge of the Organ and San Andres mountain ranges. Nearly 9,000 residents cross San Agustin Pass every day to punch timeclocks on a tree-shaded campus at its base.

In 1942, the U.S. military designated White Sands Proving Grounds to test weapons. Three years later, the world's first atomic bomb was detonated at its northern end. After the Germans destroyed parts of London with their V-2 rockets in the war, the United States decided to improve upon its own missile capability and began by enlarging the test area to include 2.7 million acres of tall grassland, displacing hundreds of ranchers and their families. Its new name, White Sands Missile Range, reflects an expanded mission: testing rockets, missiles, and payloads for the space shuttle program. To protect travelers from wayward rockets along US 70-82, which cuts through the missile range, roadblocks are erected during firings.

■ MESILLA

Although Mesilla lost out, in population and prestige, to Las Cruces in the great railroad rush of the 1880s, the sleepy town has succeeded in retaining its nineteenth-century character. From miles away, the white crosses atop two steeples of the **San Albino Church** can be seen towering above the tree-shaded town. This block-long brick church anchors the northern end of a quiet central plaza, with a white-washed gazebo in its center. Black wrought-iron benches with wooden seats are a perfect place to watch the afternoon sun transform the mud-brown walls of shops and galleries into hues of soft yellow and rose red. Sit back and muse about the days when the plaza bustled with stagecoaches in for repair at the Butterfield station and when, over shots of whiskey, cowboys impressed each other with tales of herding cattle on the untamed range. The Confederate flag flapped above the plaza for a year between 1861 and 1862, and 20 years later in a stuffy courtroom, a shackled Billy the Kid was sentenced to die for the murder of Lincoln County Sheriff William Brady. And don't forget: for a time Mesilla was the capital of the Territory of Arizona.

Today, the blacksmith shop, saddle shop, and horse stables of the Butterfield station have been turned into the dining rooms of **La Posta**, a superb Mexican restaurant. Across the street, the **William Bonney Gallery,** once the jail that housed Billy the Kid, sells Frederic Remington bronze sculptures and vases painted by R.C. Gorman. The courthouse itself is now the **Billy the Kid Gift Shop,** where the notorious outlaw is emblazoned on mugs, T-shirts, postcards, and shot glasses. On the west side of the plaza is **Mesilla Book Center**—an excellent source for books on the Southwest's history, geology, anthropology, and way of life.

Away from the plaza on Mesilla's narrow back streets, residents still live in 100-year-old adobe homes, some displaying brightly painted wooden window casings and others crumbling to the ground. It's easy to imagine horses plodding along, neighbors sharing news in rapid Spanish, Mariachi music wafting from doorways, and the delightfully greasy smell of *chicharrones* (crispy fried pork skin) cooking in oil.

THE VALLEY

South of Mesilla, with the jagged peaks of the Organ Mountains a distant backdrop, NM 28 follows the bends of the Rio Grande, passing beneath a three-mile-long (5-km) canopy created by thick groves of pecan trees. This extensive pecan

orchard, whose 180,000 trees make it the largest in the world, is owned by the Stahmann family. Deep-dug irrigation ditches filled with swiftly flowing water feed wide expanses of deep-green chile fields, white-tufted cotton plants, and pale-green heads of lettuce. Mixed in with these lush crops, clusters of grapes grow along vines that surround a tasting room at **La Vina Vineyard and Winery.** Stop in for a glass of Chardonnay or Zinfandel.

Farmers who tend these fields live in small hamlets with names like San Miguel, Chamberino, and La Mesa. They meet to share a beer and discuss local politics at **Chope's Bar and Cafe** in La Mesa. As the conversation heats up, so does the green chile that smothers plates of enchiladas and burritos served here. This chile is for palates accustomed to fire. If yours isn't, expect to leave with a runny nose and perspiring brow.

■ DEMING

Deming is a railroad town named after the daughter of an Indiana sawmill owner. Mary Ann Deming also happened to be married to Charles Crocker, a California silver baron and one of the promoters of the Southern Pacific Railroad, which in 1881 met the Atchison, Topeka & Santa Fe Railroad among creosote bush and cholla cactus north of the Little Florida Mountains. He named the resulting ramshackle gathering of tents and shanties after his wife.

She'd probably be pleased to know that the boisterous railroad camp that bore her name grew into a quiet, tidy, tree-lined town that boasts clean air and pure water. The water comes from the Mimbres River, which passes underground through town; the clear skies remain unsullied by heavy industry or auto traffic. Most Deming residents walk around their town—to work, the beauty shop, or the post office. Rarely do they lock their doors behind them. In the evening, they sit on their porches, taking in the last rays of a golden sun, or they go for a stroll through their neighborhoods. Daytime finds cows and steers outside of town, chewing on patches of desert grass that have sprouted up between mesquite trees and yuccas. Fields of waving milo and the white pods of cotton plants flourish in the intense sun.

According to some people, the best thing about Deming is the **Deming Duck Race.** It all started on a slow day in 1980 when realtor Steve Marlowe and his

Tom Day on the Culberson Ranch displays the tails of 110 rattlesnakes found on the ranch during a 12-month period. (Paul Chesley)

friend, Harold Cousland, editor of the *Deming Headlight,* were bemoaning the te-
dium of small-town life over coffee. Marlowe asked Cousland whether he thought
duck races might liven things up. He knew full well there weren't any ducks flying
around their hot, dry, landlocked hometown, but that was no obstacle. Marlowe
had heard that such races took place at the Long Branch Saloon in North Las
Vegas, Nevada.

Cousland considered Marlowe's idea daffy, but liked it because it lent itself to
endless puns, a newspaper man's dream. A week later, Marlowe scheduled a meeting to plan the first Great American Duck Race. A Saturday night Duck Ball, during which a Duck Queen would be crowned, would open the late-August weekend festivities, followed the next day by the races. Marlowe, already calling himself
the event's "chief quacker," had sent away to Las Vegas for official rules. The entry
fee would be $5 and ducks would be vying for a $1,000 purse. Billing itself as
"The World's Richest Duck Race," the event drew 184 downy competitors and
5,000 spectators.

Through the years, the wacky races have gone from a joke to the town's most
popular annual attraction, typically drawing up to 25,000 spectators on the fourth
weekend in August. More than 400 webbed entrants compete for the top prize,
now $2,000.

The 16-foot-long (5-m), eight-lane course is erected at Deming Duck Downs,
otherwise known as the Luna County Courthouse. The lanes are separated by
"duck wire," otherwise known as chicken wire. A carpeted Duck Deck atop each
lane serves as a platform upon which the trainer crawls, hollers, and threatens—
whatever it takes, short of touching his protegé, to instill a winning spirit. Throughout the weekend, ducks run in elimination heats until the final round on Sunday
afternoon. "Be a winner, or be dinner," is a common phrase trainers impart to their
contestants.

Competitors come from across the country, some renting trucks big enough to
hold portable wading pools to keep ducks content before their races. Prior to the
1981 event, Marlowe received a call from a Utah duck trainer whose entrant was
so fast that it had suffered burned breast feathers and blistered feet during practice
runs. The trainer wondered if he could use a drag chute on his duck to stop it at
the end of the race. Permission was granted, but the braggart never showed up.

Deming's main link to the past is the **Deming Luna Mimbres Museum,** located
in the old National Guard Armory. One room is dedicated to the display of more

than 500 lovingly costumed dolls; another holds a collection of intricately stitched quilts dating back to 1847. A chuckwagon conjures up the traveling kitchens of roundup days, and Mimbres pottery, arrowheads, and baskets represent the tribes that once roamed the region.

Southeast of town, the relentless sun beats down on the Little Florida Mountains, reflecting specimens of cloudy agate, blood-red jasper, shiny black perlite, and smoky quartz. Here among the granite and volcanic breccia outcroppings of **Rock Hound State Park**, people wander through the spiny thorns of yuccas, beavertail, and barrel cacti, searching for precious geodes. In an unusual twist, visitors are encouraged to take their favorite finds home.

■ COLUMBUS

This sleepy border town hasn't been the same since the early morning hours of March 9, 1916. That morning, as the townsfolk lay sleeping, Pancho Villa led a band of Mexican revolutionaries in an attack on the quiet village and burned most of it to the ground. Eighteen Americans were killed—some residents and others soldiers stationed at Camp Furlong. The following day, U.S. Army Gen. John J. Pershing headed across the border into Mexico, leading 10,000 soldiers through a desolate desert covered with thorny cactus and parched mountains. Trucks and motorcycles provided support for soldiers on horseback, and eight cloth-covered Curtis JN-3 biplanes, known as Jennys, of the First Aero Squadron took to the sky. This punitive expedition marked the introduction to warfare of motorized vehicles and aircraft. Unfortunately, the deep sand and mud in the roadless expanse of northern Mexico proved too much for the vehicles. The biplanes, worn out from long use as trainers, suffered engine breakdowns. And when running, they didn't have enough power to clear Mexico's 12,000-foot (3,658-m) mountains. The

The raid on Columbus by Pancho Villa in 1916 was the only land invasion of the U.S. in this century. (Museum of New Mexico)

planes did prove useful in speeding messages between units. Pershing spent most of a year vainly chasing Villa through Mexico. He returned to Columbus on February 5, 1917.

Despite the devastation wrought by Villa, the citizens of Columbus have named a state park after him. Apparently, they figured Pershing State Park wouldn't draw as many visitors as **Pancho Villa State Park** and they could be right because the park, dedicated in 1959 alongside the ruins of Camp Furlong, is the community's main attraction. Campsites are carved out of a dense mass of orange-tipped ocotillo, knee-high beavertails, century plants, mesquite bushes, yuccas, and yellow-budded cholla. Five thousand varieties of cactus and wildflowers are crowded into this botanical paradise.

Columbus has remained a small, slow-moving community. Residents escape the summer heat at **Norma's Cafe** and exchange gossip over a cup of coffee. Gaunt

Pancho Villa at his headquarters in Ciudad, Juarez just before his advance on Torreon in 1914. (Museum of New Mexico)

Motor trucks delivering supplies to the U.S. Army in Mexico; Pershing Punitive Expedition, 1916. (Museum of New Mexico)

dogs unhurriedly cross wide dirt streets. The entire town has been designated a National Historic Landmark, as it is the only place in the United States ever invaded by a foreign army. There aren't many architectural examples, but each one is interesting, from the wrought-iron lettering on the white-washed post office to the two-story yellow clapboard Southern Pacific Railroad depot, which has been restored as the **Columbus Historical Museum.**

As the only official port of entry into Mexico from New Mexico, people stroll across the border to the town of **Palomas** to buy liquor, sample the fresh fruit sold from a pushcart, or visit the beautiful stone **Parroquia Guadalupe Catholic Church.** If you're looking for great bargains on a wide selection of Mexican goods, you'll have to go elsewhere in Mexico, but Palomas does offer visitors a wonderful taste of the country. Few people in town speak English, but they are more than willing to communicate through a friendly exchange of hand gestures. From a distance, Palomas looks to the eye to be about the size of Columbus, yet there are 500 residents in Columbus and 12,000 in Palomas.

■ LORDSBURG

Named for a Southern Pacific engineer, Lordsburg is mainly a gas-up and stretch stop, but three miles (5 km) southwest of town a collection of tin-roofed adobe buildings is worth a longer look. Hidden among a group of small hills covered in mesquite, yucca, greasewood, and beavertail cactus, the old townsite of **Shakespeare** has gone through numerous incarnations: first as a watering hole for Apache Indians, then as a stop on the Butterfield Trail, then as a boisterous mining boomtown. In 1935, it was purchased by the Hill family. Tours are offered on the second Sunday of each month.

Shakespeare's status grew from a stopover into a destination point in 1870 after W.D. Brown, a dropout from a government survey party, discovered some promising-looking ore in the nearby Pyramid Mountains. Overnight, tents and adobe shacks shot up across the stark brown landscape. After the silver boom died down, reports drifted across the country of a diamond strike in an undisclosed location outside of town. After showing off a bag of uncut stones to California banker William Ralston, two scruffy miners convinced him to pay them $600,000 for their claim in the Pyramid Mountains. Within a few weeks, more than 3,000 prospectors converged on Shakespeare. More tents and buildings went up until the main street was lined with seven saloons, stores, a barber shop, assay office, Chinese laundry, restaurants, and boarding houses. Nobody was finding any diamonds, but nobody seemed to care. There was no church, no newspaper, and no law. Free-for-all fights and murder were commonplace. Within months, the diamond strike was determined to be a swindle: the mountainside purported to contain the rich deposit had actually been salted with a few appropriately placed diamonds and the now-wealthy miners were nowhere to be found. Within a few days, Shakespeare was nearly empty.

A bumpy dirt road cuts through greasewood and yuccas to the few remaining buildings of Shakespeare. Janaloo Hill lives in the old general store, which doubles as a museum. But don't expect her to offer you an impromptu tour if you arrive when the town is closed. It's best to call ahead. For further information, write to P.O. Box 253, Lordsburg, NM 88045 or call (505) 542-9791.

Straddling the Continental Divide in New Mexico's boot heel, the tall grasslands of the **Gray Ranch** are preserved by the Nature Conservancy, which in 1990 purchased the richly endowed 500-square-mile (1,295-sq-km) spread. Although the ranch is not yet open to the public, its reputation as one of the nation's most significant biological areas is far-reaching. The ranch, once owned by California mining and livestock baron George Hearst, father of publishing magnate William Randolph Hearst, is home to nearly 100 rare and endangered plant and animal species, including the ridgenosed rattlesnake, Sanborn's long-nosed bat, the white-sided jackrabbit, and night-blooming cereus, a spiny-stemmed bush with delicate white blooms that come out at night.

■ SILVER CITY

One prospector who traveled to Shakespeare to check out its famous silver strike took a quick look at the distinct ore, scratched his head, and headed back home north to Piños Altos, a gold-mining burg in the foothills of what today is the Gila Wilderness. John Bullard knew where there was plenty more of the valuable silver: right outside his home. Soon the pine-covered hills were covered with makeshift tents and shacks, which became known as Silver City. Banks, saloons, restaurants, billiard halls, and meat markets popped up on the dirt streets, along with the offices of doctors, lawyers, dressmakers, and tailors. Smooth-talking gamblers in wide-rimmed black hats warmed seats in gambling houses. Bow-legged cowboys swaggered up to bars, demanding shots of red eye and mescal. All of these people apparently were eager to know of the larger world, for by the end of 1882, six newspapers were being published in the mining district.

Prior to the arrival of the railroad, which reached Silver City in 1881, 12- and 14-horse teams hauled ore from the Mogollon Mountains to town, where it was shipped off by stagecoach and wagon train. Stacks of gold and silver bricks stood outside freight offices. Incredibly, the temptation to pinch one or two proved even stronger than the threat of the noose: public hangings were frequent.

Unlike civic officials in most of the boomtowns of the day, Silver City's lawmakers had the foresight to prohibit frame buildings within the town's limits, hoping to prevent widespread destruction from fires. As a result, most of the original townsite has survived. Brick and adobe buildings, which mix Victorian architecture with the flat-roofed vernacular style, line almost every street. A white-picket fence surrounds the two-story H.B. Ailman House, which is a good place to start a stroll because it serves as the **Silver City Museum.**

An example of the town's resourcefulness is the **Big Ditch Park,** a 55-foot-deep (17-m) trench that once was Main Street. As miners sought their fortunes, they loosened the soil of Silver City's hills, which, along with heavy rains, caused massive flooding between 1895 and 1903. Walls of water as high as 12 feet (4 m), raged through town, gutting Main Street down to bedrock. In 1980, it became a city park.

Silver City, like so many other cities in New Mexico, lays claim to Billy the Kid. As a pre-teen then known as Henry McCarty, the outlaw attended school and worked as a waiter at the Star Hotel. He moved there with his mother and stepfather, who had a burning desire to strike it rich in the silver mines. You can follow the outlaw's brief presence in the mining district on a self-guided **Billy the Kid tour,** which takes you past the site of his boyhood home (since torn down), the Star Hotel, his mother's grave, and the site of the jail from which he made his first escape.

Unlike many early mining districts that fizzled after the ore played out, Silver City's mines are still producing, though copper has replaced silver as the primary metal extracted from the rich earth. Thirteen miles (21 km) east of town, the village of Santa Rita has been swallowed up by a massive **open-pit copper operation.** From an observation deck, you can peer into the 1,000-foot-deep (305-m) mine that stretches more than a mile (1.6 km) across. Trucks appear small as they drive along the terraced red-brown earth.

OUTSIDE SILVER CITY

Three miles (5 km) north of Silver City amid a flat expanse of piñons and junipers sits a commanding two-story Pueblo Revival bed-and-breakfast inn that caters to naturalists. The **Bear Mountain Guest Ranch** is the vision of Myra McCormick who, ever since 1959, has led discussions at the ranch's long wooden dinner table, eager to find out about her guests. Morning meals find diners sharing their breakfast hour with piñon jays and whatever other birds come along to outside feeders. The 160-acre ranch backs up to the Gila Wilderness, which is prime country for bird watching and native plant excursions, led by McCormick, who prefers to call plants by their genus names. She also offers archaeology and Indian pottery workshops as part of weekend and week-long packages.

The old gold mining district of **Piños Altos** seven miles (11 km) north of town hasn't fared as well as Silver City. But the cozy hamlet, named for the surrounding

Panning for gold remains one of the quixotic hobbies of the Southwest. (Paul Chesley)

tall pines, has done well at preserving its frontier past. A walk along the dirt streets of town takes you past the Piños Altos Ice Cream Parlor, housed in the old Norton Store. The creaky wooden floors of the Buckhorn Saloon don't seem to bother Indian Joe, a life-sized doll who sits at one end of the bar—day and night. He's the only one who gets to drink Buckhorn Beer. At an adjacent brick-walled dining room, some of the best steaks in these parts are served atop red checkered tablecloths. Around a bend and up a hill, the Gold Avenue Methodist Episcopal Church houses an art gallery. The adobe building, with its stained glass windows and steeply pitched roof, was built in 1898 with the financial assistance of Phoebe Hearst, mother of California newspaper publisher William Randolph Hearst. Her late-husband, George Hearst, had fared well in the Piños Altos mines. Another western celebrity with an interest in Piños Altos was Roy Bean who, with his brother Sam, operated a store here before the Civil War. Roy went on to become a famous frontier judge in West Texas.

Past Piños Altos, NM 15 ends at the **Gila Cliff Dwellings National Monument.** A one-mile (1.6 km) loop trail takes you up and through 42 rock-walled rooms built into the side of a volcanic cliff. You can climb ladders to explore the dark interiors. The well-protected dwellings look pretty much like they did when the Mogollon Indians lived in them from the 1280s into the 1300s. During the day, these people cultivated squash, corn, beans, and tobacco on nearby mesas and along the West Fork of the Gila River. They also hunted deer and gathered wild berries and nuts in the nearby forest. For generations their voices and children's laughter echoed throughout the steep-walled canyon. By the early 1300s, the only sounds remaining came from birds and the gurgling river. No one knows why they left, but many think they joined other Pueblo Indians to the north and south. The monument is adjacent to the 438,360-acre **Gila Wilderness,** which was promoted by conservationist Aldo Leopold and established in 1924 as the first in the country.

Heading south, NM 35 (which turns into NM 61 through the Mimbres Valley) passes an island of house-size boulders rising from the burnt-sienna prairie. This jumble of Tertiary tuff that flowed from an erupting volcano a million years ago has been turned into **City of Rocks State Park,** where picnic tables and campsites are wedged among the boulders. The only sound in this wide plain comes from the wind, which regularly whistles through ocotillo, cholla, and yucca cacti. Slate-blue mountain ranges line the horizon in every direction.

North of Silver City, US 180 skirts the 2.7-million-acre **Gila National Forest** and passes through a few small ranching communities. **Glenwood** has the most to offer—a few motels, a bar, and the Catwalk, a two-and-a-half-mile (4 km) steel walkway anchored to a rock wall above the rushing waters of Whitewater Creek. Before gold and silver were discovered in the Mogollon Mountains above the creek, the box canyon served as a hideout for the likes of Geronimo and Butch Cassidy, who carefully picked a path along the creekbed. In the 1880s, a group of miners looking for an easier way to do things built a wooden pipeline along the wall to carry water to a millsite and mining camp at the mouth of the canyon. The pipeline, installed three miles (5 km) upstream where water was always plentiful, was needed because the creek often dried up by the time it reached the settlement. While this water supply worked just fine, the pipeline did need repairs, which in places could be done only by walking on the dangling tube, thus the name "catwalk." After the mill closed in 1913 (followed by the mines in 1942), a trail was completed on the same route in 1936. The steel catwalk came later, in 1962. Today, this steel pathway passes alongside hybrid oaks, sycamores, and alders. Golden lichen cover boulders, and farther upstream the trail meets up with others that weave through the Gila National Forest where Rocky Mountain bighorn sheep and mule deer roam the slopes.

A few miles past Glenwood is the turnoff to **Mogollon,** an old mining town wedged into a narrow canyon in the Mogollon Mountains. In 1890, it was a bustling mining camp that boasted 20 saloons and 2,000 residents, including Ben Lilly, one of the West's most adept mountain lion hunters. Lilly charged ranchers $50 for each dead mountain lion he brought them. He bagged 110 during his career. Silver and gold ore was processed at nearby mills, which produced 18 million ounces (504 million g) of silver before the mines closed at the outbreak of World War II.

A walk through town takes you past a clock that reads 4 o'clock, the time the last shift ended in the mines. Today nine hardy people live year-round in the weather-beaten hamlet along Silver Creek. They are joined in the summer by about 31 others, mostly shopkeepers, who cater to vacationers heading into the Gila Wilderness. The road leading to this rustic village is only nine miles (14 km) long, but it takes a good 30 minutes to negotiate its steep incline and sharp curves. Past Mogollon, NM 78 becomes gravel and penetrates the wilderness.

As you follow NM 12 through the ranching centers of Reserve, Aragon, and Horse Springs, you're passing through the ancient home of the Mimbres Indians. These people lived throughout the Gila National Forest, down into the Mimbres Valley southeast of Silver City. What distinguished them from their Mogollon relatives was their pottery decorated in geometric designs and surreal animal figures. Many of these pots, typically found at gravesites, have been dug up on ranches throughout the Tularosa Mountains near Reserve and Aragon. The Mimbreños abandoned their homes in the twelfth century, long before their distant Mogollon relatives left the Gila River. As you drive through this grassy mountain valley, you won't see any remains of Mimbres dwellings because none have been preserved. You can only imagine the hours of painstaking work that went into the unspoiled quality of their designs.

Wildflowers brighten the desert. (Paul Chesley)

■ THE LIGHTNING FIELD

In the middle of a high-desert sagebrush plain 30 miles (48 km) northeast of Quemado, a grid of 400 stainless steel poles rises to the sky, looking like a giant bed of nails. In this unlikely array of metal, the poles are spaced 220 feet (67 m) apart in rows that measure one-mile (1.6 km) by one-kilometer. This is the precisely calculated statement of Walter De Maria, the internationally known artist who spent five years searching for just this spot.

No cattle roam this 3,400-acre plateau that stands at an elevation of 7,200 feet (2,195 m), and not many people either. Between the months of May and October, six people at a time are permitted to visit The Lightning Field. Each pays a minimum of $65 to spend the night in a renovated homesteader's cabin on the land and share a hot meal.

Most importantly, they share the experience that De Maria envisioned when he conceived the field in the early 1970s. For five years, the artist combed remote areas in California, Nevada, Utah, Arizona, and Texas before deciding on a site in western New Mexico 11.5 miles (18 km) east of the Continental Divide. He considered the land a major part of the work, and his priorities included isolation, flat terrain, and high lightning activity. It was also important that only a few people at a time visit the site, so they could easily lose each other when walking among the 20-foot-tall (6-m) poles.

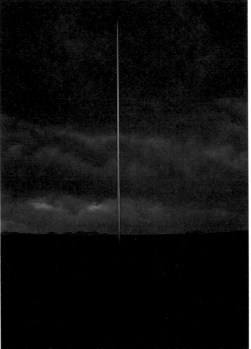

The Lightning Field—400 poles of an extraordinary landscape sculpture. (Paul Chesley)

Completed in 1977, the project was commissioned and is maintained by the Dia Art Foundation, a New York-based non-profit organization that promotes large-scale art projects. The foundation has since established a Quemado branch, which houses a few of De Maria's smaller works. The doors usually are locked, but if you'd like to ask a few questions, try Jonay's Bar a few doors down.

Despite the esoteric nature of this place, the experience is in demand. About 300 people visit the field each year, making advance reservations a must. Walk-ins typically are turned away. Those who do have reservations are picked up at 2:30 p.m. in front of Jonay's Bar. A caretaker drives them for a 45-minute ride over gravel roads to a weathered cabin where he helps unload luggage, then leaves. He returns at 11 a.m. the following day. The interval in between is completely unstructured, allowing plenty of time to walk around the field, breathe in the fresh sage, marvel at the immense sky, and wait for it to rain.

During thunderstorms, which occur most often in July and August, the poles become lightning rods and perform spectacular light shows. But most of the time the pointed steel shafts stand silent. That fits with De Maria's vision: that the light be as important as the lightning. Early in the morning and at sunset, light transforms the poles into radiant rods as they reflect the soft rays of the sun. When the sun is overhead, that dimension is lost as they seem to fade from sight.

Comments from visitors vary. Some claim a visit to the Lightning Field is a religious experience, while others say it's a total waste of time. But both agree it is an experience not soon forgotten.

For information, contact the Lightning Field, Two Wind NW, Albuquerque, NM 87120, phone: (505) 898-5602.

A FORM OF PARADISE

*B*rightest New Mexico. In that vivid light each rock and tree and cloud and mountain existed with a kind of force and clarity that seemed not natural but supernatural. Yet it also felt as familiar as home, the country of dreams, the land I had known from the beginning.

We were riding north from El Paso in my grandfather's pickup truck, bound for the village of Baker and the old man's ranch. This was in early June: the glare of the desert sun, glancing off the steel hood of the truck, stung my eyes with such intensity that I had to close them now and then for relief. And I could almost feel the fierce dry heat, like that of an oven, drawing the moisture from my body; I thought with longing of the cool water bag that hung from the hood latch over the grille in front, inaccessible. I wished that Grandfather would stop for a minute and give us time for a drink, but I was too proud and foolish to ask him; twelve years old, I thought it important to appear tougher than I really was.

When my eyes stopped aching I could open them again, raise my head and watch the highway and fence and telephone line, all geometrically straight and parallel, rolling forever toward us. Heat waves shimmered over the asphalt, giving the road far ahead a transparent, liquid look, an illusion which receded before us as fast as we approached.

Staring ahead, I saw a vulture rise from the flattened carcass of a rabbit on the pavement and hover nearby while we passed over his lunch. Beyond the black bird with his white-trimmed wings soared the western sky, the immense and violet sky flowing over alkali flats and dunes of sand and gypsum toward the mountains that stood like chains of islands, like a convoy of purple ships, along the horizon.

Those mountains—they seemed at once both close by and impossibly remote, an easy walk away and yet beyond the limits of the imagination. Between us lay the clear and empty wilderness of scattered mesquite trees and creosote shrubs and streambeds where water ran as seldom as the rain came down. Each summer for three years I had come to New Mexico; each time I gazed upon the moon-dead landscape and asked myself: what is out there? And each time I concluded: *something* is out there—maybe everything. To me the desert looked like a form of Paradise. And it always will.

—Edward Abbey
Fire on the Mountain, 1962

SOUTHEASTERN
NEW MEXICO

SOUTHEASTERN NEW MEXICO SEEMS TO STRETCH ON FOREVER, its vast plains pulling spacious skies down upon an endless horizon. A few lofty mountain ranges interrupt occasionally monotonous emptiness, across which notable and notorious figures have sallied forth, the most famous being the desperado Billy the Kid. The baby-faced outlaw roamed the region's piñon-covered hills, grama-grass plains, and heavily forested mountains, charming women and pulling his sharpshooter on others until he himself was shot with his boots off. Later notables include Smokey Bear, a tiny black bear cub who became the nation's symbol of the fight of forest fires; Peter Hurd, who captured on canvas the people, orchards, and fields of the pastoral Hondo Valley; and Norman Petty, who launched the careers of many rock-and -rollers in his Clovis music studio.

On the eastern plains, the state's border seems fused with its influential neighbor, though New Mexicans there bristle when their area is referred to as "Little Texas." But Texas-type, stretched-out terrain and the long lazy drawl that goes with it carry across the state line into the feedlots at Clovis and the oil wells at Hobbs. Sleek black pumpjacks rhythmically bob up and down beside sheep and cattle who nonchalantly munch on grass. A strong wind sweeps across boundless fields of peanuts, white bolls of cotton, tall corn stalks, and sweet-smelling onions. Between this high tableland and the mountains that rise grandly from the cactus plains, the Pecos River flows.

The cool pine-scented mountains of the Lincoln National Forest run the length of the region. From them rises solitary Sierra Blanca—at an altitude of 12,000 feet (3,658 m), the tallest peak in the range. At the southern end, Carlsbad Caverns extends more than 800 feet (244 m) below a cactus-covered ridge, revealing an underground world of skyscraper-tall limestone sculptures.

On the western fringes of the mountains, the Tularosa Basin—a vast expanse of harsh Chihuahuan desert—stretches between the rugged San Andres and Organ mountains to the west, and the Sacramento Mountains to the east. Within this flat-bottomed bowl is the world's largest surface deposit of fine gypsum granules, partially preserved as White Sands National Monument. These windswept dunes escaped the federal government's grasp in the 1940s when the military

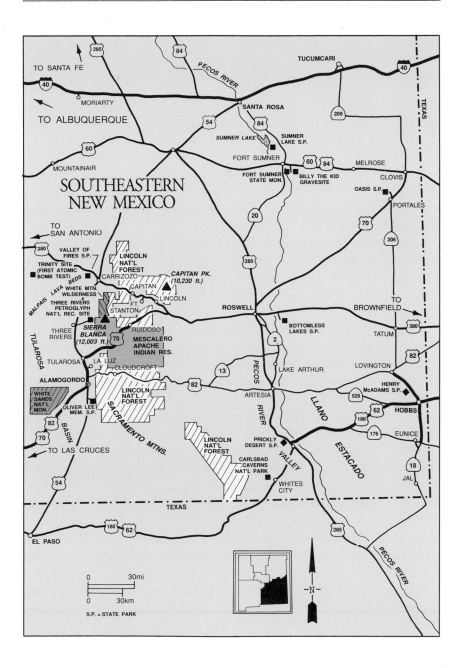

S.P. = STATE PARK

appropriated much of the surrounding range to develop weapons. The atomic bomb was first tested here, and today 2.7 million acres of this spiny cactus desert make up the top-secret defense installation of White Sands Missile Range.

■ HISTORY

Cool wetlands and forests covered much of southeastern New Mexico when the state's first inhabitants arrived from the north, pursuing mammoth and mastodon. By 10,000 B.C., the Clovis culture was stalking now-extinct forms of antelope, dire-wolves, and bison through the grasslands, eating the meat and crafting warm clothing from the hides.

Mescalero Apaches arrived in the region sometime after A.D. 1200, hunting deer and bison and harvesting berries, roots, seeds, and cacti in the forests and on the plains east of the Pecos River and west of the Rio Grande. A favorite treat was mescal, the heart of the agave cactus, which they roasted and ate. Women wove its fibers into baskets.

These roving Indians did not welcome the arrival of European settlers in the nineteenth century, who began raising sheep and growing corn and beans on Mescalero hunting lands. Comanche and Kiowa Indians came to the region and, like the Apaches, they frequently stole cattle and sheep, raided settlers' food supplies, and sometimes took captives. After the Civil War, government officials turned their attention to the problem and assigned Brig. Gen. James Carlton to put a halt to the attacks. In 1862, his men rounded up 400 Mescalero Apaches and confined them at the Bosque Redondo Reservation that had been carved out alongside the Pecos River. Two years later, famed Indian scout Kit Carson burned the fields and homes of Navajo Indians in eastern Arizona and western New Mexico, forcing their surrender. Gaunt and humbled, 8,500 Navajos then embarked on the "Long Walk," a more than 300-mile (480-km) forced march across cactus plains, rivers, and hardened lava flows to the reservation, where Fort Sumner had been built. There they lived unhappily alongside their traditional enemies, the Apaches.

Carlton, military commander in New Mexico at the time, set out to make farmers of these nomadic tribesmen. Confined on a reservation, the Indians were miserable from the outset, and Carlton's plan was a fiasco. Parasites ravaged the crops and alkaline water infected the Indians with dysentery. The general finally admitted defeat, and in 1868 the Navajos were given 3.5 million acres straddling the Arizona-New Mexico border. Additional acquisitions increased their holdings to 17 million acres, making their reservation the largest in the United States.

Today, Navajos continue their rural lifestyle—many raise sheep and plant small gardens atop red clay soil under which lie vast deposits of oil, gas, and coal. In 1873, the Mescaleros received 460,177 acres of timbered slopes and pastures in the Sacramento Mountains. (They have since turned into astute businesspeople, successfully operating a first-class resort, Inn of the Mountain Gods, and Ski Apache ski area.) In 1874, the Comanches made their peace with the military.

Once the free-roaming Indians were confined to reservations, more settlers moved into the region and established large sheep and cattle operations. In the late 1800s, the Santa Fe Railroad stretched across the region, passing through the Estancia Valley. Construction camps were erected in Willard and Encino, and Clovis on the far eastern plains. Three more lines entered the state from the south. In the early 1900s, a steady stream of homesteaders settled on the eastern plains, intending to farm 160-acre plots. In Roosevelt County, the population more than tripled between 1904 and 1910.

During World War II, New Mexico began its close relationship with the U.S. military as numerous Air Force bases were established across the creosote desert. In 1942, bases were opened at Clovis, Alamogordo, and Roswell—small towns that had plenty of room between them, where men could test out new aircraft under the wide azure skies. Only one is now closed: Walker Air Force Base at Roswell.

As weapons became more sophisticated, federal officials sought a safe place to test new rockets. In 1942, ranches in the Tularosa Basin were turned into White Sands Proving Ground. In the early hours of July 16, 1945, an atomic bomb was detonated here for the first time, melting the earth upon which it sat, and launching the world into the atomic age. Today, rockets regularly shoot skyward at what has become White Sands Missile Range, and sleek Stealth fighters swoop across the cholla and yucca-filled desert.

■ LINCOLN

Along the Rio Bonito, in a narrow valley at the edge of the Capitan Mountains, is the town of Lincoln, settled in 1849 by a small group of Hispanic farmers. Mescalero Apaches chased them out three times, but the feisty settlers kept returning. The village was known as Las Placitas del Rio Bonito until 1869, when the townsfolk renamed it after Abraham Lincoln.

Prime cattle country surrounded the town, and it became an important ranching center. As Lincoln prospered, more people wanted a piece of the business it generated, and they were willing to fight for it. One struggle escalated into a notorious period of violence, the Lincoln County War, which began in 1878.

It all started after Alexander McSween and John Tunstall opened a store to compete with already established shopkeeper Lawrence Murphy. Murphy, who didn't much appreciate the spirit of competition, attempted to crush McSween and Tunstall by filing a lawsuit against McSween pertaining to an insurance affair the previous year. A month after a guilty verdict was handed down, Tunstall, the financial backer of McSween's mercantile store, was shot to death on the road to his ranch. The same gunmen who killed Tunstall then were deputized by Sheriff William Brady and sent to search for Tunstall's killers, whom they obviously had no intention of finding.

Meanwhile, Tunstall's friends, some of whom witnessed his murder and were outraged by this hypocrisy, formed a faction to avenge his death. They called themselves the "Regulators." It wasn't long before they'd shot and killed Sheriff Brady and three of Tunstall's murderers. Pretty soon, everyone in town had taken sides. You were either a McSween man or a Murphy man. More gunfights followed, culminating in the Five Day Battle of July 1878. As McSween's men holed up inside his home, one of Murphy's supporters set the house on fire. McSween was shot and killed as he was trying to surrender. After McSween's death, the Regulators fled, but they rode around the countryside terrorizing Murphy loyalists for a few more years.

One of the McSween men was an affable, wavy-haired 19-year-old ranch hand named William Bonney (aka Henry McCarty), reckless of spirit and quick with a gun. He'd been inside the McSween house at the time it was set on fire, but escaped with the remaining Regulators. Bonney was nicknamed Billy—Billy the Kid.

Today, the tree-shaded street that cuts through Lincoln isn't much different than it was 100 years ago when Billy galloped down it. The biggest change is that it has been paved and displays a sign that reads US 380. A sleepy hamlet, Lincoln is linked to its violent past through legends. The entire town has been preserved as a state monument and is listed on the National Historic Register. A walking tour takes you past and through impeccably restored buildings, including places like the Tunstall Store, the two-story Lincoln County Courthouse (which earlier had served as the Murphy mercantile), San Juan Church, and several private homes. The Wortley Hotel, which burned down in 1936, has been rebuilt on its original foundation, and it's a rare evening's entertainment that surpasses sitting in a rocking chair on the hotel's front porch, watching the waning sunlight on nearby piñon and juniper-covered hillsides, and listening to the nighttime quiet fall upon the town.

Tunstall store in Lincoln was part of the controversy that set off the Lincoln County War.

Once a year, residents honor Billy the Kid in a folk pageant that dramatizes his last escape from the Lincoln County Courthouse. Lincoln Days is usually held the first weekend of August, and features a fiddler's contest, arts and crafts fair, and a 42-mile (67-km) Pony Express race that begins at the ghost town of White Oaks and ends at Lincoln.

VICINITY OF LINCOLN

East of Lincoln, bushy piñon and junipers give way to the orchards of the **Hondo Valley** as the Rio Bonito joins the Rio Ruidoso to become the Rio Hondo. The tiny communities of San Patricio, Hondo, Tinnie, and Picacho hide among corn and bean fields that mix with cherry and apple orchards across this narrow, fertile valley. Polo is a popular pastime.

The late Peter Hurd, a Roswell native, brought his wife, Henriette Wyeth of the Pennsylvania artist family, to live alongside the murmuring Rio Hondo in an adobe hacienda, where they both painted. Their work reflects their pastoral surroundings, capturing the simple rural life in stylized landscapes and portraits of the valley's residents.

West of Lincoln, US 380 continues on to **Fort Stanton,** which was built in 1855 to protect settlers from Mescalero Apaches. By 1896, the fort was deactivated by the

The original Smokey Bear, a cub found after a forest fire. (U.S. Forest Service)

military, and two years later it was turned into a U.S. Marine Hospital for tuberculosis patients. Since 1966, the white-washed buildings have served as a state-run school for the mentally disabled.

A few miles farther west along US 380 is **Capitan**, a village that didn't have much to brag about, especially after a devastating forest fire destroyed 17,000 acres in the Capitan Mountains in 1950. But in its smoky aftermath, firefighters discovered a badly singed black bear cub clinging to the side of a charred pine tree. The frightened cub was given the name "Hotfoot," because of his severely burned feet. His burns were treated at the nearby Flatley Ranch, then Game Warden Ray Bell flew the cub to a veterinary hospital in Santa Fe. Hotfoot soon became Smokey. Bell later kept the bear in his home, where the cub ran roughshod over the family's other household pets. Once healed, Smokey was flown to Washington, D.C. where he lived out his life at the National Zoo. The fire proved fortunate for the U.S. Forest Service, which had invented Smokey Bear six years earlier as its fire prevention symbol. The charred bear cub brought life to this campaign. When Smokey died in 1976, he was replaced by Smokey II, who also came from the Capitan Mountains.

Capitan's townsfolk have built a log museum that houses scrapbooks documenting Smokey's discovery and subsequent celebrity. Inside the nearby Smokey the Bear Historical State Park, films of the famous bear are shown. Outside, a trail leads to Smokey's grave. Down the street there's the Smokey Bear Motel, which houses the Smokey Bear Restaurant, which features the Smokey Bear Burger.

■ MOUNTAINS

Ruidoso is a popular destination for Texans hoping to cool off in the hot summer months or to ski the slopes of Sierra Blanca in the winter. Originally named for Capt. Paul Dowlin of the New Mexico Volunteers, a Union regiment, in 1885 Dowlin's Mill was changed to **Ruidoso**, which means "noisy," for the babbling river that runs through it. Dowlin's actual mill still stands and is a favorite tourist stop. It houses a gift and book shop, and the mill itself, which is still operable. Present-day owner, Carmen Phillips, grinds natural flours for sale to locals and tourists.

By the turn of the century, cabins cozied up to the banks of the Rio Ruidoso, concealed among the tall pines of the White Mountains. The town had become, and continues to be, a summer resort for flatlanders seeking relief from the

sweltering heat of southern New Mexico and West Texas. These visitors fish for trout in nearby streams, hike mountain trails, and savor the pine-scented air. When they tire of relaxing, they browse in tourist shops that line the main street, or amble down the road to the racetrack at Ruidoso Downs and raise their blood pressure betting on the quarterhorses. Every Labor Day, the horses compete for $2.5 million in the All American Futurity, the world's richest quarterhorse race.

Next door to Ruidoso is the **Mescalero Apache Reservation.** The Mescaleros didn't take well to their incarceration at Bosque Redondo in 1862, but they have adjusted quite well to the tenets of capitalism, under the leadership of tough-minded President Wendell Chino, who began his career as the tribe's first Apache minister. One of the most financially successful tribes in the country, the Mescaleros operate Ski Apache on the flanks of the 12,000-foot (3,658-m) Sierra Blanca. With a vertical drop of 1,800 feet (599 m), the resort has seven chairlifts and a gondola to whisk skiers up the mountain. In the massive peak's shadows, the tribe's flagship enterprise, Inn of the Mountain Gods, sits alongside Lake Mescalero. Golf, tennis, and horseback riding programs are available. The tribe also runs a timber operation, as well as a fish hatchery that supplies trout to a number of pueblo lakes.

Who exactly are your hosts? Here's what Oliver La Farge had to say about the Apaches in 1952: "In the Southwest, at least, it is the common observation that Indians have a delightful sense of humor, and of all the tribes, the Apaches have the keenest and quickest. . . . It is a sense of the ridiculous, kidding which is never malicious, a constant, pleased awareness that the funny side of life is also always with us and a readiness to indicate it by a quick, unexpected phrase."

Cloudcroft boasts the southernmost ski area in the United States. The town was founded after the El Paso and Northeastern Railroad Company ran out of timber for cross ties during construction of a rail route connecting El Paso with Tucumcari. The only logical solution was to build a spur into the Sacramento Mountains where wood was plentiful. This steep, winding route, known as the Cloud Climbing Railroad, rose 6,000 feet (1,829 m) in 27 miles (43 km) and passed through all of the world's life zones, from the Sonoran Desert to the Hudson Bay region of Canada. Today, a twisting road climbs the mountain.

In 1899, the year before the rail line was completed, a Victorian log lodge was constructed at the 9,200-foot (2,804-m) summit, but it was destroyed by fire in 1909. Two years later, a spectacular inn replaced it, this one built of stucco and in

Apache dancers, Lincoln.

a Renaissance revival style. Pancho Villa, Clark Gable, and Judy Garland slept here. Today, visitors seeking relief from sizzling El Paso summers are treated to a first-class experience in the cool of the Lodge, a year-round resort that features one of the highest golf courses in the world. The fairways are well-maintained and the setting is bucolic—although occasionally a bear will lope across a green just as you are trying to concentrate on your stroke. Inside, guests can belly up to a massive bullet-ridden mahogany bar that was shipped to Cloudcroft from one of Al Capone's haunts in Cicero, Illinois. The inn's restaurant is named after a resident ghost—redheaded Rebecca, a flirtatious chambermaid who was killed by a jealous lover in the 1930s. Borrow the brass skeleton key from the desk and climb a stairway to the copper-domed observatory for a panoramic view of shimmering White Sands National Monument. At night, the four-story tower is a great place to gaze at a dark sky brilliant with stars.

Speaking of star-gazing, the Sacramento Peak Observatory, one of the world's largest solar observatories, is about 20 miles (32 km) south of town at Sunspot. Open to the public from May to October, it offers self-guided tours daily, and guided tours on Saturdays. The observatory's sophisticated telescopes, one of which rises 13 stories, enable scientists to study the sun's gaseous outer envelope and sunspots.

The friendly, rustic village of Cloudcroft, which means "Cloud in a Field," caters to tourists. In the summer, something is going on nearly every weekend, from arts and crafts fairs to music festivals. But the natural beauty of 215,000 acres of national forest is enough to make a visit worthwhile: spectacular views of the white swath of gypsum sands laid out below in the Tularosa Basin, along with the fresh smell of tall pines and a profound quiet.

Southeast of Cloudcroft the Lincoln National Forest continues along a ribbon of mountains that eventually provides Texas with Guadalupe Peak, its highest at an altitude of 8,749 feet (2,667 m). The Guadalupe Mountains also provide a break in an otherwise monotonous horizon. In New Mexico, the rugged range is home to 80-foot-high (24-m) Sitting Bull Falls, west of Carlsbad. Across the border in Texas, the mountains are part of Guadalupe Mountains National Park, which includes desert lowlands, lush canyons, and forested hillsides.

■ TULAROSA BASIN

This 100-mile (16-km) desert valley flanked by two mountain ranges has been home to Mogollon Indians, Spanish colonists, and railroad and ranch families. Today, much of the area is controlled by the military—at the top-secret White Sands Missile Range, Holloman Air Force Base, and McGregor Range.

WHITE SANDS

In order to create these extensive military installations, begun as weapons testing grounds during World War II, ranchers patriotically agreed to leave their land. At White Sands, 150 families were displaced.

One place that escaped the military's condemnation was a span of glimmering white desert dunes created by erosion of the Permian rocks that form the San Andres Mountains. **White Sands National Monument** spreads across 230 square miles (598 sq km) of windswept dunes that look like ocean sand, but actually are fine granules of gypsum. Only one-half of the extensive rolling hills are included in the monument. The sweet fresh smell of gypsum permeates the air, and the fine-grained sand swirls about picnic shelters. The undulating expanse of white is interrupted only by an occasional yucca cactus shooting skyward. At the edge of the 50-foot-tall (15-m) dunes, animals have taken on the protective shade of gypsum: there are white mice, white lizards, and light-colored insects. This soft, silent, ghostly world of grit seems like an oasis in the surrounding harsh desert of sharp cactus and cracked earth. On nights when the moon is full, the glistening sands reflect an eerie glow and the effect is unearthly.

From May to September, the dunes are open until midnight on full-moon nights. Guided walks and talks are offered daily.

White Sands Missile Range is off-limits to the public, but a major highway, US 70-82, runs through it, connecting Alamogordo and Las Cruces. Travelers on this road often find themselves peripherally involved in the range's activities when they are stopped at one of the regular roadblocks erected during missile firings. In 1982, another group of bystanders witnessed the graceful landing of the Space Shuttle Columbia when it descended onto the missile range's hard-packed sand at Northrop Strip.

But very few people were on hand in the early morning hours of July 16, 1945, when the first atomic bomb was detonated near the upper edge of this sparsely

BELL RANCH

They've never seen the Northern Lights
They've never seen a hawk on the wing
They've never seen spring hit the Great Divide
They've never heard old camp Cookie sing.
—Night Rider's Lament

Leave out the Northern Lights and the Great Divide and Jerry Jeff Walker could have been a cowboy singing about the Bell Ranch when he recorded this Michael Burton song in 1975.

Bell Ranch Country is the name used by the 16 cowboys who on horseback traverse its 300,000 acres of ankle-high grama-grass pastures. This vast ranch is one of the last places in the West where cowboys round up cattle on horseback and chuck wagons bounce and rattle en route to branding operations in its far-flung corners.

Prime cattle land, the Bell's lush meadows and vermilion rock canyons are watered by shallow streams that wind toward the Canadian River, which cuts through the sprawling ranch. In 1824 when Pablo Montoya obtained a Mexican land grant for the choice pasture land, the vast holding in northeastern New Mexico stretched across 655,000 acres located northwest of present-day Tucumcari and south of Mosquero.

Montoya had been mayor of Santa Fe, but sought a place far from the congested capital. The city was, after all, already 200 years old. Leaving behind his governmental duties in the early 1800s, Montoya became a *Comanchero* who traded with Comanches throughout the northeastern plains. As he roamed the region, Montoya studied the land, searching for good grass and ample water, a place where he and his seven children could spread out and establish a ranch.

While the Bell changed hands a few times during the next 123 years, it remained intact and produced prized cattle year after year. The name comes from the bell-shaped mountain on the ranch, which also is reflected in the brand. Accompanying the rounded peak are two nearby buttes named Ding and Dong. In 1947, the ranch was divided into six sections and sold. The largest parcel was 130,000 acres and included the brand and historic headquarters with an orchard, dairy, blacksmith shop, post office, and adobe structures built by Montoya. The new owner, Harriet Ellwood Keeney, continued raising Herefords until she sold the ranch in 1970 to William Lane. Not only did Lane promise to "keep the ranch running just like it has been in the past, a real working ranch for the production of fine cattle," but the Illinois businessman acquired 176,000 more acres from the original land grant. Lane was killed in a 1978 automobile accident, but his family continues his vision.

Cowboys still rein horses atop mesas blanketed with junipers, piñons, and thorny mesquite bushes and through canyons bursting with summer sunflowers so thick and tall the riders could hide in them. Here chaps and dusters are worn for more than their rugged good looks, and sweat stains along hat brims are hard earned.

The orchard and dairy are gone, but the original ranch house, called the White House, stands sturdy, concealed by tall, broad-leafed cottonwoods. Designated in 1970 as both National and State Historic sites, ranch headquarters are located 10 miles (16 km) north of the village of Conchas.

Cowboys take a chow break on the range of the Ladder Ranch,
circa 1940. (Museum of New Mexico)

populated rangeland just west of the Oscura Mountains. The explosion vaporized everything in its path and created a blinding flash of light, followed by a shock wave that shattered windows 120 miles (192 km) away in Silver City. Even early-rising Albuquerque residents noticed a flash on the southern horizon and felt the shock waves. The massive nuclear explosion left a crater 400 yards (366 m) in diameter and eight feet (2.4 m) deep, and intense heat fused sand in the crater into a glasslike solid the color of jade. This substance was called Trinitite after the code name of the top-secret project, Trinity.

Until 1953, Trinity Site was off-limits due to dangerously high levels of radiation left behind by the blast. A lava-rock obelisk now stands at the site, which is open to visitors two days a year: the first Saturdays of April and October.

On the opposite side of the Oscura Mountains, another spectacular eruption that preceded the atomic bomb by nearly a thousand years left behind a 44-mile-long (70-km) lava flow that in some places is five miles (8 km) wide and 70 feet (21 km) deep. Indian legends tell of a volcanic eruption that caused a valley of fire five miles (8 km) west of present-day Carrizozo. Because the cracked black rock carpet isn't much good as rangeland or farmland, the state made it into a state park and appropriately called it **Valley of the Fires.** Remarkably, cholla, sotol, prickly pear, and gray-green saltbush sprout from between the dark rocks.

CARRIZOZO AND VICINITY

Five miles (8 km) west of the park is the friendly community of Carrizozo. Folks here can be thankful for the high land prices in the nearby gold-mining boom-town of White Oaks at the time the El Paso and Northeastern Railroad was looking for a terminal point. In 1899, since land was less expensive at this tree-shaded spot at the base of the Sacramento Mountains, the terminal was built here instead. Carrizozo, which grew up beside it, took its name from *carrizo,* a reed native to the surrounding plain and nearby foothills. Rumor has it that a ranch foreman embellished the name with an extra "zo" to indicate abundance. Carrizozo prospered, but booming White Oaks, which produced about $3.1 million in gold between 1879 and 1940, is now a ghost town.

As the popularity of rail travel diminished, so did the economic life of Carrizozo, but it continues to carry on as the Lincoln County seat. Residents have opened up a gift shop and bed and breakfast in hopes that tourists heading up to the mountains will stop to enjoy the peace and pace of this little New Mexico town.

The dunes glow pink in a rising sun at White Sands National Monument.

Not far away is **Three Rivers Petroglyph Site,** where more than 5,000 carvings have been preserved on an assortment of rock outcroppings along a ridge over-looking the Tularosa Basin. A 1,400-yard (1,280-m) winding path leads past etchings of stylized bighorn sheep, lizards, birds, and trees, along with hand-prints, sunbursts, and a variety of geometric designs. Archaeologists have deter-mined that the Jornada branch of the Mogollon culture was responsible for the artwork. The artists, possibly sitting at this site while serving as lookouts, lived in several villages along the Three Rivers drainage about A.D. 900. By 1400, the cul-ture had moved north, probably due to drought. One of these abandoned villages has been partially excavated and reconstructed.

TULAROSA

A welcome break in the dry basin is found at Tularosa, a peaceful, tree-shaded hamlet of simple well-tended adobe homes—some of which date from 1863. In that year, about 100 Hispanic farming families from the Mesilla Valley, which had been washed out by floods along the Rio Grande, decided to move just south of the Rio Tularosa. Here they put in orchards and planted corn, cotton, and alfalfa. Buildings on many of the original 49 blocks of the townsite have been restored or are undergoing renovation, and reveal finely crafted ornate facades, intricate wood carving, and pressed-tin trim. There is a calming ambiance to this pleasant town which, like its neighbor to the north, was named for a reed—this time a reddish one that grows on the banks of the Rio Tularosa. Irrigation ditches that were dug when the village was settled continue to carry water to tall cottonwoods and or-chards of pecan, apple, quince, peach, and cherry trees.

But Tularosa is best known as the "City of Roses." Here people take their rose bushes seriously, and they have their opinions—about when and how to prune, what fertilizer is best, which blooms are more beautiful, and which are most fra-grant. Every year during the first weekend of May as red, pink, yellow, and white roses bloom throughout town, its residents celebrate the annual Rose Festival. A queen is crowned and rides in state, surrounded by roses in the Rose Festival parade.

ALAMOGORDO AND VICINITY

In 1897, Charles Eddy, a rancher who became a major railroad developer, coaxed a group of Eastern investors to tour the Tularosa Basin. They traveled the region in horse-drawn coaches, slept in bedrolls, and ate from a chuck wagon. Eddy wanted them to see the gold, cattle, and timber that could fill rail cars. Before a month had gone by, Eddy received financing for the El Paso and Northeastern Railroad, which was to run from El Paso to Tucumcari, passing along the edge of the Sacramento Mountains. Within a year, he had purchased Alamo Ranch from Oliver Lee. The ranch served as a division point on the rail line and later grew into Alamogordo, which means "Large Cottonwood." For years, the settlement was a trading center for ranchers, farmers, and the lumber industry. Later, Alamogordo became home to one of New Mexico's favorite writers, Eugene Manlove Rhodes, and to a major branch of New Mexico State University.

But it wasn't until World War II brought the atomic bomb to the cattle country that the town began to establish its modern-day identity as a major military training and testing center. Nearby, missiles are launched and payload experiments for the space shuttle are conducted at White Sands Missile Range; pilots learn to fly Stealth jets at Holloman Air Force Base just outside of town.

In 1954, a Holloman flight surgeon became the fastest man in the world when he tested a rocket sled that blasted across the desert at 632 mph (1,011 kph). Col. John Stapp strapped himself into the one-ton contraption, powered by nine rockets with a total thrust of 40,000 pounds (18,000 kg). Stapp suffered two black eyes, burns from the straps, and bruises from bits of sand that whipped into his body. The sled today is on display at the **International Space Hall of Fame**, a $2 million mirrored, four-story gold cube set against the dry foothills of the Sacramento Mountains. Inside, try your hand at the controls of Space Station 2001, learn how an RL-10 rocket engine works, or check out the lunar rover and envision yourself behind its controls as you gather moon rocks.

Down the hill is a theater named after astronomer Clyde W. Tombaugh, who discovered Pluto in 1930. An Omnimax theater shows regularly changing films on a four-story, wrap-around screen that gives you the feeling you're an astronaut on a space shuttle mission, or a passenger aboard a raft crashing through roiling rapids in the Grand Canyon. When movies aren't showing, a special projector can recreate the heavens from any vantage point on Earth on any night of the year. And there are laser shows in which brightly colored lights are choreographed to the rhythm and mood of music.

About 10 miles (16 km) south of Alamogordo, just before the mountains give way once and for all to dry, cracked, cactus-covered earth, is **Oliver Lee Memorial State Park,** a 180-acre oasis tucked away in Dog Canyon at the base of the

Sacramento Mountains. Long ago, Apaches lived here, enjoying the seeps and springs of the lush canyon and the protection of its steep rock walls. They also lured soldiers up the dead-end gully only to ambush them. The canyon got its name in 1850, when a group of settlers pursued raiding Indians up the box canyon only to find a lone dog at the end.

In the mid-1880s, a Frenchman by the name of Francois-Jean Rochas built himself a rock house in the canyon and raised cattle and cultivated grapes, olives, and figs. Because the canyon contained the only year-round water source in the area, "Frenchy" was constantly harassed by his jealous neighbors. In 1894, his body was found in the cabin, pierced by three bullets. His death was ruled a suicide, but most folks agreed he was killed for his water. Meanwhile, a quarter mile (.4 km) south of Frenchy's cabin, cattleman Oliver Lee built his ranch headquarters. Today, the building serves as the Oliver Lee Park Museum. You can still see the remains of Frenchy's place and hike up the canyon on the old Indian trail, which climbs 3,000 feet (914 m) as it follows a steep bluff, here and there hung with dripping green moss.

South of the park the desert sprawls out and once again becomes the property of the U.S. government. **McGregor Range**, yet another missile testing ground, stretches for 1,000 square miles (2,590 sq km) to Fort Bliss, an army base in El Paso, Texas. Like its neighbor White Sands Missile Range, McGregor Range displaced about 200 ranchers when it was created in 1954. Except for one crusty character, that is, who continued to resist attempts by the government, both peaceful and otherwise, to remove him from his home. "I am not afraid of missiles," 82-year-old John Prather said. "I've raised mules all my life." By 1957, the Army admitted defeat and permitted the stubborn rancher to live out his life at his home in the middle of the missile range. He was buried there in 1965. Prather's principles inspired Edward Abbey's 1962 novel *Fire on the Mountain*.

■ PECOS RIVER VALLEY

One of New Mexico's major waterways, the Pecos River bisects the southeastern part of the state, carrying the crucial resource of water to a number of tiny farming and ranching communities. The most well-known of these is **Carlsbad,** famous for an underground environment of other-worldly limestone formations.

CARLSBAD CAVERNS

One of the largest cave systems in the world, Carlsbad Caverns comprises a three-mile (5 km) maze of concert-hall rooms whose floors and ceilings are blanketed with house-size stalagmite statues and stalagtite icicles. Filling these massive vaults are grandiose obelisks and pagodas laced with delicate tracery. A paved winding path descends through a black opening in a limestone ridge into the eerily lit bowels of the earth, leading you past dripping pale green limestone walls and into rooms that seem like they belong in a science-fiction movie, or on another planet. The names of the most spectacular formations bear witness to the lifelike shapes created by the limestone deposits: Whale's Mouth, King's Palace, Hall of Giants, Queen's Chamber Draperies. The Big Room, aptly if unimaginatively named for an expanse that could hold 14 Astrodomes, makes you feel as insignificant as an ant on a sidewalk. Its ceiling curves 256 feet (78 m) above the damp floor. The temperature of 56 degrees F (13° C) never varies here.

The sound of slowly dripping water is never far away and neither are the thousands of Mexican free-tail bats that spend their days clinging to the moist pale-green ceiling. Fortunately for visitors, the 300,000-member colony bunches together in an area away from the tour route. There are two ways to enter the chilly underground grotto: on a high-speed elevator or along a paved path through the gaping hole, also a bat route. Between May and November, a thick black cloud of them swirls up from the cool of the cave every evening at dusk at a rate of 5,000 to 10,000 a minute. Then they're on to a summertime night of feasting on flying insects.

The concealed cave remained unnoticed until 1901, when a young cowboy, James White, spotted what looked like a cloud of smoke spiraling upward near the foothills of the Guadalupe Mountains. The cloud turned out to be thousands of bats heading off to a night of hunting. Using a rope ladder, White descended into the damp cave and saw for the first time what thousands of people now see each year. By 1930 his discovery had become a national park.

If you're yearning for an adventure similar to White's, you can visit the New Cave, opened in 1973 for guided flashlight tours. While you don't need a rope ladder, you will need sturdy shoes and endurance in order to hike the strenuous one-mile (1.6 km) uphill trail to the cave's entrance. Imagine you are the first person to enter the dark interior. Flashlight beams illuminate spectacular mystical sculptures such as Christmas tree stalagmites draped in smooth limestone deposits. Reservations are required.

Each August, Carlsbad hosts its annual Bat Flight Breakfast, during which visitors eat scrambled eggs and sausage just as the world's only flying mammal, satiated after a night of hunting, swoops into its daytime haven of dark.

At the northwest end of town, a preserve for plants and animals native to the Chihuahuan Desert is a great alternative for people who prefer not to set foot inside a dank, dark cave. **Living Desert State Park** is laid out among a carpet of prickly pear, yucca, cholla, sotol, and agave cactus plants in the Ocotillo Hills overlooking Carlsbad. Here caged mountain lions pace back and forth among boulders; Mexican hawks perch atop branches; badgers and prairie dogs burrow into, and rattlesnakes slither across, the dry soil. All of these animals have been brought here because of injuries or illness. At the park, they are treated and returned to the wild. If their injuries are too extensive, they become permanent residents of the park.

A self-guided trail leads past the animals' temporary homes among gypsum hills, dusty arroyos, sand dunes, and pine trees. Every year for four days in May, park personnel re-create a Mescalero Apache tradition: a mescal roast at which the heart of a flowering agave or century plant is cooked in a special midden ring at the park and served to visitors. The taste is close to that of a sweet potato with a smoky molasses flavor.

South of town, **salt beds** litter the landscape. These beds are mined for their salt, which produces potash, an ingredient of fertilizer. At one mine, what goes into the underground chambers will be more important than the extracted potash. This is the Waste Isolation Pilot Plant (WIPP), a $1 billion federal facility built to house low-level nuclear waste generated by government nuclear weapons operations. WIPP is the first permanent repository for such wastes.

The citizens in and around Carlsbad also continue ranching, the economic base upon which the town was founded in 1888 by cattle baron Charles Eddy. The Pecos River, which runs along the edge of town, enables farmers to grow cotton and alfalfa, the area's two major crops. The river is also the source of warm-water, man-made lakes filled with white bass and catfish and a perfect temperature for waterskiing.

ARTESIA AND VICINITY

About 36 miles (58 km) upriver from Carlsbad, the smell of petroleum will probably greet your nostrils. This is an unmistakable indication you have arrived at Artesia, a small town most noted for its rich underground oil and natural gas reserves. The odor is coming from the Navajo Refining Company, the town's largest employer. Black pumpjacks, and lots of them, line the level horizon. Oil well rockers gently sway back and forth and could easily mesmerize you if you gazed at them too long. Natural gas wells are marked by an intricate arrangement of pipes, valves, and gauges called "Christmas trees." Residents say if you live here long enough, it gets so you don't even smell the oil.

Artesia has gone through numerous incarnations: it began as a homestead in the 1890s along the Chisum Trail when a Union soldier, John Truitt, settled near a spring three blocks from the heart of modern-day Artesia. It turned out there was lots of water below the parched surface and that it was easily tapped by drilling artesian wells. In the early 1900s, farmers flocked to the town, now named Artesia, where crops could survive droughts because of the bountiful water supply. The year 1923 brought yet another discovery: oil and gas. Today, there are 3,313 natural gas wells in the Permian Basin, which includes the southeast corner of New Mexico. And even though there is more natural gas under the surface than oil, black crude is still king with 14,758 operating wells.

Artesia is now also the site of a training college for Border Patrol agents.

Eight miles (13 km) north of Artesia, in a cotton belt unimpressive in natural beauty, is the hamlet of Lake Arthur. The town enjoyed a glimmer of heavenly fame in 1977 when an image of Jesus Christ appeared on a flour tortilla made by a Mrs. Rubio as she was preparing burritos for her husband's lunch. The tortilla never was eaten. Instead, it is honored inside a shrine in the Rubio home, and thousands of visitors come to view the miracle.

ROSWELL AND VICINITY

The Pecos River Valley was a favorite stopover for early Texas cattlemen driving their livestock north on the Goodnight-Loving Trail. Here there was plenty of

(following pages) Carlsbad Caverns is the largest cave complex in the United States.
(Jack Olson)

grama grass and water enough for a thousand head at the confluence of the Rio Hondo and Pecos River. One of these Texans, John Chisum, liked the area so much he built a ranch six miles (10 km) south of present-day Roswell. He then drove his cattle west across what came to be known as the Chisum Trail. Chisum himself became a cattle baron, eventually controlling the territory from Fort Sumner to the Texas border.

A primitive trading post was established in the valley in the 1860s. In 1869, a professional gambler by the name of Van Smith bought an interest in a rustic adobe hotel built nearby. Soon a town was in the making, and Van Smith decided to name it after his father, Roswell. The accidental discovery in 1891 of an artesian water source outside of town spurred irrigation efforts, which resulted in large crops of cotton, alfalfa, apples, corn, and pecans. Soon after the water was discovered, the New Mexico Military Institute, a combination high school and junior college, was established. In the 1930s, humorist Will Rogers paid a visit to the growing town. He recognized a special quality when he called it "the prettiest little town in the West."

The tree-lined town has become surprisingly sophisticated, while still serving as a major shipping and trading center for ranchers. Well-known landscape painter and portraitist Peter Hurd was born in Roswell in 1904. An extensive permanent collection of his works and those by his artist wife, Henriette Wyeth, hang in the **Roswell Museum and Art Center**, an eclectic museum with a collection that also includes paintings by Georgia O'Keeffe, Marsden Hartley, Stuart Davis, John Marin, and John Sloan.

Not content with art alone, the museum also has re-created the Roswell workshop of Dr. Robert Goddard, a rocket pioneer who spent 11 years in Roswell perfecting his liquid propulsion system. After almost single-handedly advancing the science of rocketry through experiments conducted in a rancher's field, Goddard left for Annapolis, Maryland, in 1941 to share his knowledge with the military.

On the town's outskirts, sailboats and windsurfers share the cool azure waters at **Bottomless Lakes State Park.** Canada geese, sandhill cranes, ducks, and herons rest up at **Bitter Lake National Wildlife Refuge.**

Farther upriver are the crumbling ruins of **Fort Sumner,** site of the unsuccessful incarceration of Mescalero Apaches and Navajos. The fort closed in 1868 after the military admitted defeat in its plan to make farmers and friends of the two nomadic tribes who weren't fond of each other. Some of the civilians who had moved to the area to furnish food for the fort stayed and continued to grow vegetables and raise cattle in the fertile river valley.

In 1881, Billy the Kid, by then the state's most notorious outlaw, high-tailed it to Fort Sumner after his escape from the Lincoln County Jail. By coincidence, Sheriff Pat Garrett was at Fort Sumner as well. He'd dropped by the home of Pete Maxwell, one of Billy's old friends, to check on the outlaw's whereabouts. Maxwell had turned the fort's old officer's quarters into a spacious home. As Garrett sat at the foot of Maxwell's bed in his darkened bedroom, in walked the baby-faced outlaw, looking for some food. Billy said, "¿Qué pasa?" and then Garrett shot the bullet that felled the fugitive. Billy the Kid was buried in the Fort Sumner military cemetery alongside two of his recalcitrant desperado friends, Tom O'Folliard and Charlie Bowdre. His tombstone reads: "The Boy Bandit King—He Died as He Had Lived."

Today, folks in Fort Sumner still focus on Billy the Kid: they have erected a museum in his honor and formed a historical society dedicated to their folk hero. And because people keep trying to steal Billy's tombstone, a chainlink fence now surrounds his grave marker. These attempts have inspired the Billy the Kid Tombstone Race, one of the reasons people come to **Old Fort Days**, Fort Sumner's annual celebration of its past. Another attraction is the cow plop, in which a very regular bovine is let loose to stroll in a squared-off fenced field behind a hardware store. White paint divides 425 squares, which cost $5 each. Those who contributed anxiously watch as the cow unhurriedly paces the field. They are hoping she will heed nature's call on their square. This giant outdoor bingo game nets the winner $500 and raises money for the Chamber of Commerce.

A third reason to attend Old Fort Days is the rodeo. Professionals and amateurs deftly urge their horses to lope after a calf, stop abruptly, and stand still while the rider lassos the scared calf, then dismounts and lashes its legs together. Bull riders have the toughest job: they gingerly climb on the back of a 2,000-pound (909-kg) brahma bull that isn't used to carrying around anything bigger than a horsefly. It's not easy to stay atop a heaving bull and many cowboys don't last long. The voice that booms out in between events loves to comment on the misadventures of the ring's performers. Usually, the announcer is as entertaining as the rodeo clowns whose job it is to divert an angry bull bent on giving a discarded cowboy a skyward toss. In barrel racing, the only women's event, riders run the length of the dirt arena, circle a barrel, then race back and out the chute, all in the blink of an eye.

■ LLANO ESTACADO

It's been said land doesn't get much flatter than New Mexico's eastern flank. And it's true. The Llano Estacado, or Staked Plains, is an extension of the Great Plains that stretches from Canada into Texas. In New Mexico, the grassland received its name for one of four reasons, nobody's too sure which one. It could be the multitude of tall yucca plants that sprout up from the high plateau, or the stakes early Spanish explorers pounded into the ground to tie up their horses. It could also refer to the stakes that had to be driven into the ground to give travelers a sense of direction as they traversed the vast expanse. Finally, there is the suggestion that because the literal translation of *llano estacado* is "stockaded plain," early Spanish explorers were referring to protruding mesas that rise at the northwestern edge of the plains, which they thought resembled stockades. Take your pick.

CLOVIS AND ENVIRONS

Although this area remained unsettled until the 1880s, prehistoric hunters were roaming the region 11,000 years ago. One of their more successful hunting spots was a large pond fed by the headwaters of the Brazos River, near present-day Portales. Archaeologists believe woolly mammoths, sabertooth tigers, camels, and bison used the pond as a watering hole, thus providing the hunters a perfect place to trap and butcher them. All of this finally came to light in 1932, when a highway worker discovered spearpoints and mammoth bones uncovered by gusty winds that whipped across the plains during the years of the Great Drought. The lake had dried up, leaving behind a gravel pit that proved to be rich in ancient artifacts intermingled with fossils. Modern-day man named it Blackwater Draw, and the prehistoric hunter was called Clovis, after the nearby town. Today, Blackwater Draw Museum, located between Portales and Clovis, contains many of the archaeological discoveries found at the site.

Wagons on their way to market and loaded with broom corn in Clovis, 1905. (Museum of New Mexico)

The Athabascans probably passed through the area during their fourteenth-century migrations from Canada. In the 1700s, Comanche and Kiowa Indians roamed across the vast grasslands, hunting buffalo but leaving no evidence of any permanent settlements.

It was another watering hole that attracted early European immigrants—Portales Springs, a series of cave openings through which gushed streams of fresh water. Spanish explorers thought the caves resembled *portales,* the porches of Spanish adobe homes. The first settler in Portales was Doak Good, a cattleman looking for a place to call his own in 1880.

It took the railroad to bring some definition to this endless horizon, and people as well. In the early 1900s, the town of Portales was established as a construction camp for workers on the Pecos Valley and Northern Railroad. It was followed by its close neighbor to the north, Clovis, which, until 1907, was known as Riley's Switch on the Santa Fe line. But when rail officials chose the site as a division point for the Belen cut-off, they decided to make it a proper town. A daughter of a Santa Fe Railroad official was given the honor of finding a name. She had been studying French history at the time and was taken by Clovis, King of the Franks, who converted to Christianity in A.D. 486.

The railroad helped populate the area, but the discovery years later of the massive Ogallala aquifer turned it into one of the state's premier agricultural belts. This plentiful underground water source transformed the sweeping grasslands into vast fields of alfalfa, cotton, corn, wheat, and potatoes. In Clovis, cattle are fattened at some of the largest feedlots in the Southwest; at weekly livestock auctions these healthy bovines are sold to the highest bidder.

Clovis residents like to kick up their heels to the twangs of country and western music, but back in the 1950s, one lonely musician took a detour from that genre. Norman Petty built a recording studio inside an ordinary-looking building at 1313 West Seventh Street. Instead of country singers, he encouraged rock-and-roll musicians to drop by and try their luck. His biggest catch was a young band leader from Lubbock, Texas, who wore dark-rimmed glasses, played an energetic piano, and sang in an exuberant voice. Between 1957 and his untimely death two years later, **Buddy Holly** recorded most of his greatest hit records at the Clovis studio, some with his band, the Crickets, and some on his own. "That'll Be the Day," was his first hit, followed by "Peggy Sue," "Everyday," and "Maybe Baby."

The eastern third of New Mexico's landscape is typical of high plains country. (Paul Chesley)

Young entrepeneur at Clovis Rodeo, circa 1940. (Museum of New Mexico)

Following Holly's death, Petty continued to work with local musicians, the most notable being Jimmy Gilmer and the Fireballs, who enjoyed a short-lived celebrity with their hits, "Sugar Shack" and "Bottle of Wine." Another popular 1950s musician Petty discovered was Buddy Knox ("Party Doll"). Roy Orbison, best known for "Pretty Woman," started with Petty, but left before recording any of his well-known hits. Petty died in 1984, but his inspiration is celebrated once a year at the **Clovis Music Festival,** when his widow, Vi, opens up the original Norman Petty Studio for tours. This six-day event attracts Buddy Holly fans, 1950s music stars, and rock-and-rollers of all ages.

PORTALES

Down the road, Portales is nutty for peanuts, growing 30 million pounds (13.5 million kg) of the Valencia variety every year. For three days in October, the nutty legume is honored at the Peanut Valley Festival, home of the "Peanut Olympics." Peanuts also are roasted, eaten, and displayed. At **Eastern New Mexico University,** the Jack Williamson Science Fiction Library honors the Portales author with 7,000 volumes, including the original manuscripts of most of Williamson's more than 45 novels and 150 short stories.

One Portales man, Bill Dalley, has taken the windmill off the prairie and erected 60 of the spinning antique apparati in his front yard. "A lot of old ranchers tell me that if a man wants a peaceful state of mind after a hard day of roping cattle, there's nothing better than riding up to the old windmill and listening to the groan of a wheel. It's like watching fish breathe. It's all slow motion—so slow, yet powerful," he once told a writer.

A chance meeting between two covered wagons on the *Llano* in 1907 resulted in the settlement of **Hobbs.** After being told by the oncoming party of the hardships ahead at his destination of Alpine, Texas, James Hobbs backtracked and put down his roots just inside what today is the New Mexico border. The area full of desert grasses, mesquite, and jackrabbits proved to be suited for raising cattle and growing cotton. In 1928, discovery of a major oil reserve brought an onslaught of fortune hunters, and the scrubland was transformed into a shanty town of crude shacks, metal buildings, and tents. Overnight, Hobbs became a raucous community of oil drillers. Taverns sprung up, which served as rollerskating rinks by day and dance halls by night. The town continues to be a center for the oil industry, but it has calmed down into a peaceful family community that boasts two colleges.

Because of its light winds and clear days, Hobbs attracts sailplane pilots who glide their lightweight aircraft through spacious skies. In 1983, the World Soaring Championships were held here, which spurred the creation of the Hobbs Soaring Society.

NORTHEASTERN
NEW MEXICO

A WHIPPING WIND WHISTLES THROUGH TALL GRAMA GRASSLANDS. Brown specks on the otherwise pale-green landscape materialize, upon closer view, into cattle. The Canadian and Cimarron rivers, and a section of the Pecos, are the largest and longest of the few waterways that intersect the sprawling plains of northeastern New Mexico. Simple ranch houses, whirring windmills, and the remains of long-extinct volcanoes line the horizon. Hundreds of dinosaur footprints mark the landscape near Clayton.

Chipped stone points used by Folsom Man 10,000 years ago lie protected inside Folsom Museum. In a strong wind, you can almost hear the creaking wheels of heavily loaded wagons laboring toward Santa Fe over the Santa Fe Trail, or the shrill cries of the Comanche raiding parties. For 59 years during the 1800s, cumbersome caravans linked the Spanish outpost of Santa Fe with the eastern United States. These wagon trains carried cloth and tools to the New Mexico frontier and brought back beaver pelts, silver, and gold.

In northeastern New Mexico the hunting grounds of the Apaches met those of the Comanches, and fertile plains meet the Sangre de Cristo Mountains. Here also the mountain man Lucien Maxwell became the largest single landholder in the Western Hemisphere when he inherited from his father-in-law a 1.7-million-acre land grant that included mountains and valuable rangeland stretching into present-day Colorado. And it is among these tall ponderosa pine trees and this wide-open prairie that the Marlboro Man stands tall in his saddle for photographers of cigarette advertisements.

The secluded canyons of the Sangre de Cristos proved perfect hideouts for gunfighter Clay Allison and train robber Thomas "Black Jack" Ketchum. In the late 1800s, nearly everybody who was anybody in the Wild West stayed at the St. James Hotel in the foothill town of Cimarron when passing through. Wyatt Earp, Pat Garrett, Doc Holliday, and Jesse James were frequent guests. Oklahoma oilman Waite Phillips donated 127,395 acres of these forested slopes to the Boy Scouts of America, who turned the cattle ranch into Philmont Scout Ranch, where the organization trains its young members in camping and leadership skills.

Cattle outnumber people on this vast prairie, where people take pride in all the region has to offer: from a scuba diver's oasis in the desert at Santa Rosa's Blue

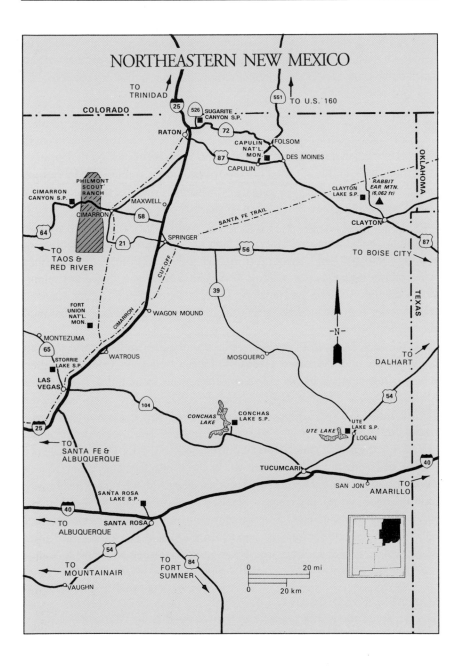

NORTHEASTERN NEW MEXICO

TO TRINIDAD

COLORADO

551 TO U.S. 160

25

526 SUGARITE CANYON S.P.

RATON

72

CAPULIN NAT'L. MON.

FOLSOM

DES MOINES

87

CAPULIN

PHILMONT SCOUT RANCH

CIMARRON CANYON S.P.

MAXWELL

CLAYTON LAKE S.P.

RABBIT EAR MTN. (6,062 ft)

OKLAHOMA

CIMARRON

58

SANTA FE TRAIL

CLAYTON

64

21

SPRINGER

56

TO BOISE CITY

87

TO TAOS & RED RIVER

CUT-OFF

39

-N-

TEXAS

FORT UNION NAT'L. MON.

CIMARRON

WAGON MOUND

MONTEZUMA

65

WATROUS

MOSQUERO

TO DALHART

STORRIE LAKE S.P.

LAS VEGAS

104

CONCHAS LAKE

CONCHAS LAKE S.P.

54

25

UTE LAKE

UTE LAKE S.P.

LOGAN

TO SANTA FE & ALBUQUERQUE

TUCUMCARI

40

SANTA ROSA LAKE S.P.

SAN JON

TO AMARILLO

40

TO ALBUQUERQUE

SANTA ROSA

54

TO MOUNTAINAIR

TO FORT SUMNER

84

0   20 mi

0   20 km

VAUGHN

Hole and the carefully preserved Victorian homes of Las Vegas to the 6,000 statuesque elk roaming the forests of Vermejo Park—once the largest privately owned ranch in the United States and now an exclusive hunting and fishing preserve.

■ HISTORY

About 100 million years ago, when the waters of an inland sea gently lapped at what today is the northeast corner of New Mexico, scores of duck-billed dinosaurs milled about near the shoreline gorging on whatever delectable plants they could find. These 10- to 15-feet-long (3-5 m) prehistoric creatures left behind 800 footprints that escaped the path of oozing lava spewed from a series of fiery volcanic explosions 10,000 years ago. Today, the footprints are embedded in sandstone 12 miles (18 km) north of Clayton. Also surviving these earth-shattering eruptions were prehistoric hunters, now referred to as Folsom Man, who stalked mastodons, woolly mammoths, bison, and antelope. Later, in the thirteenth century, scattered communities of Anasazi Indians grew squash, beans, and corn along the banks of the region's waterways.

By the time the Spanish explorer Francisco Vasquez de Coronado traipsed across the plains in 1541, these prehistoric Indians were gone. Coronado was en route to Quivira, where he was promised golden riches by an Indian guide. At his destination outside of Lyons, Kansas, the explorer found only the grass huts of the Wichita Indians. Greatly disappointed, he returned empty-handed to New Mexico and later to Mexico.

By 1700, the Jicarilla Apaches began pursuing buffalo and antelope through the region's grasslands and secluded canyons. In the 1700s, Comanches moved into this area, and the two tribes battled each other, along with a few pockets of hardy Spanish settlers, for regional control. These settlers, who lived in small communities, had received land grants from the government of Spain; the colonists had only to farm the land for four years and then they could call it their own. After Mexico gained its independence from Spain in 1821, the new government continued the practice.

MAXWELL LAND GRANT

The largest of these land grants was the Maxwell Land Grant, which Gov. Manuel Armijo issued in 1841 to Charles Beaubien, a French trapper, and

Cowboys headed back to the corral for dinner after a hard day's work on the ranges of eastern New Mexico in 1895. (Museum of New Mexico)

Guadalupe Miranda of Taos, a government official. The 1.7-million-acre grant, which included present-day Eagle Nest, Springer, and Raton and spread into southern Colorado, was three times the size of Rhode Island. It takes its name from Lucien Maxwell, a hunter and trapper who married Beaubien's daughter, Luz. After Beaubien's death in 1864, Maxwell inherited the massive landholding that included acres of minerals, timber, and some of the best pasture land in the region, upon which he administered numerous cattle and sheep ranches and even introduced beet cultivation. Although he seemed to prefer gambling and the acquisition of elaborate furnishings for the mansion he built in Cimarron, Maxwell still worked hard at developing his assets, and encouraged ranchers to lease portions of his holdings. On a handshake basis, the land baron outfitted settlers with cattle, acreage, and seed to improve upon the lush grama grass that covered the lava-rock land.

In 1870, the sale of the Maxwell grant, which by then was known to contain gold deposits, to a group of British and Dutch investors set off more than a decade of fighting between settlers and the foreigners who demanded that all squatters either buy their holdings, pay rent, or move out. During the controversy, known as the Colfax County War, farmers, ranchers, miners, and shopkeepers who had been indulged by Maxwell now claimed ownership to the land upon which they had for years carved out livings. The settlers resisted court rulings that favored the new owners, and blood occasionally was shed until 1887 when the U.S. Supreme Court once and for all confirmed the legality of the Maxwell Land Grant. Having acquired the British assets, the Dutch investors emerged as sole owners.

In 1841, the same year Beaubien and Miranda received the land grant, the town of Cimarron sprung up along the shady banks of the blue-green Cimarron River. The sheltered settlement, which began as a principal stop on a branch of the Santa Fe Trail that ended at Taos, soon became a major gathering spot for ranchers, miners, and gunslingers. Later on, it was Lucien Maxwell's center of operations.

THE CIVIL WAR

In the 1800s, when wagon trains rolled over the Santa Fe Trail, the Comanches turned their attention to the Anglo traders and the goods and tools they brought across the plains from Missouri. Both arms of the trade route entered New Mexico through this region: the Mountain Branch, which traversed southeastern Colorado before crossing rugged Raton Pass on its way to Santa Fe, and the Cimarron Cutoff, which made a beeline through southwestern Kansas and northeastern New Mexico on into the outpost capital.

New Mexico became a U.S. territory in 1848, a development that didn't much matter to the Apaches and Comanches, who considered the plains their own and continued to terrorize the wagon trains along the Santa Fe Trail. To protect the travelers and the area's settlers, Fort Union was built in 1851 near Watrous, where the Cimarron Cutoff and Mountain Branch joined. After the Civil War broke out in 1861, the military installation was fortified for a threatened Confederate invasion that didn't come that far north. A year later a regiment from the fort, along with the Colorado Volunteers, turned back Rebel forces at the Battle of Glorieta Pass, 25 miles (40 km) southeast of Santa Fe. This decisive victory, which is re-enacted every year 15 miles (24 km) south of Santa Fe at Ranchos de las Golondrinas, was the turning point in the war in the West and is referred to as the "Gettysburg of the West." The battlesite is on its way to being protected as part of the national park system.

SMOOTH RIDES AND ROUGH RIDERS

By the late 1870s, tracks laid by the Santa Fe Railroad were entering the region, first up and over the mountainous slopes of Raton Pass, then across the prairie through Springer, Wagon Mound, and Las Vegas. On the eastern plains, the Colorado and Southern Railroad connected the towns of Clayton, Des Moines, and Folsom to the tracks at Raton. The Phelps Dodge company built a line from Tucumcari north to the coal fields of Dawson, and on the way helped develop the towns of Mosquero and Roy. The railroad brought new settlers, cheaper goods, and rendered the Santa Fe Trail obsolete.

When Cuba went to war with Spain to gain its independence in 1898 and the United States went to the aid of its southern island neighbor, New Mexico's Gov. Miguel Otero, Jr. seized the opportunity to show the state's loyalty to the Stars and Stripes. In response to Otero's call for volunteers, 340 qualified horsemen signed up to ride under the leadership of Lt. Col. Theodore Roosevelt. New Mexicans made up about one-third of the future president's Rough Rider unit that charged San Juan Hill in Cuba without their horses, left behind because of a lack of transport. Said one New Mexico Rough Rider, "I was born in a dugout right here in Las Vegas, raised a cowboy, enlisted expecting to do my fighting on horseback as all the boys, but landed in Cuba afoot; marched, sweated, and fought afoot; earned whatever fame afoot."

Despite the fact that their horses were left behind, the gallantry of New Mexico's volunteers proved they supported the U.S. and not Spain—the ancestral homeland of many of them. A year later, the Rough Riders held a reunion in Las Vegas, and once again marched behind Roosevelt—this time in a parade through town. Reunions continued into the 1960s.

Arrival of the caravan at Santa Fe, 1844. (Museum of New Mexico)

■ LAS VEGAS

Las Vegas, a well-preserved but gritty town with the tall pine slopes of the Sangre de Cristo Mountains to the west and a carpet of grama grasslands spreading to the east, is often confused with the well-known Nevada gambling capital. The two couldn't be more different: flashing neon signs light the way to the gambling casinos that line the strip in the Nevada town; old-fashioned streetlamps light the quiet neighborhoods of restored Victorian homes in the New Mexico version.

New Mexico's Las Vegas (The Meadows) began as a land grant in 1821, when Luis Maria Cabeza de Baca received a grant for himself and his 17 sons along the Gallinas River, a meandering stream that forms high in the mountains. According to folklore, the river originated as a teardrop from an "eye" in the rock face of a tall peak. Persistent attacks by Comanche Indians who considered the region their hunting domain prevented the family from ever settling the land.

In 1835, after wagon trains had been rolling through the townsite on the Santa Fe Trail for 14 years, a group of 34 Spanish colonists established the town of Las Vegas and quickly planted crops, mostly beans. They also grazed sheep on nearby meadows and built simple dirt-roofed homes of adobe bricks. Men and boys worked long hours tending their herds, while the women cooked, spun thread, wove cloth, sewed clothing and bedding, and fashioned beautiful lacework and embroidery. Residents purchased tools and ribbons from caravans that regularly passed through. The town also served as a major way station on the Santa Fe Railroad, which arrived in 1879.

Early on, Las Vegas residents looked to construction materials other than adobe. **Our Lady of Sorrows Church** was the largest stone structure in New Mexico when it was built, between 1862 and 1870, of randomly fit blocks of Anton Chico sandstone. But it was the wave of settlers who arrived by train that definitely scorned the indigenous adobe homes. The newcomers preferred building styles popular in the Midwest. As a result, Las Vegas is an architectural treasure trove with 900 of its structures on the National Register of Historic Buildings.

West of the Gallinas River is the original townsite, built around a traditional tree-shaded plaza with a turquoise-trimmed gazebo sitting in the center. The finely restored **Plaza Hotel**, a showpiece when it was built in 1882, anchors the northwestern corner of the block. Streets in this part of town radiate from the plaza like spokes of a wheel and they follow the rolling terrain sliced with arroyos (usually dry, but water carved streambeds). The unspoiled appearance of Old Las Vegas in 1915 attracted Tom Mix who acted in *Never Again, The Rancher's Daughter,* and *The Country Drugstore*—films that were the forerunners of a genre that later became known as Westerns.

East of the river, neighborhoods look as if they were plucked from the Midwest or New England. Here, homes display Victorian gables, Tudor half-timbers, and Italianate bay windows. Well-kept lawns complement restored turn-of-the-century multi-story homes surrounded by precisely placed trees and shrubs. The **Carnegie Library,** built in 1903 and modeled after Thomas Jefferson's home, Monticello, is the focal point of a block of shady elms and deep green grass. It's hard to believe hundreds of miles of prairie spread east of town.

A winding road, NM 65, follows the Gallinas River into the mountains, entering the timbered **Pecos Wilderness** west of Las Vegas and passing by a few villages. One of these, **Montezuma,** is the location of the most spectacular late-nineteenth-century structure of the area, known today as Montezuma Castle. This massive 343-room edifice was built as a spa in 1888 by the Santa Fe Railroad to take advantage of nearby hot springs. A five-mile (8-km) spur led to the multi-storied wooden building with numerous turrets and balconies. For a decade, this splendid hotel was the crown jewel of the rail line, serving customers such as Ulysses S. Grant, Rutherford Hayes, Kaiser Wilhelm, and Japanese emperor Hirohito. Guests rode horses in the nearby mountains, fished for trout in the Gallinas River, played poker in oak-paneled card rooms, and soaked in the thermal baths, which reached temperatures of 110 degrees F (43° C). In 1981, the Armand Hammer Foundation turned the 110-acre complex into the United World College of the American West, a two-year institution for students 16 to 19 years old.

From Montezuma, NM 65 continues on through the rugged mountains, ending at the base of the 10,000-foot (3,048-m) **Hermit's Peak.** In 1863, Giovanni Maria Augustini, a 62-year-old Italian immigrant, moved into a cave just below the peak's eastern summit seeking solitude. Men from Las Vegas built him a small cabin, and there he carved religious emblems that he exchanged in town for cornmeal. (The hermit lived mostly on mush.) Four years later, feeling restless, the hermit moved on to southern New Mexico where he sought refuge in the Organ Mountains. There he was found dead in 1869 with a dagger in his back.

■ NORTH OF LAS VEGAS

The pointed lettuce-green leaves of an occasional yucca cactus interrupt the undu-lating prairie, its grasses taking on rust-red and yellow hues as I-25 traces the path of the Santa Fe Trail. At Watrous, today a roadside hamlet with less than 100 resi-dents, the Mountain and Cimarron branches of the Santa Fe Trail merged in the shade of leafy cottonwoods and alongside the waters of the Mora River.

FORT UNION

At the end of NM 161, the crumbling ruins of Fort Union rise like a mirage from the pastel-green prairie. These partial walls are all that remain of the largest nine-teenth-century U.S. military installation in the Southwest, which once protected settlers and travelers on the Santa Fe Trail, as well as serving as a major military supply station from 1851 until 1891. Preserved as a national monument, the fort is a reminder of the days when travel wasn't particularly convenient—or safe.

A flagstone walkway passes by what once served as officers' quarters. Brick fire-places and chimneys that tower above deteriorating walls have somehow survived the relentless wind that steadily whistles through the ruins. Press a button, and a bugle interrupts the silence of the prairie. Push another one, and an officer's wife complains to her husband about a leaky roof, or a sergeant barks out orders to his men. Close your eyes, and the fort's storehouses, offices, barracks, and corrals take shape and soldiers execute drills on the parade ground. Open them, and the soft snapping of grasshoppers rubbing their legs is all that permeates the stillness. Bees rise from hives wedged inside chimneys and shallow grass-covered indentations mark the once-busy Santa Fe Trail.

LOMA PARDA

Before the establishment of Fort Union, the small farming community of Loma Parda settled in 1830 on a secluded bend in the Mora River, was known for its juicy apples, plums, and pears, and an assortment of vegetables shipped to Den-ver and Albuquerque. The village took on a new importance, however, when the fort was built five miles (8 km) away. Prostitutes moved in, bars opened, and small orchestras, probably three-piece, played 24 hours a day in dance halls. The community became known as "Sodom on the Mora." Military commanders tried unsuccessfully to forbid their men from patronizing its haunts and even attempt-ed to buy the town.

Built in 1888 by Santa Fe Railroad, Montezuma Castle was a popular resort spa which hosted such luminaries as Ulysses Grant, Kaiser Wilhelm, and emperor Hirohito.

On one occasion, the commander sent a contingent to town to arrest a number of absentee soldiers who had left the fort without permission. Not only did the troops fail to carry out the orders, but they got sidetracked and didn't come back either. Today, all that remains of Loma Parda are wall fragments melted together from pounding rain and driving wind. Roofs are gone, and heavy *vigas* have fallen into rooms that once resounded with revelry. The commander would be satisfied.

WAGON MOUND

Heading north on I-25, traffic is sparse and cattle amble along their grama-grass dining table. Over a rise, a few volcanic mesas jut skyward. One, which resembles a covered wagon, was the last great landmark on the westward journey across the plains. When a ranching town was established on its flanks in 1850, it took the name Santa Clara, but changed nine years later to Wagon Mound. A drive through this sleepy hamlet provides a glimpse of simple tin-roofed adobe architecture. A dog lies sleepily in the middle of the street, expecting cars will go around him. Today, the highlight of the year for the town's 310 residents is Bean Day—known to outsiders as Labor Day. This harvest celebration began in 1910 when pinto beans were a big crop for area farmers. Even though beans aren't grown here anymore, past and present residents gather for bicycle and sack races and a parade in the morning, a free noon meal of barbecued beef, pinto beans, and coleslaw, followed by a rodeo and evening dance.

SPRINGER AND VICINITY

In the late 1800s, the quiet ranching centers of Springer and Maxwell grew alongside railroad tracks and riverbanks: Springer on the Cimarron River, and Maxwell on the Canadian. In Springer, other than a friendly cup of coffee at Stockman's, the town's main attraction is the **Santa Fe Trail Museum** located in the old Colfax County Courthouse. Artifacts range from Springer High School portraits to a Santa Fe Trail-era covered wagon.

About 30 miles (48 km) northeast of Springer on US 56, the imposing **Dorsey Mansion** sits tucked into the base of Chico Hill overlooking a sprawling grama grass plain. This odd-looking log and sandstone house with its Gothic-like turret was the creation of Stephen Dorsey, a U.S. senator from Arkansas who had an elaborate vision of a ranch house. He built his pretentious mansion in stages between 1880 and 1886 and made it the site of lavish all-night parties. Its indoor plumbing (a luxury in those days), billiard rooms, lily "pond" with three islands, well-stocked wine cellar, and purebred English bulls were the talk of the region. Today, a locked gate blocks the entrance, but supervised tours can be arranged by calling (505) 375-2222.

Southeast of Springer, in the late 1800s, an over-achieving lawyer and rancher turned to agriculture in the bowels of the Canadian River Canyon. Melvin Mills planted 14,000 trees—apple, peach, pear, cherry, plum, walnut, almond, and chestnut—and cultivated melons, tomatoes, grapes, and cabbages along a 10-mile-long (16-km) ribbon of shoreline. Unintimidated by thousand-foot-tall (305-m) canyon walls and a steep gravel road leading to the braided riverbed, Mills blasted underground irrigation channels, constructed cisterns, a cider press, bunkhouses, and a stone mansion on the riverplain. He hauled his crops to Springer where they were shipped to Harvey Houses along the Santa Fe Railroad. The **Mills Canyon Hotel**, now in ruins, was a popular vacation spot and served a stagecoach line that crossed the canyon here. In 1904, Mills's efforts were washed away in a disastrous flood that sent raging waters through the canyon. All that remains are partial stone walls of the hotel and a few scraggly fruit trees.

West of Springer on NM 21, at **Philmont Scout Ranch**, mule deer, stately elk, black bear, a herd of buffalo, and more than 250 head of Hereford cattle share the pine and spruce-covered slopes with thousands of Boy Scouts who practice survival skills there every summer. NM 21 follows the Mountain Branch of the Santa Fe Trail and skirts the edge of the ranch, which through later acquisitions now encompasses 137,493 acres along the Cimarron Range of the Sangre de Cristo Mountains. A raven sits atop a fence post, scanning a grassy meadow for its next meal. Nearby, a small herd of ash-gray mule deer grazes close to the road, unperturbed at passersby.

In 1845, Kit Carson built a flat-roofed adobe house and cultivated a 15-acre garden along the banks of Rayado Creek at the ranch's southeastern boundary. Four years later, Lucien Maxwell (of the Maxwell Land Grant) joined the Indian scout along the creek. But Carson's busy schedule fighting Indians and Maxwell's desire to move into the town of Cimarron forced the men to give up the operation by 1857.

At **Rayado**, young guides dressed in nineteenth-century clothing lead tours at the **Kit Carson Museum**, a reconstruction of the mountain man's home, and share tales of frontier life along the Santa Fe Trail during that era. On exhibit is a bed that reportedly was too comfortable for Carson who, after two nights, spread his buffalo robes on a hard adobe bench in the corner where he slept thereafter.

Seven miles (11 km) up the road, red tin roofs top tan stucco buildings, pristine in their manicured setting of close-cropped grass and gravel roads at Philmont's headquarters. Here between 1922 and 1927, Waite Phillips built a lavish Spanish two-story Mediterranean-style home where his family spent their summers. Skins of bear and cougars draped the walls, and a custom-made piano and shower with seven showerheads are evidence of the oilman's prosperity. Daily tours are offered throughout the summer. Across the road, the Seton Memorial Library honors Ernest Thompson Seton, an author, artist, naturalist, and the first chief scout of the Boy Scouts of America. The stucco building houses Seton's library, along with his collection of 3,000 paintings of birds, rabbits, and buffalo. Seton spent many of his years at his ranch, Seton Village, just east of Santa Fe.

■ CIMARRON

The wild and woolly town of Cimarron was settled in 1841 and served as a gathering place for the area's ranchers and miners. Set amid shady cottonwood trees and fragrant piñon pines along the shallow Cimarron River, the town served as a

Wide-open country. (Paul Chesley)

(opposite) High-plains storm looms over an abandoned farm.

principal stop on a branch of the Santa Fe Trail that led to Taos. After Maxwell relocated the headquarters of his immense land-grant holdings there in 1857, the town's popularity grew. It received another boost in 1864 when Maxwell completed a three-story adobe mansion that covered a city block. Inside were rooms for billiards, gambling, and dancing, as well as a rear section for prostitutes. Every night large sums of money exchanged hands during games of faro, roulette, monte, poker, and dice. It had a separate woman's side and men's side. Chauvinism was the order of the day!

As the years went by, Cimarron, which means "Wild" or "Untamed" in Spanish, lived up to its name. Angry gamblers who didn't like a card they were dealt often picked fights. Gunslingers who tipped one too many shots of whiskey liked to show off by shooting holes in the ceiling. Disputes were settled in the dirt streets and only the victor walked away. The *Las Vegas Gazette* once reported, "Everything is quiet in Cimarron. Nobody has been killed for three days."

Hunters, trappers, and prospectors searching for gold used the town as a jumping-off point for their excursions into the nearby mountains. At Cimarron's height, 15 saloons, four hotels, a post office, and a newspaper office lined the streets. Jesse James, Thomas "Black Jack" Ketchum, and Billy the Kid were frequent visitors. One of its more notorious residents was Clay Allison, a cattle rancher who was charming when sober and an untamed wild man when not. On one occasion in 1876, Allison, angered by an editorial in the Cimarron *News and Press,* enlisted the help of some friends to knock down the door of the newspaper office, smash the printing press with a sledgehammer, and dump cases of lead type and office materials into the river. The next day, he apologized and paid the paper's owners $200 to replace the equipment.

Having weathered a turbulent past, Cimarron today remains a ranching center, but it has quieted down. A solitary cow calls out for company, a buffalo grazes in a fenced pasture, and crows caw loudly overhead. A walk through the original townsite takes in the town's first well, in which a rusty bucket hangs from an untouched new rope; the iron bars of a stone-walled jail built in the 1870s; and small adobe homes with swings and friendly dogs in the yard. The white-washed National Hotel with its sky-blue wooden trim is now called the Santa Fe Trail Inn. A four-story stone grist mill built by Maxwell in 1864 serves as a museum containing antique surgical equipment, documents of the Maxwell Land Grant, and place settings and silverware from the original St. James Hotel that has been restored across the street.

As it heads west, US 64 winds through the twisting gorge of the Cimarron Canyon where sandstone faces meet the road and tall ponderosa pines line the gently flowing waters of the Cimarron River. This spectacular passage through the mountains emerges at the northern end of Eagle Nest Lake in the magnificently spacious Moreno Valley.

ST. JAMES HOTEL

Here's how they tell the story:

Brushing the road dust off his clothing, a polite gentleman removes his hat and inquires about lodging at the **St. James Hotel** in Cimarron. After paying for his usual room at the end of the hall on the first floor, the man swiftly signs "R.H. Howard" in the guest book. He cleans up a bit, then saunters into the hotel saloon, which hums with cocktail chatter. A sign on the wall reads: "Gents will please leave their six-guns behind the bar while in town! This will lessen the customary collections for burials." Howard abides. If it's a good night, all patrons will pay heed to the warning and no gunfights will break out in one of the most popular gathering spots in the New Mexico Territory during the late 1800s. Howard isn't looking for any fights. On the contrary, he is hoping no one recognizes him. R. H. Howard is, in fact, Jesse James.

The St. James began as a saloon, built in 1873 by Henri Lambert, a Frenchman who had served as personal chef to President Abraham Lincoln and Gen. Ulysses S. Grant. For the rest of the century, until the Santa Fe Railroad lured travelers to the growing metropolis of Raton, the St. James played host to some of the most ornery badmen around, the likes of Thomas "Black Jack" Ketchum and Clay Allison, not to mention the 26 unfortunate fellows who left the place feet first on their backs, the victims of gunfights. Many good guys of the Old West, including Garrett and David Crockett, a nephew of the famous frontiersman, slept in the hotel's comfortable beds. It was here that Buffalo Bill Cody and Annie Oakley planned his Wild West Show, Zane Grey wrote *Fighting Caravans,* and Frederic Remington based himself, sketching in the nearby piñon hills by day.

Today, a walk into the restored St. James Hotel is a walk back in time. High-backed Victorian couches and chairs enhance the lobby. Deep-brown bureaus line the walls as they did 100 years ago. Linen covers tabletops in the dining room, which was the original barroom. Despite a decor that evokes subtle elegance, a look upward reveals about 20 bullet holes in the pressed tin ceiling. The white-washed ceiling was installed in 1903 after more than 400 bullets had riddled it.

Three layers of oak floor boards were laid in the room above to protect guests, who most likely were thankful, considering the additional punctures.

Red-orange carpeted hallways lead to 15 rooms furnished with antique beds, dressers, and couches. A nameplate outside each door identifies the room with one of its famous regulars. A stairway watched over by a stuffed cougar takes guests to second-floor rooms. Near the end of the hall, a potted plant blocks the entrance to Room 18. No one sleeps here except a ghost who refuses to leave. Some claim the ghost is the restless spirit of James Wright, a gambler who was killed when trying to claim the hotel as his winnings in a poker game. They may have succeeded in carrying his body out the front door, but his spirit still stubbornly refuses to leave.

Another ghost said to drift through the second-floor hallway is Mary Lambert, owner Henri's first wife. A rush of strong perfume is a sign she is around. Additional spirits come and go from the historic hotel, adding to the ambiance of its colorful past.

For one weekend every month (except January and July), the hotel relives the days of its unsettled past, once again becoming the site of a tragic murder during Murder Mystery Weekends. Each patron is assigned a character, a late-1800s hotel guest who is either victim, investigator, suspect, or murderer. They spend their

Lassoing the "doggies" has long been a Western art form. (Paul Chesley)

Cowboys Tom Day and Simon Arreola saddle up for a day on the range. (Paul Chesley)

days gathering clues to the crime and their nights making peace with the ghosts. Murder Mystery Weekends are sponsored by Dark Deeds Afoot, 9951 Radcliffe NW, Albuquerque, 87114, or call St. James Hotel at (505) 376-2664.

■ RATON

After the Treaty of Guadalupe-Hidalgo ended the Mexican War in 1848, a 32-year-old frontiersman began digging and blasting a well-graded wagon road across the rugged 7,622-foot (2,323-m) Raton Pass. Once he had completed the road, "Uncle" Dick Wootton stretched a heavy chain across it and began charging travelers a toll: $1.50 for each wagon. (Indians went free.) "Whenever they (Indians) came along, the toll gate went up and any other little thing I could do to hurry them along was done promptly and cheerfully," he told a biographer in 1889.

Eight miles (13 km) south of the pass, travelers stopped for water and feed at Willow Springs Ranch. In 1880, after the Santa Fe Railroad laid tracks along Wootton's path, a division point was established at the ranch, which was renamed Raton. The rail line's highest point traverses Raton Pass, and its only tunnel burrows through layers of sandstone and shale there. Within a year, the new village boasted 3,000 residents. Attracted by the area's luxuriant rangeland and rich coal deposits, folks called it the "Pittsburgh of the West." Early citizens lived in boxcars parked on sidings next to the railroad. As the years passed, brick and stone buildings were erected to house stores, restaurants, hotels, and a newspaper.

A row of fast-food restaurants and gas stations attests to the town's continued role as a major stopover for travelers crossing Raton Pass into Colorado. Downtown, however, about 70 historical buildings compactly squeezed into a five-block district beckon explorers. A variety of architectural designs is represented, ranging from the Spanish Mission-Revival style of the Santa Fe depot to the terra-cotta-trimmed windows of the Raton Realty Building and Corinthian pilasters of the Roth Building. Most spectacular is the Shuler Theatre with its European Rococo interior. When completed in 1915, the ornate building housed an opera house, fire station, and city offices. Elaborate woodwork, gold-trimmed box seats, and a high ceiling painted to resemble a cloud-filled sky decorate the 480-seat theater.

South of downtown, the thoroughbreds and quarterhorses run from late June through Labor Day on weekends and holidays at La Mesa Park, a pari-mutuel racetrack. Ten miles (16 km) farther south, the National Rifle Association operates the most comprehensive shooting facility in the United States. Located on 33,000 acres dotted with piñon and junipers, the Whittington Center contains 14 shooting ranges and hosts annual national championship events. Public tours are offered daily.

Ten miles (16 km) northeast of town on NM 526, **Sugarite Canyon State Park** sits between two mesas along the banks of Chicorico Creek. Three mountain lakes are stocked with rainbow trout, and hiking trails lead onto Little Horse Mesa and among the ruins of an early twentieth-century coal mining camp.

Forty-five miles (72 km) to the west of Raton is **Vermejo Park Ranch,** a private hunting and fishing resort that sprawls across nearly 400,000 acres of pine- and aspen-covered slopes. Once part of the Maxwell Land Grant, the ranch was sold in 1926 to Harrison Chandler of the Los Angeles Times Mirror Corp. who organized the Vermejo Club. The club's $5,000 initiation fee ensured a rather select membership that included Douglas Fairbanks, Herbert Hoover, F.W. Kellogg, Cecil B. DeMille, Andrew Mellon, and Mary Pickford, for whom Mary's Lake and Mary's Cabin are named. The club disbanded during the Depression, and the ranch went through a series of owners until Pennzoil purchased it in 1973. Nine years later, the oil company donated to the U.S. Forest Service 100,000 acres of towering pines, golden aspens, and grassy meadows brimming with wildflowers. Today, Vermejo Park is still a working cattle ranch, and this outdoor paradise accommodates fishermen in the summer who come in search of rainbow, brown, brook, and cutthroat trout in 21 of the ranch's clear blue lakes. In the fall, hunters scout for deer, elk, antelope, and bear.

CAPULIN VOLCANO
Sweeping upward from a yellow-grass prairie, about 30 miles (48 km) east of Raton is a gently rounded forested mound—the remains of a once-violent volcano responsible for much of the lava rock that caps the terrain in northeastern New Mexico. The last time Capulin Volcano erupted was 10,000 years ago when red-hot lava, cinders, ash, and rock debris shot skyward and fell back upon the crater, piling up to create the 1,000-foot-tall (305-m) conical mound. After the eruptions ceased, grasses, junipers, mountain mahogany, and gambel oaks gained a foothold on slopes, which today are blanketed with vegetation.

The volcano is preserved as a national monument, and a paved two-mile (3-km) road spirals to its summit. Two short trails begin at a parking lot: one follows the rim, providing a panorama that takes in the snowcapped peaks of the Sangre de Cristos, distant volcanic hills and mesas, and the sprawling rangeland that reaches to the horizon. The second trail descends into the center of the volcano, partially filled with pumice that has slid down its sides. Lupine, penstemon, golden pea, and bright yellow sunflowers dot the slopes, and lilting songs from grosbeaks, gold finches, and bluebirds fill the air.

One group of people who probably witnessed the fiery eruptions of Capulin Mountain was Folsom Man, a people who hunted bison, camels, musk oxen, and giant sloths throughout northeastern New Mexico 10,000 years ago. Long gone, their presence remained unknown until 1908 when George McJunkin, a cowboy and former slave, discovered some stone spearpoints among large bleached bones scattered in an arroyo near the tiny community of Folsom, a shipping point on the Colorado and Southern Railroad. In 1926, after years of persistent pestering, McJunkin finally convinced a group of skeptical archaeologists to inspect the site. They determined that the bones belonged to an extinct strain of giant bison and the spearpoints were those chipped by Folsom Man, one of the state's earliest inhabitants, preceded by Clovis Man and Sandia Man by about 1,000 years. Some of the spearpoints are displayed at the **Folsom Man Museum**, which is open only in the summer on Main Street in Folsom.

■ CLAYTON AND VICINITY

Two volcanic mounds, the first foothills of the Rocky Mountains, have served as a landmark since the early 1700s when Comanche Indian Chief Orejas de Conejo (Rabbit Ears), so named because he once froze his ears, roamed the grasslands of northeastern New Mexico. After the chief was killed in battle and buried on the largest peak, the mountains were named after him. In 1717, the knobby hills north of Clayton were the site of one of the bloodiest battles of the Spanish-Comanche War, when a volunteer army of 500 Spaniards surprised the Indians, killing hundreds and taking 700 of them prisoner. In the 1800s, Rabbit Ears Mountain served as a major landmark on the Cimarron Cutoff of the Santa Fe Trail, which passed nearby. Ruts still can be seen, and six famous watering holes along the trade route can be reached within a 50-minute drive from town.

Since 1887, when the Colorado and Southern Railroad established Clayton, rail cars have been hauling fat cattle from the area's abundant grazing land to market. Named for Senator Stephen Dorsey's son, the town is mostly remembered for the celebrated hanging of Thomas "Black Jack" Ketchum in 1901.

Along with his brother, Sam, and two other partners, the Texas-born outlaw with dark, beady eyes and a habit of wearing black, murdered a few men and robbed a few trains, mostly in New Mexico. Abandoned by his gang because of his uncontrollable temper, Ketchum attempted to rob the same train he and his partners had held up three years earlier. Unfortunately for the outlaw, Conductor Frank Harrington was armed with a shotgun, which he fired into Ketchum's heart (or so he thought). The outlaw fell with a shattered arm and escaped, only to be apprehended the next day. He lived, but lost his right arm.

The next spring, after being convicted of train robbery, a crime punishable by hanging, Ketchum was prepared for his fate in Clayton, which was abuzz with newspaper reporters and spectators who bought tickets to the event. Ketchum remained calm as officers slipped the noose around his neck, but Sheriff Salome Garcia was so nervous he missed the rope with his hatchet. The second attempt was a clean cut; the trap door fell open and Ketchum fell through. His body quivered, then collapsed onto the ground. The outlaw was dead, but not by hanging: his head had been jerked off his body! A local doctor adeptly sewed it back on so Ketchum could be properly buried. No mourners accompanied the plain pine coffin to the cemetery east of town, but flowers occasionally adorn the frequently visited grave.

Few trees shade the flat streets of Clayton, which bills itself as the carbon dioxide capital of the world. Bravo Dome, the world's largest and purest carbon dioxide reserve, is embedded in sandstone 50 miles (80 km) southwest of town. On the surface, cows dominate and thousands can be seen contentedly eating the grama grass. Tawny antelope and quail often share the feast.

Throughout the eastern plains, interrupted only by tiny communities with names like Bueyeros, Amistad, Mosquero, Roy, and Nara Visa, clusters of brown bovines are all that interrupt a swell of pale-green prairie that stretches to the sky in all directions. A pickup truck whizzes by and a jackrabbit hops past. One of these small towns, **Logan**, is experiencing an influx of retirees attracted to the refreshing and well-stocked waters of nearby Ute Reservoir. In town, a faded mural depicting events in the history of New Mexico graces an outside wall of the Casa Blanca Motel. Scenes on the 25-foot-long (8-m) wall include Indians and conquistadors. The colorful aging work of art was painted by Manuel Acosta, a former pupil of Peter Hurd, a famous portraitist who was born in Roswell and produced most of his work at his home in the Hondo Valley.

■ TUCUMCARI

Situated at the edge of the Llano Estacado, near the base of a flat-topped mountain by the same name, this tree-lined community got its start in 1901 as a construction camp on the Rock Island Railroad. Known briefly as Six-Shooter Siding, the settlement attracted homesteaders who tried for years to coax crops from the sandy soil. In 1908, when the railroad decided to turn the camp into a division point, a more respectable name was needed. The name came from the nearby mountain, which reportedly had served as a Comanche lookout in years past. Most likely, Tucumcari is a derivation from the Comanche *tukamukaru*, which means to lie in wait for someone or something to approach. The more popular meaning derives from a folktale credited to Geronimo in which Tocom, the sweetheart of an Apache Indian maiden named Kari, was slain by Tonapon, a rival. Grieving for her lover, Kari killed Tonapon and then took her own life. This action caused Kari's father, Wautonomah, to stab himself, crying out "Tocom! Kari!" as his last words. But because this was Comanche country, the first derivation is probably correct.

In the mid-1900s, Route 66 sliced through the center of town, with its tourist courts, cafés, and gift shops. Today known as Tucumcari Boulevard, this strip still boasts most of the town's 26 motels (about 2,000 rooms—billboards hundreds of miles away on I-40 claim). The **Tucumcari Historical Museum,** located in a two-story brick building, houses Folsom spearpoints, mammoth teeth, antique bottles, petrified wood, a pre-1900 windmill, a covered wagon, and old saddles.

During summer months, many of the cars and trucks that pass through Tucumcari are heading to **Conchas Lake,** 32 miles (51 km) northwest of town. The clear, blue-green waters of this desert oasis on the Canadian River provide irrigation waters to area farmers and cool relief to swimmers. Water-skiers dip and lean as they slice through the calm water, and fishermen cast lines from boats and the rocky shoreline.

Also in the summer, a musical drama centered around the legendary life of Billy the Kid unfolds at the **Caprock Amphitheatre,** about 40 miles (64 km) southeast of Tucumcari. Every weekend from mid-June through mid-August, as a searing sun slips below the western horizon, gunfighters, singers and dancers transform into a stage the natural theater carved from red sandstone cliffs at the edge of the Llano Estacado.

■ SANTA ROSA

In 1865, when he was traveling around the state as an officer in Col. Kit Carson's First Regiment of New Mexico Volunteers, Don Celso Baca noticed a fertile plain wedged between the Pecos River and El Rito Creek. Baca set up a cattle operation that grew into one of the area's largest. He built a *hacienda* and in 1879 constructed an adobe chapel nearby to honor his mother. The tiny chapel was dedicated to Santa Rosa de Lima, the first canonized saint of the New World.

When 4,000 workers converged on the site in 1901 to build tracks that would connect the Rock Island Railroad with the Southern Pacific, the emerging town took its name from the chapel. After rail workers moved on to their next assignment, farming and ranching sustained the community until Route 66 was paved through its center.

Sleepy Santa Rosa continues to serve travelers on I-40 at an assortment of cafés and motels. But it also has gained a reputation among scuba divers who travel hundreds of miles to immerse themselves into the Blue Hole, a 90-foot-deep (27-m) artesian well carved into sharp limestone. The bell-shaped pool of crystal-clear deep-blue water is fed by a subterranean river that supplies 3,000 gallons (11,400 l) a minute and is inhabited by goldfish, catfish, and snails that cling to the walls. The diving den maintains a constant temperature of 60 degrees F (16° C), enabling year-round use. Nine miles (14 km) north of town, the still waters of Santa Rosa Lake beckon windsurfers, waterskiers, swimmers, and fishermen in search of prize walleye.

Possibly, Francisco Vasquez de Coronado camped at Puerto de Luna as he traveled across northeastern New Mexico en route to the imaginary Quivira said to lie in Kansas. Ten miles (16 km) south of Santa Rosa on NM 91, Puerto de Luna grew up on a bend of the Pecos River where his men probably built a bridge. A wonderful insight into this village and Santa Rosa is found in "Bless Me, Ultima," written by Albuquerque author Rudolfo Anaya, who grew up in the area. This tale of growing up in the 1940s on the *llano* abounds with descriptions of the river, the spring-fed lakes, and the faith by which people live.

(following pages) Mountains and dunes merge into a purple sunset glow over White Sands National Monument.

PRACTICAL INFORMATION

■ ORIENTATION

New Mexico, with 121,666 square miles (315,114 sq km), is the fifth-largest state in the United States. The combined area of Delaware, Maine, Massachusetts, New Hampshire, New Jersey, New York, and Rhode Island could fit neatly within its borders. Although the almost-square state is wedged between Arizona and Texas, many first-time visitors inquire whether or not a passport is required to pass through its borders and whether they need to exchange their money into pesos. Neither is necessary, for New Mexico joined the Union in 1912 as the United States' 47th state.

Only 1.5 million people live in New Mexico, one-third of them in the Albuquerque area, which leaves plenty of elbow room for the rest of the population. Las Cruces is the second-largest city with 59,000 residents, followed by Santa Fe with 56,000 people. The rest of the cities are small, with populations ranging from 43,000 at Roswell to a few dozen at Grenville.

When the wheel on their carriage broke near Taos in 1898, artists Ernest Blumenschein and Burt Phillips ended up staying and founding the Taos art colony. (Museum of New Mexico)

■ CLIMATE

	ELEVATION	AVERAGE TEMPERATURE				TEMPERATURE EXTREMES		AVERAGE ANNUAL	
		JULY		JANUARY					
		MAX.	MIN.	MAX.	MIN.	HIGH	LOW	PRECIP.	SNOW
Albuquerque	5,311	92	65	47	24	105	-17	7.8	11
Carlsbad	3,120	96	68	59	31	112	- 7	12.4	5
Chaco Canyon	6,175	91	55	43	12	102	-38	8.5	19
Cimarron	6,540	83	55	47	19	99	-35	15.3	33
Santa Fe	7,200	85	56	42	18	98	-18	13.8	29

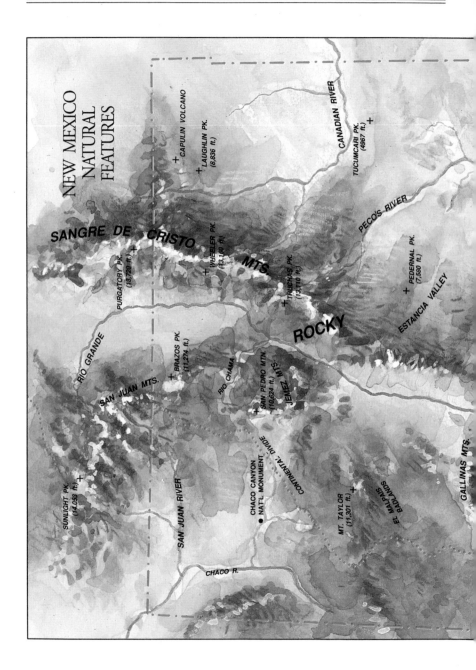

NEW MEXICO NATURAL FEATURES

CAPULIN VOLCANO

LAUGHLIN PK. (8,836 ft.)

CANADIAN RIVER

TUCUMCARI PK. (4967 ft.)

SANGRE DE CRISTO

WHEELER PK. (13,140 ft.)

MTS.

PECOS RIVER

PURGATORY PK. (13,720 ft.)

TRUCHAS PK. (13,110 ft.)

PEDERNAL PK. (7,580 ft.)

ESTANCIA VALLEY

ROCKY

RIO GRANDE

BRAZOS PK. (11,274 ft.)

RIO CHAMA

SAN PEDRO MTN. (10,624 ft.)

JEMEZ MTS.

SAN JUAN MTS.

SUNLIGHT PK. (14,053 ft.)

SAN JUAN RIVER

CONTINENTAL DIVIDE

CHACO CANYON NAT'L MONUMENT

GALLINAS MTS.

MT. TAYLOR (11,301 ft.)

EL MALPAIS BADLANDS

CHACO R.

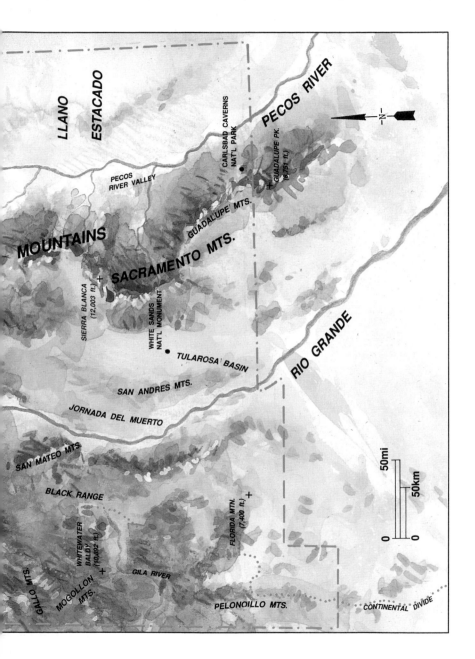

■ WHEN TO VISIT, WHAT TO WEAR

Sunshine spreads across New Mexico at least 75 percent of the year, which makes the state a great place to visit any time. Because of altitudes that range from 3,000 feet (919 m) to 13,000 feet (3,962 m), temperatures widely vary: from 98 degrees F (37° C) in Deming to 70 degrees F (21° C) in Chama in the summer, and 65 degrees F (18° C) in Roswell, compared to 32 degrees F (0° C) in Taos during the winter. Consistent dry air prevents either extreme from being too unpleasant.

Precipitation also can vary—it's not unusual for the northern mountains to receive 300 inches (762 cm) of snow during the winter, compared to one inch (2.5 cm) annually in the southern desert. Rain usually comes in the form of afternoon thunderstorms, which unleash torrents and can cause dangerous flash floods. From mid-June through mid-September, campers should not pitch tents along streambeds and should stay on high ground until the storms have passed.

The combination of high altitude and intense sun requires use of sunscreen every day. Dressing in layers is also recommended any time of the year, and no matter where you are, casual wear is acceptable, except for the dinner meal at a few Santa Fe resorts.

■ TRANSPORTATION

Albuquerque International Airport provides almost the only commercial airline access to New Mexico, which is served by 10 major carriers. Two commuter airlines, Mesa Airlines (800-933-6372) and Ross Aviation (505-844-1885), fly from Albuquerque to the state's other cities.

Despite the major role the railroad played in New Mexico's settlement, only two routes now pass through the state. AMTRAK **trains** run once daily, east-west and west-east, between Raton and Gallup, passing through Las Vegas, Lamy (17 miles [27 km] south of Santa Fe), and Albuquerque. Another route travels from El Paso through Deming and Lordsburg before exiting the state. For information on AMTRAK, call (800) 872-7245.

The **Greyhound/Trailways** bus line serves the state, connecting towns from Hobbs to Farmington. For further information, call (505) 243-4435. **Shuttlejack** also provides service between Santa Fe and Albuquerque International Airport. For rates and schedule, call (800) 452-2665 or (505) 982-4311.

The best way to see New Mexico is by car, which can be rented at most of the state's small airports, as well as in Albuquerque.

■ ACCOMMODATIONS

B = Budget; under $30   M = Moderate; $30-$80   L = Luxury; over $80

■ A B I Q U I U
Abiquiu Inn; US 84; (505) 685-4378; roadside lodging amid spectacular multi-hued cliffs; M

■ A L A M O G O R D O
Holiday Inn; 1401 S. White Sands; (505) 437-7100; standard lodging; M
White Sands Inn; 1020 S. White Sands; (505) 434-4200 quiet, comfortable motel; M

■ A L B U. Q U E R Q U E
Adobe & Roses Bed and Breakfast (B & B); 1011 Ortega NW; (505) 898-0654; serene rural valley setting with lily ponds and fruit trees; M
Albuquerque Hilton; 1901 University NE; (505) 884-2500 or (800) 821-1901; tradition with a tasteful Southwest flair; L
Albuquerque International Hostel; 1012 Central SW; (505) 243-6101; a friendly place to meet foreign visitors; B
Albuquerque Marriott; 2101 Louisiana NE; (505) 881-6800 or (800) 228-9290; high-rise elegance with great views of the Sandia Mountains; L
Casas de Suenos Bed and Breakfast (B & B); 310 Rio Grande SW; (505) 247-4560; rambling compound surrounds landmark "snail house" designed by local architect Bart Prince; M
Corrales Inn Bed and Breakfast (B & B); 4763 Corrales Rd.; (505) 897-4422; walk to shops or read in bookcase-lined library; M
De Anza Motor Lodge; 4301 Central NE; (505) 255-1654; cozy tourist court on Route 66; B
El Vado Motel; 2500 Central SW; (505) 243-4594; remnant of Route 66 heyday, great neon; B
Elaine's Bed and Breakfast; (B & B); 72 Snowline Estates, Cedar Crest; (505) 281-2467; European antiques fill this warm hillside mountain home 30 minutes east of Albuquerque; M-L

Hyatt Regency Hotel; 330 Tijeras NW; (505) 842-1234 or (800) 228-1234; Albuquerque's most luxurious hotel; L

La Posada de Albuquerque; 125 Second NW; (505) 242-9090 or (800) 777-5732; built in 1939, one of native New Mexican Conrad Hilton's early hotels and restored beautifully to its original splendor; L

Yours Truly; 160 Paseo de Corrales, Corrales; (505) 898-7027; caters to hot air balloon enthusiasts and other fun-loving folks; M

■ ANGEL FIRE

The Inn at Angel Fire; (505) 377-2504 or (800) 666-1949; overlooking ski slopes and vast Moreno Valley; M

■ ARTESIA

Best Western Pecos Inn; 2209 W. Main; (505) 748-3324 or (800) 528-1234; standard motel lodging; M

■ AZTEC

Enchantment Lodge; 1800 W. Aztec; (505) 334-6143; quiet comfort in traditional inn; M

The Hightower Motel does not appear on our list of recommended accommodations. (Paul Chesley)

The deserts and plains of the West seem to provide bumper crops of abandoned automobiles.
(Paul Chesley)

■ C A R L S B A D
Carlsbad Inn; 601 S. Canal; (505) 887-3541; traditional motel; M
Motel Stevens; 1829 S. Canal; (505) 887-2851; standard American lodging; M

■ C H A M A
Corkins Lodge; Brazos River; (505) 588-7261; rustic full-service resort in shadows of dramatic Brazos Cliffs; L
Oso Ranch & Lodge (B & B); (505) 756-2954; situated in the high country near the scenic Chama River; L

■ C I M A R R O N
St. James Hotel; (505) 376-2664; historic gathering spot for famous and infamous cowboys; M
Santa Fe Trail Inn (B & B); (505) 376-2916; once known as the National Hotel, its front door faces the Santa Fe Trail; M

■ C L A Y T O N
Clayton Motel; 422 Monroe; (505) 374-2544; traditional; M
Sunset Motel; 702 S. 1st; (505) 374-2589; clean and basic; B

■ C L O U D C R O F T
The Lodge; (505) 682-2566 or (800) 842-4216; elegant mountain resort; M-L
Pine Crest Cabins; (505) 682-2631; secluded wooded setting; M

■ C L O V I S
La Vista Inn; 1516 Mabry; (505) 762-3808; clean and quiet; M
Sands Motel; 1400 Mabry; (505) 762-3439; traditional American lodging; M

■ C O L U M B U S
Motel Columbus; (505) 531-2489; simple, white-washed lodging; B

■ D E M I N G
Chilton Inn; 1709 E. Spruce; (505) 546-8813; comfortable and quiet; M
Grand Motor Inn; US 70-80 E.; (505) 546-2632; traditional comfort; M
Wagon Wheel Motel; 1109 W. Pine; (505) 546-2681; meeting basic needs; B

■ D U L C E
Jicarilla Inn; (505) 759-3663 or (800) 528-1234; convenient stopover; M

■ E S P A Ñ O L A
Casa del Rio (B & B); Hernandez; (505) 753-2035; adobe comfort tucked into pink cliffs; M

■ F A R M I N G T O N

Abe's Motel; Navajo Dam; (505) 632-2194; quiet lodging near great fishing; B

Holiday Inn; 600 E. Broadway; (505) 327-9811 or (800) HOLIDAY; standard quiet comfort; M

The Inn; 700 Scott; (505) 327-5221 or (800) 528-1234; traditional American lodging; M

■ G A L L U P

El Rancho Hotel; 1000 E. US 66; (505) 863-9311; stay in rooms once occupied by Hollywood stars in this historic showpiece; M

Holiday Inn; 2915 W. US 66; (505) 722-2201 or (800) 432-2211; M

■ G R A N T S

Holiday Grants; I-40 East interchange; (505) 287-4426; traditional American lodging; M

The Inn; I-40 East interchange; (505) 287-7901; basic comfort; M

■ H O B B S

Leawood Best Western; 1301 E. Broadway; (505) 393-4101; traditional American lodging; M

■ L A S   C R U C E S

Las Cruces Hilton; 705 Telshor; (505) 522-4300; comfort on bluff overlooking city; M

Meson de Mesilla (B & B); 1803 Avenida de Mesilla, Mesilla; (505) 525-9212; quiet inn with one of the area's best gourmet restaurants; M

■ L A S   V E G A S

Carriage House (B & B); 926 6th; (505) 454-1784; antique-filled Victorian home; M

Pendaries Lodge; 26 miles (42 km) northwest of Las Vegas; (505) 425-6076; exclusive golf and fishing resort; M

Plaza Hotel; 230 Old Town Plaza; (505) 425-3591; 100-year-old Italianate bracketed-style showpiece; M

■ L I N C O L N

Casa de Patron (B&B); (505) 653-4676; airy home in historic town; M

Wortley Hotel; (505) 653-4500; rebuilt historic lodging complete with rocking chairs on front porch; M

■ **L O R D S B U R G**
American Inn; 944 E. Motel Dr.; (505) 542-3591; traditional lodging; M

■ **L O S   A L A M O S**
Hilltop House Hotel; Trinity at Central; (505) 662-2441; mountain vistas from centrally located lodging; M
Orange Street Inn (B & B); 3496 Orange St.; (505) 662-2651; comfortable lodging set among pine trees; M

■ **M E S C A L E R O**
Inn of the Mountain Gods; (505) 257-5141 or (800) 545-9011; secluded resort run by Mescalero Apache Tribe; M-L

■ **O J O   C A L I E N T E**
The Inn at Ojo (B & B); (505) 583-2428; peaceful accommodations next door to mineral baths; M

■ **P E C O S**
Pecos River Cabins; (505) 757-8760; riverside cabins; M
Los Pinos Ranch; Terrero; (505) 757-6213; rustic Pecos River lodging; M

■ **P O R T A L E S**
Portales Inn; 218 W. 3rd; (505) 359-1208; basic, simple, and quiet; M

■ **R A T O N**
Colt Motel; 1160 S. 2nd; (505) 445-3681; Longboy beds; B
Melody Lane Motel; 136 Canyon; (505) 445-3655 or (800) 421-5210; in-room steam baths; M
Vermejo Park Ranch; (505) 445-3097; exclusive hunting and fishing resort; L

■ **R E D   R I V E R**
Bitter Creek Guest Ranch; (505) 754-2587; cabins in national forest seclusion; M
Red River Inn; (505) 754-2930; walk to shops from this centrally located modern motel; M

■ **R O S W E L L**
El Rancho Palacio; 2205 N. Main; (505) 622-2721; traditional lodging; M
Roswell Inn; 1815 N. Main; (505) 623-4920; standard American lodging; M

■ **R U I D O S O**
Carrizo Lodge; (505) 257-9131; historic lodge; M
Dan Dee Cabins; (505) 257-2165; fireplaces and ski packages; M

Monjeau Shadows Country Inn (B & B); Nogal; (505) 336-4191; hidden among pine forest; M-L

Shadow Mountain Lodge; (505) 257-4886 or (800) 441-4331; motel tucked into tall pines; M

Storybook Cabins; (505) 257-2115; fireplaces in upper canyon units; M

■ S A N T A   F E

Alamo Lodge; 1842 Cerrillos; (505) 982-1841; simply kept tourist court; M

Alexander's Inn (B&B); 529 E. Palace; (505) 986-1431; cozy rooms near downtown; M-L

Bishop's Lodge; Bishop's Lodge Rd.; (505) 983-6377; Southwest elegance in foothills a few miles north of downtown; L

La Fonda; 100 E. San Francisco; (505) 982-5511 or (800) 523-5002; where the Santa Fe Trail ends and lodging elegance begins; L

La Posada de Santa Fe; 330 E. Palace; (505) 986-0000 or (800) 727-5276; six secluded acres speckled with adobe cottages; L

Rancho Encantado; Tesuque; (505) 982-3537; secluded resort in foothills of Sangre de Cristo Mountains five miles (8 km) north of Santa Fe; L

Territorial Inn (B & B); 215 Washington; (505) 989-7737; elegantly remodeled 100-year-old home; L

■ S A N T A   R O S A

Adobe Inn; (505) 472-3446; traditional Best Western; M

■ S I L V E R   C I T Y

Bear Creek Cabins; Piños Altos; (505) 388-4501; tucked into tall pines; M

Bear Mountain Guest Ranch (B & B); Bear Mountain Rd.; (505) 538-2538; two-story ranch house with wonderful rooms; M

Copper Manor; 710 Silver Heights; (505) 538-5392; standard motel lodging, friendly folks; M

D-Bar Guest Ranch; Mimbres Valley; (505) 772-5563 (April through November); peace at the edge of the Gila Wilderness; M-L

Holiday Motor Hotel; US 180 E.; (505) 538-3711; no-frills motel lodging; M

■ S O C O R R O

Casa Blanca (B & B); San Antonio; (505) 835-3027; Victorian farmhouse at edge of wildlife bird refuge; M

Eaton House (B & B); 403 Eaton; (505) 835-1067; former army colonel's home is today a haven for birdwatchers and travelers; M

■ T A O S

Casa de las Chimeneas (B & B); Los Pandos and Cordoba roads; (505) 758-4777; three charming rooms open onto bountiful English garden; L

Hotel St. Bernard; Taos Ski Valley; (505) 776-2251; experience the soul of European hospitality; L

La Posada de Taos (B & B); 309 Juanita Ln.; (505) 758-8164; small cozy compound tucked into quiet neighborhood; M

Mabel Dodge Luhan House (B & B); Morada Ln.; (505) 758-9456; If adobe walls and giant cottonwoods could talk!; L

Sagebrush Inn; Paseo del Pueblo Sur; (505) 758-2254 or (800) 428-3626; great lounge that features local live music; M-L

Taos Inn; 125 Paseo del Pueblo Norte; (505) 758-2233 or (800) 826-7466; historic downtown gathering spot tastefully adorned; L

■ T R U T H   O R   C O N S E Q U E N C E S

Ace Lodge; 1014 N. Date; (505) 894-2151; simple and clean; M

Black Range Lodge; Kingston; (505) 895-5652; sleepy mountain getaway; M

Elephant Butte Inn; NM 195, Elephant Butte; (505) 744-5431; situated on New Mexico's largest lake; M

Enchanted Villa (B & B); Hillsboro; (505) 895-5686; adobe retreat in old mining town; M

■ T U C U M C A R I

Holiday Inn; E. Tucumcari Blvd.; (505) 461-3780; basic comfort; M

■ RESTAURANTS

B = Budget; less than $7   M = Moderate; $7-$15   E = Expensive; $15 and up

■ A B I Q U I U
Café Abiquiu at the Abiquiu Inn; (505) 685-4378; international menu; M

■ A L A M O G O R D O
Angelina's Italian Restaurant; 415 S. White Sands; (505) 434-1166; family Italian restaurant; M
Cattleman's Steakhouse; 2904 N. White Sands; (505) 434-5252; M

■ A L B U Q U E R Q U E
ASIAN
Bangkok Café; 5901 Central NE; (505) 255-5036; M
India Kitchen; 6910 Montgomery NE; (505) 884-2333; M
Japanese Kitchen; 12 Winrock Center NE; (505) 884-8937; E
Minato Restaurant; 10721 Montgomery NE; (505) 293-2929; E
Saigon Far East; 901 San Pedro SE; (505) 255-7408; B
Shalimar; 8405 Montgomery NE; (505) 275-7949; M

CARIBBEAN
Fofo's Caribbean Cuisine; 107 San Pablo SE; (505) 255-3925; M

ITALIAN
Casa Vieja; 4541 Corrales Rd.; (505) 898-7489; E
Dion's Pizza; five locations; (505) 265- 6919; B
Mama Mia Ristorante Italiano; 1430 Carlise NE; (505) 265-4557; M
Nunzio's Pizza; five locations; (505) 265-8888; B
Scalo Northern Italian Grill; 3500 Central SE; (505) 255-8781; M
Paisano's Italian Restaurant; 1935 Eubank NE; (505) 298-7541; M

MEDITERRANEAN
Gyros Diner; 106-A Cornell SE; (505) 255-4401; B
Michelle's Old World Café; 6205 Montgomery NE; (505) 884-7938; M
Oasis Restaurant; 5400 San Mateo NE; (505) 884-2324; M

MEXICAN
Acapulco Tacos & Burritos; 840 San Mateo SE; (505) 268-9865; B
Adobe Rose Café; 6724 Central SE; (505) 255-7673; B

Barelas Coffee House; 1502 4th SW; (505) 843-7577; B
Duran Central Pharmacy; 1815 Central NW; (505) 247-4141; B
El Patio; 142 Harvard SE; (505) 268-4245; B
Garcia's Kitchen; three locations; (505) 247-9149; B
La Esquina; First Plaza Galeria; (505) 242-3432; B
La Placita Dining Rooms; 302 San Felipe NW; 247-2204; B
M & J Sanitary Tortilla Factory; 403 2nd SW; (505) 242-4890; B
Monroe's Restaurant; 6021 Osuna NE; (505) 881-4224; B
Pollo Fiesta; 1124 Edith Blvd. NE; (505) 247-4999
Sadie's Dining Room; 6132 4th NW; (505) 345-5339; B-M
Teofilo's Restaurant; 144 Main St, Los Lunas; (505) 865-5511; B

NEW AMERICAN CUISINE
Artichoke Café; 424 Central SE; (505) 243-0200; E
Prairie Star; 1000 N. Jemez Dam Rd.; (505) 867-3327; E
Restaurant Andre; 1100 San Mateo NE; (505) 268-5354; E
Stephen's; 1311 Tijeras NW; (505)842-1773; E

TRADITIONAL AMERICAN
Central Delicatessen; 3118 Central SE; (505) 266-3003; B
Dee's Cheesecake Emporium; 3300 Menaul NE; (505) 884-1777; B
Double Rainbow; 3416 Central SE; (505) 255-6633; B
Frontier Restaurant; 2400 Central SE; (505) 266-0550; B
Gin Mill; 6300 San Mateo NE; (505) 821-6300; B
Model Pharmacy; 3636 Monte Vista NE; (505) 255-8686; B
Owl Café; 800 Eubank NE; (505) 291-4900; B
66 Diner; 1405 Central NE; (505) 247-1421; B
Soho Eatery; 2423 San Pedro NE; (505) 884-5368; M
Yester-Daves; 10601 Montgomery NE; (505) 293-0033; B

■ AZTEC
Aztec Restaurant; (505) 334-9586; hearty American and Mexican fare; B

■ CHIMAYO
Rancho de Chimayo; (505) 351-4444; featuring Chimayo red chile and frosty margaritas; M

Some good old boys in a good old bar in Silver City. (Paul Chesley)

■ CIMARRON
St. James Hotel; (505) 376-2664; coffee shop and dining room, American; M-E
Cimarron Art Gallery Soda Fountain; (505) 376-2614; great milkshakes; B

■ CLAYTON
Eklund Hotel Dining Room; 15 Main; (505) 374-2551; historic steakhouse; B-M
La Paloma Blanca Café; 22 Pine; (505) 374-2201; great breakfasts; B

■ CLOUDCROFT
Rebecca's at the Lodge; (505) 682-2566; continental cuisine in historic inn; M-E

■ CLOVIS
El Monterrey; 118 Mitchell; (505) 763-4031; American dining; M

■ COLUMBUS
Norma's Café; New Mexican and American cooking; B

■ DEMING
K-Bob's Steakhouse; 316 E. Cedar; (505) 546-8883; M

■ ESPAÑOLA
Angelina's; Paseo de Oñate; (505) 753-9913; New Mexican fare and steaks in
  rambling adobe; B
El Paragua; Santa Cruz Rd.; (505) 753-3211; New Mexican fare and steaks in
  elegant setting; M
Matilda's Café; Corlett Rd.; (505) 753-3200; New Mexican specialties; B

■ FARMINGTON
KB Dillon's; 101 W. Broadway; (505) 325-0222; steak and seafood; M-E

■ GALLUP
El Sombrero; 1201 W. US 66; (505) 863-4554; New Mexican specialties; B
La Ventana; 1644 S. 2nd; (505) 722-5822; steaks and seafood; M
Ranch Kitchen; 3001 W. US 66; (505) 722-2537; New Mexican specialties; B

■ GRANTS
Grants Station; 200 W. Santa Fe; (505) 287-2334; American fare; B

■ HOBBS
K-Bob's Steakhouse; 108 W. Bender; (505) 392-8796; M

■ JEMEZ SPRINGS
Los Ojos Restaurant; (505) 829-3547; great green chile cheeseburger; B
Timber Ridge Restaurant; La Cueva; (505) 829-3322; basic American fare; B

■ L A S   C R U C E S

Brown Bag Deli; El Molino and Alameda; (505) 524-2857; great sandwiches; B

Dick's Café; 2305 S. Valley; (505) 524-1360 diner fare and New Mexican specialties; B

Great American Food and Beverage Co.; 503 S. Solano; (505) 524-7033; pizza and sandwiches; B

Hacienda; 2605 S. Espina; (505) 522-6380; New Mexican specialties; M

La Posta; Mesilla; (505) 524-3524; New Mexican food in former stagecoach station; M

Mesón de Mesilla; 1803 Avenida de Mesilla; (505) 525-2380; gourmet specialties change daily; E

My Brother's Place; 336 S. Main; (505) 523-7681; spicy New Mexican fare; B

Ranchway; 604 N. Valley; (505) 523-7361; B

Spanish Kitchen; 129 E. Madrid; (505) 526-4275; B

Tatsu; 930 El Paseo; (505) 526-7144; Japanese specialties; M

Tegmeyer's Salad Works; 2001 E. Lohman; (505) 525-2332; B

■ L A S   V E G A S

El Rialto; 141 Bridge; (505) 454-0037; New Mexican specialties; B-M

Hillcrest Restaurant; 1106 Grand; (505) 425-7211; American all the way; B

Plaza Hotel Restaurant; 203 Old Town Plaza; (505) 524-3591 continental and New Mexican food next to a great saloon; M

■ R A T O N

Chicago Joe's; 1281 S. 2nd; (505) 445-2095; Italian dinners and pizza; B

Colt; 1160 S. 2nd; (505) 445-5991; New Mexican specialties and 24-hour breakfast; B-M

La Cosina; 745 S. 3rd; (505) 445-9675; New Mexican fare; M

■ R E D   R I V E R

Redwood Café; (505) 754-2951; New Mexican and American fare; M

Texas Red's Steakhouse; (505) 754-6348; M

■ R O S W E L L

Cattle Baron; 1113 N. Main; (505) 622-2465; M

Claim, The; 1310 N. Main; (505) 623-4021; steakhouse; M

Club House, The; West of Roswell; (505) 622-1158; American fare; M

El Toro; 102 S. Main; (505) 622-9280; New Mexican specialties; B

Mario's; 200 E. 2nd; (505) 623-1740; American and New Mexican specialties; M

■ R U I D O S O

Blue Goose; 2811 Sudderth; (505) 257-5271; American fare; B-M
Casa Blanca; 501 Mechem; (505) 257-2495; New Mexican specialties; M
La Lorraine; 2523 Sudderth; (505) 257-2954; classic French cuisine; M
Tinnie's Silver Dollar; US 70 E.; (505) 653-4425; steakhouse; M

■ S A N T A   F E

Bobcat Bite; Las Vegas Hwy.; (505) 983-5319; meat-lover's paradise; B-M
Coyote Café; 132 W. Water; (505) 983-1615; the imagination knows no bounds
in this most exclusive eatery; E
Dave's Not Here; 1115 Hickox; (505) 983-7060; no-frills American and Mexican
fare; B
Guadalupe Café; 313 S. Guadalupe; (505) 982-9762; hearty New Mexican and
American; B
La Choza; 905 Alarid; (505) 982-0909; pretensions are left at the door of this
New Mexican restaurant; B
Maria's New Mexican Kitchen; 555 W. Cordova; (505) 983-7929; M
Old Mexico Grill; 2434 Cerrillos; (505) 473-0338; elegant fare from south of the
border; M-E
Natural Café; 1494 Cerrillos; (505) 983-1411; vegetarian; M
Pink Adobe; 406 Old Santa Fe Trail; (505) 983-7712; New Mexican and
continental cuisine; E
Pranzo; 540 Montezuma; (505) 983-8333; Northern Italian; M-E
Santacafé; 231 W. Washington; (505) 984-1788; contemporary cuisine; E
Shed, The; 113½ E. Palace; (505) 982-9030; red chile is featured; M
Tia Sophia's; 210 W. San Francisco; (505) 983-9880; great breakfast burritos; B
Zia Diner; 326 S. Guadalupe; (505) 988-7008; great homemade pie; M

■ S A N T A   R O S A

Club Café; Old Route 66; (505) 472-3631; favorite local gathering spot features
New Mexican and American fare, great salsa; M

■ S I L V E R   C I T Y

Buckhorn Saloon and Opera House; Piños Altos; (505) 538-9911; steakhouse; E
Corner Café; 204 N. Bullard; (505) 388-2056; great breakfasts; B
Red Barn; 708 Silver Heights; (505) 538-5666; steak and salad bar; M
Silver Café; 514 N. Bullard; (505) 388-3480; spicy New Mexican fare; B

■ SOCORRO
Armijo's; 602 US 85; (505) 835-1686; New Mexican fare; B
Capitol Bar; 110 Plaza; (505) 835-1193; burgers and sandwiches in local
gathering spot on central plaza; B
El Sombrero; 210 Mesquite; (505) 835-3945; New Mexican specialties; B
Owl Bar; San Antonio; (505) 835-9946; renowned green chile cheeseburgers; B
Val Verde Steak House; 203 Manzanares; (505) 835-3380; steaks and salads in
historic hotel; M

■ TAOS
Apple Tree; 123 Bent St.; (505) 758-1900; creatively prepared seafood, pasta, and
salad; M-E
Casa Cordova; Arroyo Seco; (505) 776-2200; Northern Italian cuisine; E
Lambert's; 309 Paseo del Pueblo Sur; (505) 758-1009; contemporary American
food; E
Michael's Kitchen; Paseo del Pueblo Norte; (505) 758-4178; local gathering spot,
great breakfast; B-M
Roberto's; Kit Carson Rd.; (505) 758-2434; traditional New Mexican fare; B-M

■ TRUTH OR CONSEQUENCES
Cuchillo Café; NM 52 in Cuchillo; New Mexican specialties in roadside hamlet; B
La Cocina; 220 Date; (505) 894-6499; New Mexican fare; B
Los Arcos; 1100 N. Date; (505) 894-6200; steak and seafood; M

■ TUCUMCARI
Piñon Tree Restaurant in the Ramada Inn; 1302 W. Tucumcari; (505) 461-3140;
standard American and New Mexican fare; B-M

■ ALBUQUERQUE NIGHTLIFE

Beyond Ordinary; 211 Gold SW; (505) 764-8858; wild hair and clothes mix with innovative tunes
Cooperage; 7220 Lomas NE; (505) 255-1657; rock and rhythm-and-blues
El Rey; 624 Central SW; (505) 242-9300; rock, reggae, rhythm-and-blues
La Posada; 125 2nd St. NW; (505) 242-9090; local jazz favorite Linda Cotton belts out tunes weekend evenings
Midnight Rodeo; 4901 Mcleod NE; (505) 888-0100; country-western
Sundance Saloon; 12000 Candelaria NE; (505) 296-6761; country-western

■ MUSEUMS AND GALLERIES

Museums and galleries are listed below in the following geographical order: Albuquerque, Santa Fe, Taos, North-central New Mexico, Northwestern New Mexico, Southwestern New Mexico, Southeastern New Mexico, and Northeastern New Mexico.

■ ALBUQUERQUE

Albuquerque Museum; 2000 Mountain NW; (505) 242-4600
American International Rattlesnake Museum; 202 San Felipe NW; (505) 242-6569
Andrews Pueblo Pottery and Art Gallery; 400 San Felipe NW; (505) 243-0414
Café Gallery; 516 Central SW; (505) 242-8244; contemporary art by local artists
Ernie Pyle Memorial Branch Library; 900 Girard NE; (505) 256-2065
Geology and Meteoritic Museum; UNM campus; 505) 277-4204
Indian Pueblo Cultural Center; 2401 12th NW; (505) 843-7270
Jonson Gallery; 1901 Las Lomas NE; (505) 277-4967; collection of late-modernist painter Raymond Jonson
Los Colores; Corrales; (505) 898-5077; historic weaving gallery
Mariposa Gallery; 113 Romero NW; (505) 842-9097; contemporary art, crafts, and jewelry
Maxwell Museum of Anthropology; UNM campus; (505) 277-4404
National Atomic Museum; Kirtland Air Force Base, Wyoming gate; (505) 844-8443

Navajo Gallery; 323 Romero NW; (505) 843-7666; exclusively the work of
   Indian painter R. C. Gorman
New Mexico Museum of Natural History; 1801 Mountain NW; (595) 841-8837
Spanish History Museum; 2221 Lead SE; (505) 268-9981
Tamarind Institute; 108 Cornell SE; (505) 277-3901; tours on the first Friday
   afternoon of the month; internationally renowned lithography studio
Tinkertown Museum; Sandia Park; (505) 281-5233; one man's colossal collection
   of animated, miniature wood carvings that combine into a Western town
University Art Museum; UNM campus; (505) 277-4001
Weyrich Gallery; 2935-D Louisiana NE; (505) 883-7410; contemporary art
   and crafts

■ SANTA FE
Center for Contemporary Arts; 291 Barcelona; (505) 982-1338
Davis Mather Folk Art Gallery; 141 Lincoln; (505) 983-1660
Dewey Galleries; 74 E. San Francisco; (505) 982-8632; early and contemporary
   Southwest art and furniture
El Rancho de las Golondrinas; (505) 471-2261; restored Spanish colonial ranch
   that operates as a living museum
Institute of American Indian Arts Museum; 1369 Cerrillos; (505) 988-6281;
   contemporary Native American art
Museum of Fine Arts; Lincoln and Palace; (505) 827-4455
Museum of Indian Arts and Culture; 708 Camino Lejo; (505) 827-8941
Museum of International Folk Art; 706 Camino Lejo; (505) 827-8350
Palace of the Governors; Santa Fe Plaza; (505) 827-6483; Southwest history
Randall Davey Audubon Center; Upper Canyon Rd.; (505) 983-4609
Santa Fe Children's Museum; 1050 Old Pecos Trail; (505) 989-8359
School of American Research; 660 Garcia; (505) 982-3584; anthropology study
   center with Southwest Indian art; by appointment only
Wheelwright Museum of the American Indian; 704 Camino Lejo;
   (505) 982-4836

■ TAOS
Governor Bent Home; 117A Bent; (505) 758-2376
Ernest L. Blumenschein Home; 222 Ledoux; (505) 758-0330
Kit Carson Home; E. Kit Carson; (505) 758-4741
Nicholai Fechin House; 227 Paseo del Pueblo Norte; (505) 758-1710

Martinez Hacienda; (505) 758-1000; fully restored Spanish colonial hacienda
Millicent Rogers Museum; (505) 758-2462; art of northern New Mexico from
old to new

■ N O R T H - C E N T R A L   N E W   M E X I C O
Bradbury Science Museum; Diamond Dr., Los Alamos; (505) 667-4444
Florence Hawley Ellis Museum of Anthropology; Ghost Ranch; (505) 685-4333
Ghost Ranch Living Museum; Ghost Ranch; (505) 685-4312
Hand Artes Gallery; Truchas; (505) 689-2443; Southwest arts and crafts
Los Alamos Historical Museum; 2132 Central, Los Alamos; (505) 662-4493

■ N O R T H W E S T E R N   N E W   M E X I C O
Aztec Museum; 125 N. Main, Aztec; (505) 334-9829; historical
Farmington Museum; 302 N. Orchard, Farmington; (505) 327-7701; historic
artifacts
Jicarilla Apache Museum; Dulce; (505) 759-3515
Navajo Trading Company; 232 W. US 66, Gallup; (505) 863-6131
New Mexico Museum of Mining; 100 Iron, Grants; (505) 287-4802
Tanner's Indian Arts; 1000 W. US 66, Gallup; (505) 863-6017
Tobe Turpin's Indian Trading Company; 1710 S. 2nd, Gallup; (505) 722-3806

■ S O U T H W E S T E R N   N E W   M E X I C O
Black Range Museum; Hillsboro; (505) 895-5233; historical
Branigan Cultural Center; 106 W. Hadley, Las Cruces; (505) 524-1422
Deming Luna Mimbres Museum; 301 S. Silver, Deming; (505) 546-2382;
regional historical artifacts
Gadsden Museum; Mesilla; (505) 526-6293; artifacts from early Indian, Spanish,
and Anglo settlers
Geronimo Springs Museum; 325 Main, Truth or Consequences;
(505) 894-6600; mostly historic pieces, but highlight is Ralph Edwards Wing
Las Cruces Museum of Natural History; Mesilla Valley Mall, Las Cruces;
(505) 522-3120
Mineralogical Museum; New Mexico Institute of Mining and Technology
campus, Socorro; (505) 835-5420
New Mexico State University Art Gallery; NMSU campus, Las Cruces;
(505) 646-2545

New Mexico State University Museum; NMSU campus, Las Cruces; (505) 646-3739

Silver City Museum; 312 W. Broadway; (505) 538-5921; historic

■ S O U T H E A S T E R N   N E W   M E X I C O

Billy the Kid Museum; Fort Sumner; (505) 355-2380

Blackwater Draw Museum; Portales; (505) 562-2254; evidence of Clovis Man

Confederate Air Force; New Mexico Wing, Hobbs Lea County Airport, Hobbs; (505) 393-9915

Lea County Cowboy Hall of Fame; Hobbs; (505) 392-4510, ext. 371

Roswell Museum; 100 W. 11th, Roswell; (505) 624-6744

Smokey Bear Museum; Capitan; (505) 354-2612

Space Center; Alamogordo; (505) 545-4021

■ N O R T H E A S T E R N   N E W   M E X I C O

Cleveland Roller Mill Museum; (505) 387-2645; operating mill and art gallery

Dorsey Mansion; Springer; (505) 375-2222; palatial late-nineteenth-century home of former Arkansas senator Stephen Dorsey

Folsom Museum; Folsom; (505) 278-2155; fossils and spearpoints from discovery of Folsom Man

Hand Artes Gallery; Truchas; (505) 689-2443; Southwest arts and crafts

Herzstein Memorial Museum; 2nd and Walnut, Clayton; (505) 374-9508; historical artifacts from Union County

Old Mill Museum; Cimarron; (505) 376-2466

Raton Museum; Raton; (505) 445-8979; historic artifacts

Rough Riders Memorial and City Museum; 727 Grand, Las Vegas; (505) 425-8726

Santa Fe Trail Museum; Springer; (505) 483-2341

Tucumcari Historical Museum; 416 S. Adams, Tucumcari; (505) 461-4201

■ OUTDOORS

In New Mexico, more than one-half of the state's 777,766 acres is public, and much of that is open to hunting, fishing, skiing, snowmobiling, hiking, camping, birdwatching, sailing, windsurfing, water skiing, horseback riding, rafting, and canoeing.

Licenses are required to hunt and fish and can be obtained at nearly 300 stores throughout the state, as well as from the state **Game and Fish Department**, 408 Galisteo Street, Santa Fe, 87503. The phone number is (505) 827-7911. For information on hunting guides, contact the New Mexico Council of Outfitters and Guides, 160 Washington SE, #175, Albuquerque, 87108; or call (505) 243-4461.

For folks who would rather view wildlife, seven **national wildlife refuges** are scattered throughout the state. Most serve as feeding areas for waterfowl. At Bosque del Apache, whooping cranes, sandhill cranes, and thousands of snow geese spend each winter. For further information, call (505) 835-1828.

A surprisingly large number of good-sized reservoirs have been created in New Mexico, perfect for swimming, fishing, and boating. Santa Rosa, Conchas, Cochiti, and Abiquiu lakes are managed by the **U.S. Army Corps of Engineers,** (505) 766-2738. An assortment of 20 more lakes are state parks. Shaded campsites abut most shorelines. For further information on these and other state recreational offerings, contact the **State Park and Recreation Division,** 408 Galisteo, Santa Fe, 87504; (505) 827-7465.

Additional picnic and camping facilities, and hiking trails are found on 30 million acres managed by the **Bureau of Land Management.** These include the Three Rivers Petroglyph Site, Wild Rivers Recreation Area, El Malpais National Monument, and Valley of Fires Recreation Area. For further information, contact the New Mexico State Office of the BLM, 120 South Federal Place, Santa Fe, 87504; (505) 988-6000.

The BLM also supervises boaters on the Rio Grande and the Chama River. A dozen commercial outfitters ply the roiling waters during the late-spring-to-early-summer season on the Rio Grande and the summer-long season on the gentler Chama. For information on outfitters and how to do it yourself, contact the BLM's Taos Resource Center, 224 Cruz Alta Road, Taos, 87571; (505) 758-8851.

The **Forest Service** controls more than 10 million acres that include remote mountain wilderness and the Kiowa National Grasslands. Backpackers, snowmobilers, skiers, and hang gliders share this vast space. For further information, contact the Southwestern Regional Office, Public Affairs Office, 517 Gold Avenue SW, Albuquerque, 87102; (505) 842-3292.

New Mexico is also famous for its **world-class skiing** at Taos Ski Valley, which boasts a vertical drop of 2,612 feet (784 m) and some of the steepest slopes and lightest powder in the West. Eight more downhill ski areas are carved into the northern and central mountains, most geared to intermediate skiers. Snowboards are permitted at most areas. From November 1st until the ski areas close in April, the New Mexico Snophone provides up-to-date conditions on the slopes and the roads leading to them. The number is (505) 984-0606.

■ PARKS AND MONUMENTS

Alameda Park Zoo; Alamogordo; (800) 826-0294 in state or (800) 545-4021, ext. A-1 out of state

Aztec Ruins National Monument; Aztec; (505) 334-6174; remains of Anasazi village

Bandelier National Monument; near Los Alamos; (505) 627-3861; ancient Indian village

Bandera Crater and Ice Caves; near Grants; (505) 783-4303; volcanic crater and lava tubes

Bosque del Apache National Wildlife Refuge; (505) 835-1828

Caballo Lake State Park; (505) 743-3942

Capulin Volcano National Monument; near Raton; (505) 278-2201

Carlsbad Caverns National Park; (505) 885-8884

Chaco Culture National Historic Park; (505) 988-6727

City of Rocks State Park; south of Silver City; (505) 536-2800; house-size rock formations

Coronado State Monument; Bernalillo; (505) 867-5351; where the Spanish explorer wintered during New Mexico visit

El Malpais National Monument; near Grants; (505) 285-5405; volcanic badlands

El Morro National Monument; near Grants; (505) 783-4226; inscription rock contains centuries-old messages

Elephant Butte Lake State Park; (505) 744-5421

Fort Selden State Monument; Radium Springs; (505) 526-8911; nineteenth-century fort

Fort Sumner State Monument; Fort Sumner; (505) 355-2573

Fort Union National Monument; (505) 425-8025

Gila Cliff Dwellings National Monument; (505) 536-9461

Jemez State Monument; Jemez Springs; (505) 829-3530; remains of Spanish mission and Indian village

Kiowa National Grasslands; (505) 374-9652

Lincoln State Monument; Lincoln; (505) 653-4372; historic village

Living Desert State Park; Carlsbad; (505) 887-5516; animals and plants indigenous to Chihuahua Desert

Oliver Lee Memorial State Park (Dog Canyon); near Alamogordo; (505) 437-8284; former Indian stronghold

Pancho Villa State Park; Columbus; (505) 531-2711; botanical garden on remains of border fort

Pecos National Monument; Pecos; (505) 757-6414; Spanish mission alongside Indian village

Petroglyph State Park; 6900 Unser NW, Albuquerque; (505) 823-4016

Rio Grande Nature Center; 2901 Candelaria NW, Albuquerque; (505) 344-7240; river ecosystem

Rio Grande Zoological Park; 903 10th NW, Albuquerque; (505) 843-7413

Rock Hound State Park; Deming; (505) 546-1212; where collecting rocks is encouraged

Salinas National Monument; Mountainair; (505) 847-2585; Spanish missions and Indian villages in three sections

Salmon Ruins; Bloomfield; (505) 632-2013; ancient Indian village

Smokey Bear Historical State Park; Capitan; (505) 354-2748

Sugarite Canyon State Park; Raton; (505) 445-5607

Villanueva State Park; Villanueva, on Pecos River; (505) 421-2957

Western New Mexico University Museum; WNMU campus, Silver City; (505) 538-6386

White Sands National Monument; (505) 437-1058

■ SPORTS

Even though New Mexico is home to no top-of-the-line professional sporting teams, the state still breeds serious, outspoken fans. Mostly, they turn out to cheer on the University of New Mexico Lobos basketball team, the New Mexico State University Aggies basketball team, and the Albuquerque Dukes, the Los Angeles Dodgers' top Triple-A minor league team.

Betting on the horses also is popular at eight racetracks statewide. (There are even mule races in Ruidoso.) And even though Albuquerque is home to the famous Unser race-car-driving family, fans must travel outside the state to watch them in action.

■ HORSERACING

The Downs at Albuquerque; (505) 262-1188
The Downs at Santa Fe; (505) 471-3311
La Mesa Park; Raton; (505) 445-2301
Ruidoso Downs; (505) 378-4431
San Juan Downs; Farmington; (505) 326-4551
Sunland Park; Sunland Park; (505) 589-1131

■ SKI AREAS

Angel Fire; (800) 446-8117
Enchanted Forest; (505) 754-2374; cross-country
Pajarito Mountain; Los Alamos; (505) 662-7669
Red River; (505) 754-2382
Sandia Peak; Albuquerque; (505) 296-9585
Santa Fe; (505) 982-4429
Sipapu; Peñasco; (505) 587-2240
Ski Apache; Ruidoso; (505) 336-4356
Ski Cloudcroft; (505) 682-2333
Taos Ski Valley; (505) 776-2291

■ GOLF COURSES

For a more complete list, contact the Sun Country Golf Association, 10035 Golf Course Lane NW, Albuquerque, 87114; (505) 897-0864.

Albuquerque Country Club; (505) 243-7156
Angel Fire Country Club; Angel Fire; (505) 377-2301, ext. 400
Four Hills Country Club; Albuquerque; (505) 296-1122
Inn of the Mountain Gods; Mescalero; (505) 257-5141, ext. 7444
Lodge Golf Course, The; Cloudcroft; (505) 682-2098
Pendaries Village Golf and Country Club; Rociada; (505) 425-6018
Picacho Hills Country Club; Las Cruces; (505) 523-2556
Piñon Hills Golf Course; Farmington; (505) 326-6066
Portales Country Club; Portales; (505) 356-8943
Santa Fe Country Club; (505) 471-0601
Santa Teresa Country Club; Santa Teresa; (505) 589-5401
Spring River Golf Course; Roswell; (505) 622-9506
Tanoan Country Club; Albuquerque; (505) 822-8433

■ VINEYARDS

For a complete directory, write New Mexico Vine and Wine Society, P.O. Box 26751, Albuquerque, 87125.

Alamosa Cellars; Elephant Butte; (505) 744-5319
Anderson Valley; 4920 Rio Grande NW, Albuquerque; (505) 344-7266
Blue Teal; Mesilla; (505) 524-0390
Domaine Cheurlin; Elephant Butte; (505) 744-5418
La Chiripada; Dixon; (505) 579-4437
Madison; Ribera; (505) 421-8028
Sandia Shadows; 11704 Coronado NE, Albuquerque; (505) 298-8826

■ FESTIVALS AND EVENTS

Despite its vast spaces, something is going on in New Mexico nearly every weekend. A small sample of what's available is listed below. For a more complete listing, contact the State Tourism Division at (505) 827-0291 or (800) 545-2040.

JANUARY
Sled Dog Races; Chama; (505) 756-2306

FEBRUARY
Chama Chile Classic; Chama; (505) 756-2306; cross-country skiing
Mt. Taylor Winter Quadrathlon; Grants; (505) 285-6969
Snow shovel races; Angel Fire; (800) 446-8117

MARCH
Columbus Memorial Service; Columbus; (505) 531-2708; service honoring those
  killed during Pancho Villa raid
Good Friday pilgrimage to Chimayo; (505) 753-2831
Rockhound Roundup; Deming; (505) 546-6209

APRIL
Dinosaur Days; Clayton; (505) 374-8361; tour of dinosaur tracks
Trinity Site Tour; Alamogordo; (505) 437-6120
Winston Fiesta; Winston; (505) 743-2736; parade, Pony Express ride, barbecue,
  flea market

MAY
Cinco de Mayo; celebrations across the state
Farmington Balloon Festival; (505) 326-7602
Memorial Day; Angel Fire; (800) 446-8117; ceremonies at Vietnam Veteran's
  Memorial
Mesilla Wine Festival; (505) 646-4543
Railroad Days; Lordsburg; (505) 542-9864
San Felipe Fiesta; Old Town Plaza, Albuquerque; (505) 243-4628
Santa Rosa Days; (505) 472-3763; parade, raft races
The Great Rio Grande Raft Race; Albuquerque; (505) 768-3490; floating
  bathtubs compete with inner-tubes and rafts
Truth or Consequences Fiesta; (505) 894-2946; with Ralph Edwards

Tularosa Rose Festival; (505) 585-2855

JUNE

Anasazi Pageant; Farmington; (505) 884-9043; through Labor Day; musical pageant celebrating the Southwest's multicultural heritage

Annual Flight Festival; Alamogordo; (505) 437-2840, out-of-state (800) 545-4021; International Space Hall of Fame

Aztec Fiesta Days; (505) 334-9551

Billy the Kid; San Jon; (505) 576-2455; Caprock Amphitheatre

Elfego Baca Shoot; Socorro; (505) 835-1550; one-hole golfing tournament

New Mexico Arts and Crafts Fair; Albuquerque; (505) 884-9043

Old Fort Days; Fort Sumner; (505) 355-7705; featuring world's richest tombstone race

Spring Festival; La Cienega; (505) 471-2261; Rancho de las Golondrinas,

Summerfest; Albuquerque; (505) 768-3490; every summer weekend through August, Civic Plaza

JULY

Clovis Music Festival; (505) 763-3435

Fourth of July; fireworks across the state

Old Lincoln Days and Pony Express Race; Lincoln; (505) 653-4025

Spanish Market; Santa Fe Plaza; (505) 983-4038

Rodeo de Santa Fe; Santa Fe Rodeo Grounds; (505) 988-3044

Santa Fe Chamber Music Festival; (505) 983-2075; through mid-August

Santa Fe Opera; (505) 982-3851; through mid-August

Smokey Bear Stampede; Capitan; (505) 354-2224; parade, rodeo, Western dances

AUGUST

Bat Flight Breakfast; Carlsbad Caverns; (505) 785-2232

Connie Mack World Series Baseball; Farmington; (505) 327-9673

Deming Duck Races; (505) 546-2674

Fiesta de San Lorenzo; Bernalillo; (505) 867-3311

Indian Market; Santa Fe Plaza; (505) 983-5220

SEPTEMBER

Bernalillo Wine Festival; (505) 867-3311

Fiestas de Santa Fe; (505) 988-7575

Hatch Chile Festival; (505) 267-4847

Hillsboro Apple Festival; (505) 895-5328
New Mexico State Fair; Albuquerque; (505) 265-1791
Old Taos Trade Fair; (505) 758-0505

OCTOBER
Albuquerque International Balloon Fiesta; (505) 821-1000
Greek Festival; Albuquerque; (505) 247-9411
Harvest Festival; Rancho de las Golondrinas; (505) 471-2261
Peanut Valley Festival; Portales; (505) 356-8541
Trinity Site Tour; Alamogordo; (505) 437-6120
Whole Enchilada Fiesta; Las Cruces; (505) 524-1968

NOVEMBER
Indian National Finals Rodeo; Albuquerque; (505) 265-1791

DECEMBER
Las Posadas; across the state; re-enactment of Joseph and Mary's search for shelter
   in Bethlehem
Red Rock Balloon Rally; Gallup; (505) 863-3841

■ INDIAN EVENTS

Call Indian Pueblo Cultural Center in Albuquerque for up-to-date dance
   information at (505) 843-7270.

Jan. 1: Turtle Dance; Taos Pueblo; (505) 758-8626
Jan. 6: Deer or Buffalo Dance; Taos Pueblo; (505) 758-8626
Jan. 23: San Ildefonso Pueblo Feast Day, dances; (505) 843-7270
Feb. 2: Candelaria Day dances at San Felipe and Picuris pueblos;
   (505) 843-7270
Easter weekend: Basket and Corn dances at most pueblos; (505) 843-7270
Mid-April: Gathering of Nations Powwow; Albuquerque; (505) 836-2810
May 1: San Felipe Feast Day; Cochiti and Taos pueblos; (505) 843-7270
Mid-May; Mescal Roast; Living Desert State Park, Carlsbad; (505) 887-5516
Late May: Santa Fe Powwow; (505) 983-5220
Memorial Day through Labor Day: Evening dances at Red Rock State Park;
   Gallup; (505) 722-3839

Late May: Blessing of the Fields; Tesuque Pueblo; (505) 843-7270

June 24: San Juan Feast Day; Taos Pueblo; (505) 758-8626

June 29: San Pedro Feast Day; San Felipe, Santa Ana, and Santo Domingo pueblos; (505) 843-7270

July: Mescalero Apache Girls' Puberty Ceremonial; Mescalero; (505) 671-4494

July 4: Powwow and rodeo; Window Rock, Arizona; (602) 871-6702

Early July: Annual Powwow; Taos Pueblo; (505) 758-8626

July 25-26: Corn Dance; Taos Pueblo; (505) 758-8626

Aug. 4: Santo Domingo Feast Day; Santo Domingo Pueblo; (505) 843-7270

Early August: Inter-Tribal Ceremonial; Gallup; (505) 863-3896

Aug. 15: San Antonio Feast Day; Laguna and Zia pueblos; (505) 843-7270

Sept. 2: San Esteban Feast Day; Acoma Pueblo; (505) 843-7270

Early September: Navajo Nation Fair; Window Rock, Ariz.; (602) 871-6702

Sept. 15: Jicarilla Apache Gojiiya Feast; Dulce; (505) 756-2306

Sept. 30: San Geronimo Trade Fair; Taos Pueblo; (505) 758-8626

Early October: Shiprock Navajo Nation Fair; Shiprock; (505) 368-4679

Nov. 12: San Diego Feast Day; Jemez and Tesuque pueblos; (505) 843-7270

Early December: Shalako Dances at Zuni Pueblo

Dec. 25: Christmas dances at most pueblos; (505) 758-8626

■ SPAS

Ojo Caliente Mineral Springs; Ojo Caliente; (505) 583-2233

Ten Thousand Waves; Hyde Park Rd., Santa Fe; (505) 988-1047

■ TOURS

Art Tours of Santa Fe; 301 E. Alameda, Santa Fe; (505) 988-3527

Discover Santa Fe; Santa Fe; (505) 982-4979

Ghost Tours; Santa Fe; (505) 983-0111

Old Town Walking Tours; Albuquerque Museum; 2000 Mountain NW, Albuquerque; (505) 243-7255

Santa Fe Detours; 100 E. San Francisco, Santa Fe; (800) 338-6877

■ BOOKSTORES

Bookroom, The; 606 Canyon Rd., Santa Fe; (505) 988-5438
Bookworks; 4022 Rio Grande NW, Albuquerque; (505) 344-8139
Cobean Stationery Company; Roswell; (505) 622-1922
Collected Works; 208-B W. San Francisco, Santa Fe; (505) 988-4226
Dana Bookstore; Socorro; (505) 835-3434
Living Batch; 106 Cornell SE, Albuquerque; (505) 262-1619
Los Artesanos Bookstore; Old Town Plaza, Las Vegas; (505) 425-8331
Los Llanos Bookstore; 500 Montezuma, Santa Fe; (505) 982-8542
Mesilla Book Center; Mesilla Plaza; (505) 526-6220
Salt of the Earth Books; 2128 Central SE, Albuquerque; (505) 842-1220

■ PERIODICALS

Nearly every town in New Mexico puts out its own newspaper, either daily semi-weekly, weekly, or bi-weekly. The *Albuquerque Journal* is the largest and most comprehensive, and is circulated throughout the state. Every Friday, its entertainment section focuses on events for the upcoming weekend. The weekly *Santa Fe Reporter* comes out on Thursdays and is a good source for weekend happenings in the capital city. The *Taos News,* also printed on Thursdays, lists area weekend events. *New Mexico Magazine* is a glossy monthly publication full of articles about the state's people, places, and history. The month's events, ranging from theater presentations to rodeos, are listed in the magazine's Sundial section.

■ ADDITIONAL ATTRACTIONS

Acoma Pueblo; (505) 552-6604
Cumbres & Toltec Scenic Railroad; Chama; (505) 726-2151
DAV Vietnam Veteran's Memorial Chapel; Angel Fire; (505) 377-6900
Salmon Raspberry Ranch; La Cueva, 25 miles (40 km) north of Las Vegas on NM 518; best in late summer to early fall
Taos Pueblo; (505) 758-8626

■ USEFUL ADDRESSES

New Mexico Game and Fish Department; 408 Galisteo, Santa Fe; (505) 827-7911

State Parks and Recreation; 408 Galisteo, Santa Fe; (505) 827-7465

State Tourism Division; 1100 S. St. Francis, Santa Fe; (505) 827-0291 or (800) 545-2040

G L O S S A R Y

ACEQUIA: Irrigation ditch.

BULTO: Small wooden carved sculpture usually of a saint.

CARRETA: Rudimentary two-wheeled wooden cart hauled by oxen. They were the only vehicles used in New Mexico in the 1700s and early 1800s.

CHAMISA: Shrub with slender, flexible branches that display small yellow blooms in the fall. Also known as rabbitbrush.

FAROLITO: Small brown paper sacks in which votive candles are placed in sand. On Christmas Eve, *farolitos* line rooftops, doorways and sidewalks in celebration of Christmas.

FRIJOLES: Beans.

HORNO: Beehive-shaped outdoor oven used by rural Hispanics and Pueblo and Navajo Indians, mostly for baking bread.

KACHINA: Spiritual guide of an anthropomorphic nature that manifests itself in dancers at Pueblo ceremonies. Also, small wooden figurines that resemble the costumed dancers.

KIVA: Circular or rectangular ceremonial chamber, usually subterranean, built apart from dwellings at pueblos. Off limits to visitors.

JACALES: Rudimentary buildings in which vertical poles were lashed close together and covered with mud plaster. Roofs were dirt supported by *vigas* and *latillas*.

LATILLAS: Small peeled poles used as ceiling beams, placed in between larger *vigas*. Sometimes they are arranged in herringbone patterns.

LLANO: Plains, as in Llano Estacado.

LUMINARIA: Small bonfire set ablaze on sidewalks in neighborhoods that display *farolitos* on Christmas Eve. Hands are warmed at small fires. In most parts of the state, *farolitos* are referred to as *luminarias*.

PETROGLYPH: Figure carved into rock wall by ancient Indians.

PICTOGRAPH: Figure painted on rock wall by ancient Indians.

PUEBLO: Community, village. Early Spanish explorers named the first Indians they encountered "Pueblo Indians" because their towns resembled Spanish villages.

RETABLO: Two-dimensional line painting of a saint or holy person on a flat board that is designed to hang on a wall.

REREDOS: Altar screen.

RISTRA: String of red chiles hanging from *vigas* outside homes.

SANTO: Image or statue of a holy person or saint, such as a *retablo* or *bulto*.

VIGAS: Exposed roof beams, usually made of pine, that jut from the sides of adobe buildings.

(above) Dry deserts of New Mexico contrast with its lush highlands (opposite). (Paul Chesley)

FOLK MEDICINES OF NEW MEXICO

Twenty years ago, the late Tibo J. Chavez, author of *New Mexican Folklore of the Rio Abajo,* interviewed hundreds of Hispanic residents up and down the Middle Rio Grande Valley to document herbal remedies that have been passed down through the centuries. Some of these traditional medicines were introduced by both Pueblo and Apache Indians, while others came with early Spanish colonists who brought with them plants and herbs when they made their new homes in New Mexico. Today, many of these plants still sprout from gardens along the river corridor and stock medicine cabinets in homes. In addition to regular folk, Chavez talked to seven women known as *curanderas,* or female healers versed in the uses of herbs as home remedies. (The following was included with permission of Tibo Chavez, and reprinted here for its historic interest only. Neither the author nor the publisher are making any medical claims for these folk medicines.)

AGUA DE SANDIA: Watermelon juice
Agua de sandia is considered very effective as a wash for sore eyes.

AJO: Garlic
Ajo is considered an excellent remedy for stomach disorders. The ajo is roasted in the oven and then placed in water. Sugar is added and the contents are boiled. The boiled water is then strained and ingested as tea. Raw ajo is recommended for controlling high blood pressure.

AMOL: Yucca root
The root of the yucca is mashed with a hammer and placed in a tub of water to soak overnight. From the pulverized plant rise suds that serve as an excellent dandruff shampoo.

ANISE
One of the most common spices in a Hispanic kitchen, anise is a major ingredient in traditional *biscochitos* (sugar cookies). Mashed and boiled in water, the spice is used to treat a bad cough.

CALAVERA DE PERRO: Dog skull
An old dog skull is pounded into a fine powder, which then is heated in an oven until it turns a brownish color. The powder is applied with grease to the skin of a sprained or broken bone after the bone has been set. A splint is then applied. In time, the bone will heal with no further difficulties.

CEBOLLA: Onion
Eaten raw, onion works to calm nerves. Raw onions sliced and soaked in vinegar can be applied to a temple on the side of the head to relieve headaches.

CONTRA YERBA: Caltrop family
This is one of the most basic and widely used remedies of the Rio Abajo. The root of the contra yerba is ground into a fine powder and applied to open wounds to prevent infection. The plant's root water is boiled as a cure for stomach ulcers.

FLOR DE SAUCO: Honeysuckle
The seeds or white flower of the honeysuckle bush are boiled into a tea that works to reduce fever.

HEDIONDILLO: Greasewood
Old-timers believed tea brewed from hediondillo prevented and even cured cancer. Hediondillo baths are recommended for rheumatism, arthritis and swelling of the joints.

MASTRONZO: Horehound
In addition to being cultivated in gardens, this remedy grows wild along ditch banks. As a tea, mastranzo is used to cure stomach and respiratory ailments.

OSHA: Parsley family
Osha is the most multi-purpose plant of the valley. Cowboys carry the dry root in their pockets as a first-aid kit. The root is taken for stomach disorders and headaches, applied as a poultice when mixed with flour and other remedies, and used as an enema.

YERBA BUENA: Spearmint
The most popular of the Rio Abajo remedies, yerba buena tea soothes stomach disorders. Its dry leaves in a powder form are used to treat open wounds and infections.

LOW RIDERS

Displaying a fresh coat of fire-engine red paint, a 1967 Chevrolet Impala inches along, its tinted windows hiding the identities of those inside—and possibly a television set and bar. Not far behind is a 1950 Chevrolet pickup truck with a multi-colored design of red, blue, and yellow stripes of varying widths and lengths painted on its side, cruising along precariously close to the ground. Then there is a 1958 sea-foam green Volkswagon with matching tire rims. A welded chainlink steering wheel can be seen inside a 1956 Chevrolet painted in cobalt blue and white. Burgundy crushed velvet covers the seats, dashboard, ceiling, and door panels.

As you pass by a parking lot, you might spot two drivers showing off the detached beds of their shiny Nissan pickup trucks. By pressing a button, these beds gyrate up, down, and sideways in a flash. Low riders call these informal hydraulic displays "bed dancing" contests. While waiting at stoplights, drivers flip a toggle switch, which causes the 3,000-pound (1,363-kg) car to "scrape" its frame on the pavement or "hop" the rear end of the car 29 inches (74 cm) into the air. The hydraulic pumps that enable a driver to "juice it all around" are powered by eight storage batteries.

While Española is New Mexico's most concentrated pocket of low riders, the phenomenon is not unique to the state. In fact, low riding originated in the early 1950s in Texas and California among Hispanic teenagers who enjoyed disparaging the hot-rods driven by lower-middle-class Anglos. The image of Mexican-Americans cruising around in "mean and clean" automobiles also helped counter the perception that all Hispanic youths congregated in "pachuco gangs," which were popular in the 1930s and 1940s. By driving at the speed limit, or in many cases, slower than the limit, low riders present themselves as law-abiding, energy-conserving citizens. And many customizers refuse to give up the hobby even after they grow up, marry, and acquire gray hair.

Many of these low riders belong to car clubs where they share their design concepts and hydraulic technology. In addition, they regularly compete with members of car clubs in Santa Fe and Albuquerque in contests at which automobiles are judged on appearance and their "scraping" and "hopping" abilities.

A classy chassis.

RECOMMENDED READING

Following is a brief list of the many wonderful books available on New Mexico.

Abbey, Edward. *The Brave Cowboy* and *Fire on the Mountain*. Albuquerque: University of New Mexico Press, 1956, 1962. Fiction. Both novels describe a stubborn man rooted to the state.

Anaya, Rudolfo. *Bless Me, Ultima* and *Heart of Aztlan*. Berkeley: Tonatiuh International, 1972, 1976. Mixes Hispanic folklore with fiction in two books about growing up Hispanic in New Mexico.

Bandelier, Adolf. *Delight Makers*. San Diego: Harcourt, Brace and Jovanovich, 1971. Re-creates Indian life along Bandelier National Monument's Frijoles Creek.

Bradford, Richard. *Red Sky at Morning*. Philadelphia: Lippincott, 1968. A coming-of-age story about a young boy who is shipped off to relatives in rural New Mexico when his father is called away to serve in World War II.

Bunting, Bainbridge. *John Gaw Meem, Southwestern Architect*. Albuquerque: University of New Mexico Press, 1983. A look at the man behind some of the state's best examples of Spanish-Pueblo architecture.

Chilton, Lance (et al.). *New Mexico, a New Guide to the Colorful State*. Albuquerque: University of New Mexico Press, 1984. An overall primer to the state, providing complete, up-to-date information including history, flora and fauna, architecture, and religion, organized around 18 tours.

Chronic, Halka. *Roadside Geology of New Mexico*. Missoula, Montana: Mountain Press Publishing Co., 1987. A good book to have handy when cruising the state's highways. It discusses the state's fascinating geology route-by-route.

Church, Peggy Pond. *The House at Otowi Bridge*. Albuquerque: University of New Mexico Press, 1959. Tells the story of Edith Warner, who lived alongside the Rio Grande, maintaining friendships with the San Ildefonso Indians and the scientists who were developing the world's first atomic bomb at nearby Los Alamos.

Dutton, Bertha. *American Indians of the Southwest.* Albuquerque: University of New Mexico Press, 1983. An exhaustive study of the region's Native Americans.

Hillerman,Tony. *Dance Hall of the Dead, People of Darkness, Dark Wind, Ghostway, Skinwalkers, Thief of Time,* and *Talking God.* New York: Harper & Row, 1973, 1980, 1982, 1984, 1986, 1988, 1989. Takes readers along on the fictitious crime-solving paths of Jim Chee and Joe Leaphorn, officers with the Navajo Tribal Police. His series of murder mysteries are a wonderful introduction to Navajo culture.

Horgan, Paul. *Great River: the Rio Grande in North American History.* New York: Holt, Rinehart and Winston, 1968. Deep, beautifully descriptive, and wonderful insight into the state as it matured from a primitive hunting ground to statehood.

Lavender, David. *The Trail to Santa Fe.* Boston: Houghton Mifflin, 1958. A compact book that traces the birth and death of the Santa Fe Trail.

Lisle, Laurie. *Portrait of an Artist, a Biography of Georgia O'Keeffe.* New York: Washington Square Press, 1980. A well-researched biography.

Looney, Ralph. *Haunted Highways.* Albuquerque: University of New Mexico Press, 1979. Ghost towns revisited.

Nichols, John. *The Milagro Beanfield War, The Magic Journey,* and *Nirvana Blues.* New York: Holt, Rinehart & Winston, 1974, 1978, 1981. Taos resident and writer, Nichols, shares his love and reverence for New Mexico in this trilogy.

O'Keeffe Georgia. *Georgia O'Keeffe, a Studio Book.* New York: Viking Press, 1976. A full-color collection of O'Keeffe's work with accompanying text written by the artist.

Pearce, T.M. *New Mexico Place Names.* Albuquerque: University of New Mexico Press, 1965. Indispensable quick reference: for instance, it tells the origin of Gut-Ache Mesa and the location of Bathtub Draw.

Piper, Ti. *Fishing in New Mexico.* Albuquerque: University of New Mexico Press, 1989. Written for the fishing fanatic. It details the state's stream and lake offerings, best bait, and best time to go.

Richter, Conrad. *Sea of Grass.* New York: Alfred Knopf, 1936. A slice of life on the eastern New Mexico plains at the turn of the twentieth century

Roads of New Mexico. Fredericksburg, Texas: Shearer Publishing, 1990. Atlas with historical data, weather information, a list of movies filmed here, and incredible detail showing unnamed gravel roads, water tanks, and fence lines.

Roberts, Susan and Calvin. *New Mexico.* Albuquerque: University of New Mexico Press, 1988. A comprehensive and readable history.

Schaafsma, Polly. *Indian Rock Art of the Southwest.* Albuquerque: University of New Mexico Press, 1980. The definitive book on Indian petroglyphs and pictographs.

Simmons, Marc. *New Mexico, an Interpretive History* and *Albuquerque, a Narrative History.* Albuquerque: University of New Mexico Press, 1977, 1982. These accounts are lively and easy to read.

Spears, Beverley. *American Adobes.* Albuquerque: University of New Mexico Press, 1985. A Santa Fe architect documents New Mexico's rural indigenous architecture.

Utley, Robert. *Billy the Kid, a Short and Violent Life.* Lincoln, Nebraska: University of Nebraska Press, 1989. Among the more accurate texts on the subject.

Varney, Phillip. *New Mexico's Best Ghost Towns.* Flagstaff, Arizona: Northland Press, 1981.

This much photographed ladder at Acoma Pueblo is a work of art in its own right.

COMES THE ARCHBISHOP

*T*ravelling with Eusabio [an Indian guide] was like travelling with the landscape made human. He accepted chance and weather as the country did, with a sort of grave enjoyment. He talked little, ate little, slept anywhere, preserved a countenance open and warm, and . . . had unfailing good manners. The Bishop was rather surprised that he stopped so often by the way to gather flowers. One morning he came back with the mules, holding a bunch of crimson flowers—long, tube-shaped bells, that hung lightly from one side of a naked stem and trembled in the wind.

"The Indians call rainbow flower," he said, holding them up and making the red tubes quiver. "It is early for these."

When they left the rock or tree or sand dune that had sheltered them for the night, the Navajo was careful to obliterate every trace of their temporary occupation. He buried the embers of the fire and the remnants of food, unpiled any stones he had piled together, filled up the holes he had scooped in the sand. . . . Father Latour judged that, just as it was the white man's way to assert himself in any landscape, to change it, make it over a little (at least to leave some mark of memorial of his sojourn), it was the Indian's way to pass through a country without disturbing anything; to pass and leave no trace, like fish through the water, or birds through the air.

It was the Indian manner to vanish into the landscape, not to stand out against it. The Hopi villages that were set upon rock mesas were made to look like the rock on which they sat, were imperceptible at a distance. The Navajo hogans, among the sand and willows, were made of sand and willows. None of the pueblos would at that time admit glass windows into their dwellings. The reflection of the sun on the glazing was to them ugly and unnatural—even dangerous. Moreover, these Indians disliked novelty and change. They came and went by the old paths worn into the rock by the feet of their fathers, used the old natural stairway of stone to climb to their mesa towns, carried water from the old springs, even after white men had dug wells.

In the working of silver or drilling of turquoise the Indians had exhaustless patience; upon their blankets and belts and ceremonial robes they lavished their skill and pains. But their conception of decoration did not extend to the landscape. They seemed to have none of the European's desire to "master" nature, to arrange and re-create. They spent their ingenuity in the other direction; in accommodating themselves to the scene in which they found themselves. This was not so much from indolence, the Bishop thought, as from an inherited caution and respect. It was as if the great country were asleep, and they wished to carry on their lives without awakening it; or as if the spirits of earth and air and water were things not to antagonize and arouse. When they hunted, it was with the same discretion; an Indian hunt was never a slaughter. They ravaged neither the rivers nor the forest, and if they irrigated, they took as little water as would serve their needs. The land and all that it bore they treated with consideration; not attempting to improve it, they never desecrated it.

As Father Latour and Eusabio approached Albuquerque, they occasionally fell in with company; Indians going to and fro on the long winding trails across the plain, or up into the Sandia mountains. They had all of them the same quiet way of moving, whether their pace was swift or slow, and the same unobtrusive demeanor: an Indian wrapped in his bright blanket, seated upon his mule or walking beside it, moving through the pale new-budding sagebrush, winding among the sad waves, as if it were his business to pass unseen and unheard through a country awakening with spring.

North of Laguna two Zuni runners sped by them, going somewhere east on "Indian business." They saluted Eusabio by gestures with the open palm, but did not stop. They coursed over the sand with the fleetness of young antelope, their bodies disappearing and reappearing among the sand dunes, like the shadows that eagles cast in their strong, unhurried flight.

—Willa Cather, *Death Comes for the Archbishop,* 1927

I N D E X

MacArthur, Gen. Douglas   181
Madrid   71-72
Marin, John   125
Martinez Hacienda   *30-31, 95,* 142
Martinez, Maria   47, 93, *107,* 133, 144
Martinez, Paddy   162
Maxwell Land Grant   185, 250-51, 262, 267
Maxwell Museum of Anthropology   46
Maxwell, Lucien   250, 262
McCarty, Henry   *see Billy the Kid*
McGregor Range   234
McSween, Alexander   220-221
Meem, John Gaw   40
Mendoza, Antonio de   20
Mescalero Apache   31, 178-79, 218, 219, 222, 225
Mescalero Apache Reservation   224, 236, 240
Mesilla   199
Mesilla Valley   194
Mesquite Street   194
Mexican-American War of 1848   28, 181, 266
Millenium Turquoise Mine   73
Millicent Rogers Museum   144
Mills Canyon Hotel   259
Mills, Melvin   259
Mimbres   17-18, 177, 178, 212
mining   71, 72, 73, 110, 162-163, 167, 169, 188, 207, 208
Miranda, Guadalupe   251
Mission de Nuestra Señora de los Angeles de Porciuncula   107
Mission de San Buenaventura   76
Mix, Tom   53, 255
Mogollon   211
Mogollon Indians   17-18, 74, 178, 196, 210, 212, 227
Momaday, N. Scott   170-171
Montezuma   64, 70
Montezuma Castle   255, *256*
Mountainair   76
movie stars   53, 164, 225
Mrs. Rubio's tortilla   237
Mt. Taylor   34, 152
Mudheads   157-158
Murder Mystery Weekends   265

Museum of Fine Arts   132
Museum of International Folk Art   132
museums and galleries   132, 141, 294-297

Nambe Pueblo   136
National Atomic Museum   42
National Rifle Association   266-267
Native American tribes   *see individual tribes*
Navajo   18, 24, 28, 29-30, 132, 133, 146, 149, 218-219, 240
Navajo Reservation   52, 146, 149
New Mexico Institute of Mining and Technology   188
New Mexico Mining Museum   162
New Mexico Museum of Indian Arts and Culture   132
New Mexico Museum of Natural History   45
New Mexico State University, Las Cruces   198
nightlife   52, 152, 294

O'Keeffe, Georgia   97-98, 112-113, *113,* 125, 132, 140
Ojo Caliente Mineral Springs   98
Old Coal Mine Museum   72
Old Fort Days   241
Old Man Gloom   126
Old Town   44
Oliver Lee Memorial State Park   233
Oppenheimer, J. Robert   106
Organ Mountains   194, 196, 197
Our Lady of Sorrows Church   254
outdoor activities   298-299

Palace of the Governors   88, 120, 131
Paleozoic Era   16
Palomas   205
Pancho Villa   203-204, *204*
Pancho Villa State Park   204
Parker, Peter "Shorty"   39
parks and monuments   299-300
Parroquia Guadalupe Catholic Church   205
Pecos National Monument   108
Pecos River Valley   216, 235-237
Pecos Wilderness   108, 138
Penasco   138

COMPASS AMERICAN GUIDES

WRITTEN FOR THE "LITERATE TRAVELER," this series of guides conjures up the images, explores the myths and legends, and reveals the spirit of America, its cities and states, and Canada.

Compass American Guides are available in general and travel bookstores, or may be ordered directly by calling 1-800-733-3000; or by sending a check or money order, including the cost of shipping and handling, payable to: Random House, Inc. 400 Hahn Road, Westminster Maryland 21157. Books are shipped by USPS Book Rate (allow 30 days for delivery): $2.00 for the 1st book, $0.50 for each additional book. Applicable sales tax will be charged. All prices are subject to change. Or ask your bookseller to order for you.

> *"Books can make thoughtful (and sometimes even thought-provoking) gifts for incentive travel winners or convention attendees. A new series of guidebooks published by Compass American Guides is right on the mark."*—SUCCESSFUL MEETINGS *magazine*
>
> Consider Compass American Guides as gifts or incentives for VIP's, employees, clients, customers, convention and meeting attendees, friends and others. Quantity discounts and customized editions are available.

Chicago   Veteran newsman and inveterate Chicagoan, Jack Schnedler, who writes regularly for the *Chicago Sun-Times,* captures the essence of this brawny, exuberant city, covering its history from swamp to skyscrapers, its architecture and urban essences.
Author: Jack Schnedler—Photographer: Zbigniew Bzdak
ISBN 1-878867-28-8; 320 pp; Price $16.95 (paper). ISBN 1-878867-29-6; Price: $24.95

Las Vegas   Deke Castleman's rollicking introduction to the capital of glitz, with a tale of fifty hotels, a celebration of tacky museums, a guide to quick weddings and sign language, and, of course, a system for playing slots, craps, blackjack, poker, and other games of chance.
Author: Deke Castleman—Photographer: Michael Yamashita
ISBN 1-878867-18-0; 304 pp; Price $14.95. Second edition.

Los Angeles   A hip and fast-moving tour of Los Angeles with special attention to those places where movies were filmed, movie stars lived and loved, and legends were born.
Author: Gil Reavill—Photographer: Mark S. Wexler
ISBN 1-878867-17-2; 324 pp; Price $14.95.

San Francisco and the Bay Area   San Francisco has something for everyone, whether your taste runs to cappuccino or dim sum, to downtown honky tonk or Davies Symphony Hall. Special emphasis on the surrounding Bay Area, from the Napa Valley to the markets of the East Bay.
Author: Barry Parr—Photographer: Michael Yamashita
ISBN 1-878867-16-4; 400 pp; Price $14.95. Second edition.

Arizona   From hidden canyons to museums of archaeology, from the civilized pleasures of Phoenix to jagged wildlands, author Larry Cheek reveals Arizona's scenic, cultural, and historical attractions and colorful eccentricities.
Author: Larry Cheek—Photographer: Michael Freeman
ISBN 1-878867-32-6; 288 pp; Price $16.95. Second edition.

Colorado   Champagne powder and cattle ranches, deserts and mountains, clean civilized cities, and classic American small towns—author Klusmire describes them all with wit, folksy humor, and a native's insight.
Author: Jon Klusmire—Photographer: Paul Chesley
ISBN 1-878867-07-5; 318 pp; Price $14.95 (paper). ISBN 1-878867-20-2; Price $22.95 (cloth)

Hawai'i   Some credit Hawai'i's magic to climate and scenery, others to its handsome people and spirit of *aloha*—but all are stirred by its royal history and its connection to the cultures of Polynesia. This guide helps you discover Hawai'i's magic for yourself.
Author: Moana Tregaskis—Photographers: Wayne Levin and Paul Chesley
ISBN 1-878867-23-7; 364 pp; Price $15.95 (paper). ISBN 1-878867-24-5; Price $22.95 (cloth)

Montana   Love of land and sky runs deep in Montana. Mountain ranges with names like the Crazies and the Sapphires. Legendary rivers—the Madison, Big Hole, and Yellowstone. Curiouser creeks—Froze-to-Death, Stinking Water, and Hellroaring. High plains, once home to buffalo, still offer wide vistas to the eye and soul. This land of the Big Sky may well be the last best place.
Author: Norma Tirrell—Photographer: John Reddy
ISBN 1-878867-10-5; 320 pp; Price $14.95 (paper). ISBN 1-878867-13-X; Price $22.95 (cloth)

New Mexico   Space, light, purity—New Mexico has cast a magical spell of mystery over its inhabitants for centuries. Rich in history, New Mexico has seen the sophisticated Anasazi culture, Spanish conquistadors searching for gold, 16th century colonists, and Pancho Villa. This truly is a Land of Enchantment.
Author: Nancy Harbert—Photographer: Michael Freeman
ISBN 1-878867-06-7; 336 pp; Price $15.95 (paper). ISBN 1-878867-22-9; Price $22.95 (cloth)

Utah   Unspoiled as the day Brigham Young proclaimed "this is the right place," this land of red-rock canyons and snow-capped mountains offers glorious scenery and a glimpse of the magnificent cliff-dwellings of the ancient Anasazi Indians. Special emphasis on outdoor recreation.
Author: Tom & Gayen Wharton—Photographer: Tom Till
ISBN 1-878867-31-8; 352 pp; Price $16.95. Second edition.

Wyoming   High, wide, and handsome, a land where tales of Indians, pioneers, gun slingers, cattle barons, cowboys and other characters of the Old West still cling to life. Nat Burt, son of pioneering dude ranchers, roams the state where the myth of the cowboy was born.
Author: Nathaniel Burt—Photographer: Don Pitcher
ISBN 1-878867-04-0; 392 pp; Price $14.95 (paper). ISBN 1-878867-03-2; Price $22.95 (cloth)

Canada   Veteran journalist Garry Marchant approaches the second largest country in the world as not one, but six different nations. Special sections on the Inuits, Canadian sports, rail hotels, 'Newfies,' Quebecois culture and the Calgary Stampede.
Author: Garry Marchant—Photographer: Ken Straiton
ISBN 1-878867-12-1; 308 pp; Price $14.95

■ ABOUT THE AUTHOR

Nancy Harbert has rafted and canoed New Mexico's rivers, hiked its trails, fished its streams, and skied its slopes. A resident since 1979, she has traveled to the state's far reaches and talked to ranchers, miners, Indians, governors, and regular folk as a reporter for the *Albuquerque Journal* and *United Press International.* She now lives in Albuquerque after stints in Santa Fe and Las Cruces. Currently editor of the *New Mexico Lawyer* and a stringer for *Time* Magazine, she continues to enjoy the state's natural and cultural wonders whenever she can.

■ ABOUT THE PHOTOGRAPHER

Michael Freeman is a noted photographer and writer who has traveled all over the globe for book and magazine publishers, both British and American. His work has appeared in the *Sunday Times* of London and *Smithsonian* magazine. Most recently, for the large-picture format book *Angkor,* published by Houghton-Mifflin, he has undertaken the first study of this ancient Cambodian city in two decades.